Contemporary Perspectives
on Constitutional Interpretation

Contemporary Perspectives on Constitutional Interpretation

EDITED BY

Susan J. Brison and Walter Sinnott-Armstrong

Westview Press

BOULDER • SAN FRANCISCO • OXFORD

Copyright © 1993 by Westview Press, Inc.

Published in 1993 in the United States of America by Westview Press, Inc., 5500 Central Avenue, Boulder, Colorado 80301-2877, and in the United Kingdom by Westview Press, 36 Lonsdale Road, Summertown, Oxford OX2 7EW

A CIP catalog record for this book is available from the Library of Congress.

ISBN 0-8133-8393-5 (hc.) ISBN 0-8133-8394-3 (pbk.)

Printed and bound in the United States of America

The paper used in this publication meets the requirements
of the American National Standard for Permanence of Paper
for Printed Library Materials Z39.48-1984.

10   9   8   7   6   5   4   3   2   1

To Martha and Robert Brison
S. J. B.

To Walter Armstrong, Jr.,
and in memory of Alice McKee Armstrong
W. S-A.

Contents

Acknowledgments

This anthology grew out of the Humanities Research Institute on Constitutional Interpretation that we directed at Dartmouth College in the fall of 1991. The institute brought together for a term scholars from various disciplines, including history, law, literature, philosophy, politics, and religion. It also sponsored a series of talks by legal theorists, which included presentations by five of the contributors to this anthology. Generous funding for the institute was provided by the Andrew W. Mellon Foundation, the National Endowment for the Humanities, the Nelson A. Rockefeller Center for the Social Sciences, and Lawrence Newman (Dartmouth Class of 1952). Additional support and encouragement came from Dean James Wright, Associate Dean Bruce Duncan, and President James Freedman of Dartmouth College. Assistant Dean Sandra Gregg provided much helpful administrative assistance.

We learned a great deal from all of the participants in the institute, and we are especially grateful to Frederick Schauer, who was the William H. Morton Distinguished Professor of the Humanities at Dartmouth in the fall of 1991 and has continued to provide invaluable advice on this project since that time.

In assembling this anthology, we were aided by the editors of the *Boston University Law Review* and by our research assistants, Ted Brader, Amy Candido, and Ann Marshall. We would like to thank the Presidential Scholars Program and the Faculty Research Committee at Dartmouth for funding these assistants. Spencer Carr, Shena Redmond, Marykay Scott, and Jennifer Watson, our editors at Westview Press, gave us welcome suggestions throughout the project. Nancy Davies of Humanities Computing and Gonzalo Lira, our compositor, provided expert technical assistance with the preparation of the final typescript.

Finally, we would also like to thank Thomas Trezise and Liz Sinnott-Armstrong for their patience, understanding, and companionship.

Susan J. Brison
Walter Sinnott-Armstrong

Credits

A Philosophical Introduction to Constitutional Interpretation

Walter Sinnott-Armstrong and Susan J. Brison

In 1992, the Supreme Court handed down opinions in controversial cases involving abortion, school prayer, hate speech, airport solicitation, environmental regulation, and many other issues.[1] These opinions raise important questions about how to interpret specific constitutional provisions, and they also raise more general questions of method. How should the Court interpret the Constitution? Is there any single method of constitutional decision making that could justify all of these decisions? If only some of these decisions are justified, which are they, and how can we tell? If such decisions cannot be justified by any general method, is constitutional law no more than passing politics or even blind luck?

These questions have practical importance for judges who decide cases, for lawyers who advise clients, for presidents and senators who nominate and confirm judges, for police who investigate crimes, for attorneys-general who decide which cases to pursue, for city clerks who issue parade permits, for teachers who decide whether to silence racist views in class, and even for private citizens who want their personal decisions to conform to constitutional ideals. Constitutional interpretation also has theoretical interest for academics in many fields. It has been compared with the interpretation of literature, art, religious texts, and historical periods. Methods and theories drawn from such fields as literary theory, philosophy, political science, and economics have been used to illuminate constitutional interpretation, making it a paradigm of interdisciplinary study.

In order to understand constitutional interpretation, it is helpful to separate several issues. We will begin by discussing the nature and purpose of constitutional interpretation in general. Then we will look at each of the main kinds of reasons that are used to justify interpreting the Constitution one way rather than another. Only then can we return to the questions of whether and how these factors fit together into a general method of constitutional interpretation.

1

What Is Constitutional Interpretation?

Constitutional interpretation can best be understood by looking at its goal and function. Most people who interpret the Constitution do so in order to reach some kind of decision. Different interpreters use the Constitution for different kinds of decisions at different levels of government as well as in different areas of private life. Despite this variety, it is common to focus on judges who need to decide whether a given state action is constitutional.[2]

In order to argue for such a decision, a judge needs premises about the facts of the case and about what exactly is in the Constitution. The judge also needs some test of what is necessary and sufficient to violate the relevant constitutional provision. For example, the Fourteenth Amendment says, "No state shall . . . deny to any person within its jurisdiction the equal protection of the laws." The problem is that all state actions create some kinds of inequality, so a judge needs a more precise test of which inequalities violate the equal protection clause. Some interpreters claim that a state denies equal protection of the laws whenever its actions have a disproportionate adverse *effect* on an underprivileged group. Others claim that a state denies equal protection only if the state's *motive* is to cause a disproportionate adverse effect on an underprivileged group or on anyone else. The point of such interpretive premises, or "interpretations,"[3] is to provide tests that make it easier to apply constitutional provisions to particular cases.

The problem is that there are always alternative interpretations that support different decisions, and judges need to choose among the alternatives. This is where a theory of interpretation comes in. In this role, a theory of interpretation is about how people do or should decide among possible tests or interpretations.

Theories of constitutional interpretation can be either descriptive or prescriptive. Some theories merely describe how people *do* in fact interpret the Constitution. Other theories prescribe how judges and others *ought* to interpret the Constitution. The latter imply that some constitutional interpretations are good or correct and others are bad or wrong or that certain reasons or grounds are adequate or inadequate to justify interpretations. These theories might even provide practical rules that people are supposed to follow consciously when making their interpretations and decisions. Prescriptive and descriptive theories might be connected indirectly, but, since our courts are not always right, descriptions of how courts do reason do not directly imply prescriptions about how they should reason. In the end, most of us who study constitutional interpretation want to know how we should interpret the Constitution because we want theories to help us make decisions and evaluate others' decisions. That is why most of the theories in this anthology are prescriptive.

Although all prescriptive theories say that someone ought to interpret something in some way, they differ in the people they address and in the areas of law they cover. Some theories assume that everyone ought to interpret all parts of the Constitution in the same way. Others claim or allow that different methods should be used by different levels of courts and officials or for different parts of the Constitution.[4] In any case, most theories focus on interpretations by the Supreme Court of the Bill of Rights and the Fourteenth Amendment (which together will be referred to as the extended Bill of Rights). Consequently, the main question is, How should Supreme Court justices choose among alternative interpretations when they apply the extended Bill of Rights to a particular case?

One way to answer this question is to survey the kinds of reasons that can support or oppose constitutional interpretations. When judges argue for their interpretations and when others criticize or praise judicial decisions, they usually base their arguments on:

(i) the meanings of words in the Constitution,

(ii) the intentions of the authors of the Constitution,

(iii) precedents set by past judges, and

(iv) value judgments.

Of course, each of these factors is complex in itself and in its interactions with the others.

Many of the controversies about constitutional interpretation can be understood as being about the nature of these reasons and about how much weight, if any, each reason should have. Advocates of judicial restraint criticize judicial activists for basing their decisions on illegitimate reasons, such as the judge's own value judgments. Similarly, interpretivists argue that their opponents are not really interpreting when they use precedents that go beyond the Constitution itself. And advocates of a living constitution oppose restricting judges to reasons that reflect the distant past. All of these debates, then, are essentially about which reasons judges may or should use in interpreting the Constitution.

Choosing among these reasons amounts to deciding how to distribute power in our society. Judges will have tremendous power if, for example, they are allowed to use their own values to overturn legislative actions. It will be harder for judges to overturn legislation if judges are restricted to other reasons, such as original intent. Thus, the basic issue is about how much and what kinds of power judges should have.

One way to resolve this issue is to apply a background political theory. Some theorists argue that all legitimate authority comes from the people or the majority. On this view, since Supreme Court justices are not elected, they should not use their own value judgments unless they are explicitly authorized to do so by the meaning or intention of the Constitution. Opponents respond that the extended Bill of Rights is supposed to protect minorities and individuals against majorities, but these rights cannot be protected if judges are not allowed to go beyond what the majority explicitly approves. The proper distribution of power also hinges on how likely various institutions are to make mistakes. Some theorists argue that judges have less access to general information, expertise, and time than legislators. Opponents respond that legislators are subject to some kinds of political pressures that do not affect judges with life tenure and that judges receive more detailed information about the particular cases before them. A third issue concerns stability. Some theorists argue that judges must be empowered to adapt constitutional law to changing circumstances. Their opponents emphasize that too much change can create chaos and shatter legitimate expectations. All of these factors need to be considered in determining how much power judges should have and, thus, what kinds of reasons judges should use in reaching their decisions.

Meanings

One of the best-known approaches to constitutional interpretation is originalism. Originalists claim that the Constitution should be interpreted solely or mainly according to certain facts about the time of its origin—either the original meanings of its words or the original intentions of its authors.

The original meanings of words are emphasized by many judges and theorists.[5] Justice Hugo L. Black wrote, "I prefer to put my faith in the words of the written Constitution itself rather than to rely on the shifting, day-to-day standards of fairness of individual judges."[6] Similarly, in this anthology, Robert Bork writes, "What is the meaning of a rule that judges should not change? It is . . . what the public of that time would have understood the words to mean."[7] The main point in both cases is to exclude reliance on judicial value judgments.

This commitment to meaning comes in various strengths. Some theorists claim that judges should never base their interpretations on anything other than meaning. Others allow that, when meaning is indeterminate, interpretations can be based on other reasons. A still weaker view is that meaning always has some force but can be overridden by other factors in conflicts. All of these views agree that meaning provides a reason that should be considered in evaluating possible interpretations.

There is much common sense behind this general approach. Just as we cannot interpret a newspaper without reading its words, so we cannot interpret the Constitution without reading its words. And words are useless without meanings. One cannot adequately interpret the Second Amendment "right of the people to keep and bear arms" if one assumes that the word "arms" means "appendages extending from the upper body." The meanings of words might not be the end of interpretation, but they are at least part of the beginning.

Nonetheless, this simple appeal hides a host of complications. To interpret the Constitution solely by the common meanings of its words leads quickly to absurdity. The Eighth Amendment reads, "Excessive bail shall not be required, nor excessive fines imposed, nor cruel and unusual punishments inflicted." According to the common meaning of the word "and," a punishment that is cruel but not unusual is not both cruel and unusual. Thus, if we interpret the Eighth Amendment according to common meanings, it allows states to torture as long as they torture often enough! Similarly, the First Amendment reads, "Congress shall make no law . . . abridging the freedom of speech." If this were interpreted strictly according to the common meanings of the words "no" and "freedom" and "speech," it would rule out laws against perjury and false advertising. Finally, the Fourteenth Amendment reads in part, "No State shall . . . deny to any person within its jurisdiction the equal protection of the laws." If we interpret this clause according to the common meaning of the word "protection," it would not rule out a state law that provides goods or services (such as transportation) to one group but not to another, as long as both groups are equally protected from injury and loss.

Of course, none of these amendments is or should be interpreted in these ways. The question is how to avoid these absurdities. There are several possibilities.

First, even though common meaning cannot be the sole basis or an absolute basis for constitutional interpretation, one still can argue that it provides a reason for interpretation that can be overridden by other reasons when it points to absurd results. But then we need to know how strong this reason is and what other kinds of reasons there are in order to determine when common meaning is overridden.

A second way to avoid the above absurdities is to turn from common meaning to technical meaning. A technical meaning is just a common meaning within a smaller community, such as the legal community. The law is famous for its technical meanings, and the Constitution does include many technical terms, such as "Grand Jury" in the Fifth Amendment and "Suits at common law" in the Seventh Amendment. If the phrase "cruel and unusual" is interpreted as a single unit with a technical meaning, the Eighth Amendment might rule out cruel punishment even when it is not unusual. But then we face another question: *Which* technical meaning? The relevant technical meaning seems clear in some cases, but not in others. If "freedom of speech" is not abridged by perjury laws, what does abridge this freedom? If "protection" in the equal protection clause does not mean just protection against injury or loss, what exactly does have to be equal? There are many alternatives, none is defined in the amendment, and none is agreed on throughout the legal community, so judges have to decide among alternative technical meanings in order to decide among alternative interpretations. The notion of technical meaning alone provides no guidance, so we need to turn to other kinds of reasons in order to justify an interpretation according to any particular technical meaning.

A third possibility is to interpret the Constitution according to speaker's meaning instead of word meaning. Word meaning, which we have been discussing so far, is the conventional meaning of a word throughout a community across a variety of contexts. In contrast, speaker's meaning refers to what a speaker meant to say by the words, which is often analyzed as the beliefs that the speaker intended to cause in an audience by uttering those words on that particular occasion. For example, if George says, "The president is an idiot," George does not mean to say that the president has the mental capacity of a three year old, even if this is what his words mean. All he means to say is that the president makes many serious mistakes.

The notion of speaker's meaning helps to avoid the absurd interpretations mentioned above. Although the framers said "cruel and unusual," they probably meant to say "cruel or unusual." They intended to create the belief that cruel punishments are forbidden even if they are not unusual. And even though the First Amendment says, "Congress shall make no law . . . abridging the freedom of speech," the framers and ratifiers might have meant to say something less absolute. These examples suggest that speaker's meaning should sometimes take precedence when it conflicts with word meaning. But it is not clear that speaker's meaning should always take precedence. After all, what was ratified were the words of an amendment, not any particular speaker's meaning. And people who want to follow the law often read the words in the law rather than doing the historical research necessary to determine a speaker's meaning on a particular occasion. Finally, since speaker's meaning is a kind of intention (an intention to create a belief in an audience), it suffers from the same general problems as other intentions, which will be discussed in the next section.

Before turning to intentions, we need to ask whether appeals to meaning really do allow judges to avoid value judgments. The avoidance of value judgments is not the only reason to base interpretations on meanings, but it is one of the main goals of originalists who emphasize meaning.

The trickiest cases occur when the words of the Constitution are evaluative, as they often are, especially in the extended Bill of Rights. The terms "unreasonable" in the Fourth Amendment, "due" and "just" in the Fifth Amendment, "excessive" and "cruel" in the Eighth Amendment, "rights" in the Ninth Amendment, and "due" again in the Fourteenth Amendment are all explicitly evaluative. Even phrases like "free exercise" and "freedom of speech" in the First Amendment and "liberty" and "equal" in the Fourteenth Amendment seem to be implicitly evaluative, especially if they are interpreted according to technical or speaker's meanings.

Consider the word "cruel" in the Eighth Amendment. Although this position is controversial, let us assume that the ratifiers agreed that a punishment is cruel only when it causes unnecessary physical suffering and that hanging is not cruel by this standard. How then should we interpret the evaluative term "cruel"?

One possibility is that present judges should interpret the term "cruel" to apply to and only to those particular cases that the ratifiers explicitly considered. Then hanging is not unconstitutional. On this theory, it does not matter whether present judges believe that hanging is cruel. Judges are required to apply the standards and beliefs of the ratifiers instead of imposing their own.

Another option is for judges to interpret the Eighth Amendment by the general standards of the ratifiers without necessarily applying those standards in the same way. A judge would then have to find a punishment cruel only when it causes unnecessary physical suffering, but the judge need not accept the ratifiers' view that hanging meets this standard if new evidence shows that hanging causes physical suffering, and if less painful methods (such as lethal injection) are now available.

A third possibility is that a judge should find hanging unconstitutional if it is cruel, regardless of whether hanging meets the standards of the ratifiers. In applying this interpretation of the amendment to cases, judges will have to use their own best judgment of the proper standards of cruelty.[8] They will have to make their own value judgments.

Which approach fits the words of the amendment? It is striking that the Eighth Amendment does not mention the ratifier's beliefs, intentions, or standards. It uses the word "cruel" without elaboration. One still might claim that the speaker's standards or common standards at the time are part of the meaning of evaluative words like "cruel." But this claim cannot be right. If I say that something is cruel, and you deny that it is cruel, because we use different standards of cruelty, then we are not using the word "cruel" with different meanings. We are disagreeing substantively about the proper standards of cruelty. In order to understand such disputes, the meaning of the word "cruel" cannot be tied to any particular standard of cruelty. Consequently, the meanings of the words in the Eighth Amendment seem to direct judges to use their own standards of what is cruel.[9]

Originalists would object that judges must remain neutral in order to ensure impartiality, legitimacy, and stability. However, even originalists should admit that there is nothing wrong with judges using their own value judgments *if* they are authorized by law to do so. If the framers or the ratifiers wanted future judges to follow the framers' or the ratifiers' standards, then they could have said so explicitly and specified those standards. But they did not. In fact, many of the framers and ratifiers kept their memoirs secret. Their silence suggests that the ratifiers wanted to authorize future judges to use their own standards instead of the standards of the framers or ratifiers. Another possible explanation for this silence is that the ratifiers could not agree on specific standards, but that hardly speaks in favor of restricting future judges to any particular standards.

Still, there are limits. This argument applies only to the extent that a constitutional provision includes evaluative language. The Eighth Amendment refers to cruelty, so judges can rule out punishments for being cruel, but not for being ugly or expensive. There are other arguments for allowing judicial value judgments (which we will discuss below), but the language of the Constitution cannot authorize any use of judicial value judgments except where the language is evaluative.

In any case, appeals to meaning cannot avoid *all* judicial value judgments. Some words in the Constitution seem to direct judges to use their own best moral judgment. Value judgments are also necessary to determine when to override common meaning or to choose a technical meaning. We will also see how value judgments are needed to determine speaker's meanings, as with other intentions. In all of these ways, meaning does not exclude, but rather requires, value judgments by judges.

Intentions

Originalists also often try to avoid judicial value judgments by appealing to original intentions. For example, in a public school prayer case, Chief Justice Rehnquist wrote, "As drafters of our Bill of Rights, the Framers inscribed the principles that control today. Any deviation from their intentions frustrates the permanence of that Charter and will only lead to the type of unprincipled decisionmaking that has plagued our Establishment Clause cases since Everson."[10] Similarly,

Bork argued in an early article that the primary way to derive rights from the Constitution is "to take from the document rather specific values that text or history show the framers actually to have intended and which are capable of being translated into principled rules."[11]

Such appeals to intention are often run together with appeals to meaning. After all, the language of a constitutional provision is strong evidence of the intention behind it. Nonetheless, intention and meaning can conflict. Whenever words are used to reach a goal, there can be cases where following the common meanings (or even the intended meanings) of the words will frustrate the intended goal. In addition, meaning and intention are determined by different kinds of evidence. Legislative debates have a special place in establishing legislative intent but not in establishing common word meaning, and statements by private citizens about other topics can be evidence of word meaning but not of legislative intention. For all of these reasons, intentions must be distinguished from word meanings.

Appeals to intention can vary in strength. Some claim that the only way to justify any interpretation of the Constitution is to show that it matches the framers' intentions. A weaker position is that judges must never interpret the Constitution so as to conflict with original intent, but, when alternatives are consistent with original intent, judges may base their decisions on other factors.[12] A still weaker position sees original intent as just one factor that can be overridden by others in making judicial interpretations and decisions.

There is much common sense behind such appeals to intentions. When asked, "Do you know the time?" it is obnoxious to overlook the speaker's intentions and just answer "Yes." To some, it seems just as obtuse to interpret the Constitution apart from its underlying intentions. Intent theorists also argue that legislative intentions provide the only way to avoid value judgments by judges when they interpret the Constitution. And following original intent is also supposed to bring stability to constitutional law, since past intentions cannot be changed by present judges.

As with meaning, this seemingly simple appeal to intention hides a host of complications. For one thing, an intention is a mental state.[13] But the Constitution was written and ratified by many people, not just one, and it is hard to see how groups can literally have minds, mental states, or intentions. Admittedly, everyone in a group can intend the same thing at some level. Each member of an orchestra can intend to play *some* notes in a performance of a symphony even if they play different notes. This makes it natural to say that the orchestra intends to play the symphony even though no single member of the orchestra intends to play the whole symphony. Still, there are special problems with constitutional intentions. The groups that originated the Constitution were not as unified as an orchestra. Several groups were involved, and they disagreed deeply both among and within themselves. So we need to look more carefully at the groups whose intentions are at issue.

The first question is, Whose intentions are relevant? Many intent theorists claim that provisions of the Constitution should be interpreted according to the intentions of the people who wrote them, namely, the framers. However, it was the ratifiers who turned the words of the framers into a part of the Constitution, and it is the ratifiers, not the framers, who represent the majority. Consequently, the concerns with democracy and with the creators of the Constitution, which provide the main rationales for original intent theories, should lead original intent theorists to emphasize the intentions of the ratifiers.

Whichever group we focus on, we still run into the problem of discord. Like the framers, the ratifiers were numerous and contentious. Even those who voted for an amendment disagreed in many ways. The resulting provisions were often compromises that did not fully satisfy anyone.[14] Some ratifiers undoubtedly voted for clauses that they did not like because they liked the rest of the amendment or the rest of the Bill of Rights. Probably, some of those who voted for a clause hoped that it would not be interpreted literally or strictly, while others hoped that it would be. Furthermore, the historical records are often too incomplete or conflicting to tell what the original intent was, or even whether there was one.

These problems do not show that all appeals to intentions are pointless. The ratifiers did sometimes agree on general goals and on some applications. It seems clear that the ratifiers of the First Amendment intended the free speech and press clauses to secure open debate about governmental officials and policies (at least) and that the ratifiers of the Eighth Amendment intended its cruel and unusual punishment clause to rule out some forms of physical torture then being practiced. The Second Amendment even includes an explicit statement of its intention: The right to bear arms is retained in order to protect "the security of a free State." These clear intentions, admittedly, do not resolve many (if any) controversial cases, but intention theorists can still insist that ratifiers' intentions should be respected at least when they are clear.[15] Some intent theorists go further and claim that judges should not overturn any legislation unless it violates the clear intent of a constitutional provision. This theory might permit some horrendous legislation, but these intent theorists respond that it is not the job of the courts to correct every mistake made by the legislature. Usually legislatures have to clean up their own acts, or the people must clean them up through elections.

Another serious problem for intent theorists is that, even when intentions are clear, they are multileveled. Presumably, all ratifiers of the

Fourteenth Amendment intended to add the words "equal protection of the laws" (among others) to the Constitution and to create the belief that states would not be allowed to deny equal protection of the laws. But the ratifiers also differed in some intentions. Some ratifiers probably intended only to reduce the number of physical attacks on former slaves and to enable them to achieve greater political equality. Others probably also intended to increase social and economic equality for former slaves and possibly also for some other groups or for all individuals.[16]

Which of these intentions should ground constitutional interpretation? How one answers this question determines what is ruled out by the equal protection clause. If an interpreter focuses on the intention to secure political equality for former slaves, then the equal protection clause would not be taken to apply at all to social and economic inequalities, and it would not be considered to protect other disadvantaged groups. If an interpreter sees the equal protection clause as intended to protect all disadvantaged groups and to protect them against social and economic harms, then it would be seen to rule out many more state actions, while allowing affirmative action quotas (unless such quotas harm disadvantaged groups). And if the clause is seen as intended to guarantee equal treatment in all areas to all citizens as individuals, then it would be taken to rule out affirmative action quotas because of how they affect members of groups that are not disadvantaged. Thus, the force of the equal protection clause depends directly on the intention used to interpret it.

How can we decide which intention to apply? We cannot determine what the ratifiers "really" intended[17] because individual ratifiers had real intentions at several levels of generality and different ratifiers intended different things. We cannot determine which intention they would have considered to be most important because it is too hard to answer questions about what they would have done if they had foreseen the problem.[18] So we have to turn to political considerations about the best distribution of power. Those who want to limit judicial power will want to limit judges to basing decisions on the most concrete intentions and/or on cases that were talked about in legislative debates. But judges will have much more power if they are allowed to base their interpretations on more abstract intentions. As its preamble tells us, the most general intentions of the whole Constitution are "to form a more perfect Union, establish Justice, insure domestic Tranquillity, provide for the common defence, promote the general Welfare, and secure the Blessings of Liberty to ourselves and our Posterity." If judges are allowed to interpret the Constitution according to these general goals, then they can overrule any statute that interferes with "the general Welfare" in their opinion. If neither extreme seems plausible, one might try to specify some intermediate level of intention or maybe some minimal level of agreement among the ratifiers. But it will not be easy to specify or apply such a compromise, and one will need some reason to pick one intermediate level instead of another. In the end, even original intent theorists must implicitly base their interpretations on their own value judgments about who should have power in our society.

Value judgments also enter into decision making in other ways. Once an intended goal has been identified, judges have to ask which decision in the present case provides the best means to further that goal. Judges must also use their value judgments when different goals from different parts of the Constitution come into conflict. In the case of conflicts between the First and Fourteenth amendments, which were ratified at different times, there was no single group of ratifiers. A judge relying on original intent, therefore, would have to choose between the goals of the different groups. In the case of conflicts within the Bill of Rights, the ratifiers did not provide any way to weigh the relative importance of the conflicting goals. Since judges have to take into account the whole Constitution and not just its parts,[19] they cannot avoid weighing these conflicting intentions. For all these reasons, original intent theories cannot avoid judicial value judgments. These problems do not show that intentions never count at all, but they do demonstrate that judges have to look beyond intentions alone when they interpret the Constitution.

Precedents

Instead of looking back to original meaning and intention, judges often base their interpretations and decisions on judicial precedents. In fact, the doctrine of *stare decisis*, which says that established precedents should usually be allowed to stand, is often claimed to be essential to law in general. For example, in a recent case on abortion, *Planned Parenthood of Southeastern Pennsylvania v. Casey*, the Supreme Court said, "We recognize that no judicial system could do society's work if it eyed each issue afresh in every case that raised it. Indeed, the very concept of the rule of law underlying our own Constitution requires such continuity over time that a respect for precedent is, by definition, indispensable."[20]

At the same time, as the Court also acknowledged in *Casey*, a precedent may on occasion be overturned. A ruling can be seen as an error if it is simply unworkable, if the doctrine informing the ruling was abandoned in light of developing principles of law, or if the ruling depended on factual claims that are viewed as mistaken. In *Casey*, the Court ruled that the relevant precedent, *Roe v. Wade*,[21] was not unworkable in practice, was not dependent on obsolete constitutional doctrine, and was not undermined by new empirical findings. Thus, the Court concluded, the precedent should be allowed to stand.

This reliance on precedent might seem unwarranted to those who distrust judges and want to limit their power. The judges who wrote the opinions and made the decisions in past cases were not elected, so their authority is just as questionable as that of present judges. Past judges also faced the same limits on their expertise and time, so there is little reason to believe that they were less likely to make mistakes than present judges.

Nonetheless, following precedent promotes several goals. First, the law becomes more stable. Legitimate expectations are disappointed less often since many people try to determine the legal consequences of their actions by seeking advice from lawyers, who base their counsel on their reading of prior cases. Second, large numbers of decisions can be made more efficiently by following precedent, since judges do not have to decide each case individually. And, finally, judges who follow precedent are supposed to avoid value judgments of their own and thus remain impartial about the particular case at hand.

To say that it is desirable, or even imperative, for judges to follow precedent does not, however, indicate *how* judges are supposed to do this. How are judges to decide which precedents to follow and how to apply them to the case at hand?

Some arguments from precedents are based on analogies. If a statute was found unconstitutional in a past case, and if there are important similarities between the past case and a present case, and if there is no important difference between the past case and the present case that could justify a different decision in the present case, then the past decision is seen as reason to find the statute in the present case unconstitutional as well.[22] Such an argument need not depend on any general rule of law, since the judge need not give a complete list of the kinds of similarities and differences that might justify a decision in the present case.

Opponents of an argument from analogy have two ways to respond. They can distinguish the precedent by finding an important difference between the past case and the present case, or they can overturn the precedent by arguing that it was a mistake. But these responses are not always easy to defend. Although it is easy to find some difference between a past case and a present case, it is not as easy to show why this difference is important enough to justify a different decision in the present case and in others like it. And most judges are very reluctant to overturn precedents (especially multiple, long-standing ones by respected justices) and accept the burden of showing why the precedents were mistaken. Thus, arguments from analogy do put some pressure on opponents to come up with independent reasons to distinguish or over-turn the precedent.

Such arguments from analogy occur often in common law where no statute or constitution applies, and they can also be found less often in constitutional law. Richard Epstein's contribution to this anthology is an argument for applying the analogical method used in the common law to constitutional cases.[23] Epstein discusses the desirability of using this approach to interpret passages of the Constitution dealing with searches and seizures, takings, free speech, and the free exercise of religion.

Instead of drawing analogies to single precedents, judges often survey a large number of precedents and look for general legal principles that underlie or justify the group as a whole. For example, in a case concerning the establishment of religion, *Lemon v. Kurtzman*, the majority stated:

> Every analysis in this area must begin with consideration of the cumulative criteria developed by the Court over many years. Three such tests may be gleaned from our cases. First, the statute must have a secular legislative purpose; second, its principal or primary effect must be one that neither advances nor inhibits religion . . . ; finally, the statute must not foster "an excessive government entanglement with religion."[24]

This kind of argument is discussed by Dworkin in this anthology. Dworkin compares a judge who tries to make his decisions fit groups of precedents to a chain novelist who tries to write a new chapter that fits previous chapters written by other people. In both cases, past materials are supposed to constrain what can be done in the present. Of course, groups of precedents often do not point to a single simple principle. Precedents can conflict, and then judges have to decide which one to uphold and justify. Even when precedents are consistent and correct, judges can always construct more than one principle to justify them.[25] Some of these principles will seem unreasonable, but to tell which ones are unreasonable requires judges to make value judgments. And sometimes judges must decide among several apparently reasonable principles. Thus, groups of precedents alone do not always determine a judge's decision.

Yet another form of argument from precedent occurs when judges apply a formula from an opinion in a past case.[26] Many cases after *Lemon* were decided simply by applying the three-pronged test from the *Lemon* opinion.[27] Such tests or interpretations are supposed to elaborate the meaning or purpose of the Constitutional provision and to provide guidance in deciding subsequent cases.

It is striking that the formulas used to decide future cases can come from dissenting opinions, inessential dicta, or even footnotes. One extremely influential dissent was in *Abrams v. United States*, where Holmes argued that "the ultimate good desired is better reached by free trade in ideas."[28] Another important free speech precedent, the "fighting words" doctrine, was introduced in dicta in *Chaplinsky v. New Hampshire* and was not found in the statement of the decision itself.[29] And one of the most famous precedents is footnote four in *United States v. Carolene Products Co.*, where Justice Stone argued that the mere rationality of a statute may not be enough to justify a law in cases involving "discrete and insular minorities" where the possibility of prejudice "may call for a correspondingly more searching judicial inquiry."[30] This statement, in a mere footnote in a case about interstate shipments of filled milk, has been cited as a precedent in cases dealing with subjects as diverse as freedom of religion and affirmative action.[31]

As the use of the *Carolene Products* footnote illustrates, judges who apply a formula from a prior opinion do not assume that the past case is closely analogous to the present case. They need not even assume that the prior decision was correct. For example, in the *Bakke* decision on affirmative action, Justice Powell quoted the majority opinion in *Korematsu*: "[A]ll legal restrictions which curtail the rights of a single racial group are immediately suspect. That is not to say that all such restrictions are unconstitutional. It is to say that courts must subject them to the most rigid scrutiny."[32] Powell relied heavily on this passage, despite strong criticisms of the *Korematsu* decision, which allowed the internment of Japanese Americans during World War II, and despite many important differences between the internments reviewed in *Korematsu* and the affirmative action programs reviewed in *Bakke*. Thus, Powell's argument rested completely on the quoted formula.

The sources of these formulas raise questions about why judges should follow them. In addition to the usual arguments for *stare decisis* outlined above and the attractiveness of the formulas themselves, some formulas seem to carry more weight because they were announced by judges who are especially esteemed and trusted. In his contribution to this anthology, Mark Tushnet suggests that assessment of a justice's character *should* play a crucial role in determining the merit of his or her interpretation of the Constitution.

Since formulas drawn from precedent opinions are written in general language, the formulas themselves often have to be interpreted. Later decisions can then explain or refine the formulas, and can, in turn, be used as reasons for even later decisions. This whole process seems desirable to those who trust judges and want a living constitution to respond to contemporary problems and circumstances. Opponents, however, argue that it is the job of the legislature to make new laws.

Judges are not elected, so too much reliance on judicial precedents can systematically frustrate the will of the majority. Moreover, if judges make mistakes, and future judges follow their lead just because the precedents are "established," then they can lead our legal system and our society down a blind alley. These dangers will convince those who distrust judges to give less weight to precedents, especially precedents that have no independent basis in the meaning or intent of the Constitution. The issue of how much weight judges should give precedents is, viewed in this way, simply the issue of how much power judges should have relative to legislators.

Even if it is granted that the judiciary should follow precedents, it is not clear how much, if at all, precedents really can constrain or guide judges. Numerous problems arise in any appeal to precedent, whether it involves the use of analogy, the derivation of a general principle from a series of cases, or the application of a previously stated formula. One common problem is being unable to find and agree on an appropriate description of the issue in the present case. For example, in *Bowers v. Hardwick*, the Supreme Court upheld Georgia's antisodomy law because the majority considered the issue to be "whether the Federal Constitution confers a fundamental right upon homosexuals to engage in sodomy," and they found no precedents supporting such a right. The dissent, in contrast, argued that *Bowers* was not about homosexual sodomy in particular, but rather "about 'the most comprehensive of rights and the right most valued by civilized men,' namely, 'the right to be let alone',"[33] and they found many precedents for that more general right. *Bowers* thus shows that the proper level of generality is crucial for precedents, as it was for intentions. Whether Georgia's anti-sodomy law violated a constitutionally protected right depends on how one describes the right. And the appropriate level of description is not determined by the precedents themselves. Indeed, which precedents are relevant depends on how the issue in question in the present case is described.

Another problem with appeals to precedent is that prior rulings can (and sometimes should) be overturned.[34] How can the Court decide *which* precedents to overturn? Some precedents are overruled because they depend on factual claims that are later refuted. Other precedents are overturned because they conflict with recent developments in constitutional law that the Court endorses. Some justices want to overturn precedents that go beyond the original meaning or intention of the Constitution. And some precedents seem to be overruled mainly because they are seen to be at odds with justice. Many of these decisions to overrule precedents, therefore, rely on value judgments by the Court. Furthermore, if the Court always has the power to overturn precedents that are bad enough, then, even when the Court decides not to overturn a precedent, its decision must be based implicitly on the value judgment that the precedent is not bad enough to be overturned.

All of these considerations suggest that judges cannot simply apply precedents without relying on their own value judgments. In drawing analogies to precedents, judges need to decide which similarities and differences are important. In deriving general principles from groups of precedents, judges must decide which principle best justifies the precedents overall. When judges cite formulas from precedent opinions, they need to decide which formulas should be given force. Judges also need to decide how the present issue should be described. And, finally, they have to decide whether a precedent is bad enough to be overturned.

Values

As we have seen, judges often base their interpretations on value judgments. But which kinds of values? Most often, judges appeal to moral values, but some judges also appeal to special institutional values and to efficiency or other economic values that are not clearly moral in nature. Some important formulas, such as Holmes's "clear and present danger" test,[35] even seem to be accepted partly because they are so pithy. Although all of these kinds of values can be relevant, moral values usually have the most force, and we will have them primarily in mind in the following discussion.

Moral values affect constitutional interpretation in many ways. Judges invoke moral values when they decide whether to base their interpretations on meanings or on intentions or on precedents. Judges also use moral values to determine the meanings, intentions, or precedents in a particular case. And they must appeal to moral values when meanings, intentions, and precedents fail to yield a satisfactory or determinate interpretation.

Judges depend most clearly on moral values when they appeal to "unenumerated rights"—rights that are not mentioned explicitly in the Constitution. The most famous and controversial example of an unenumerated right is the supposed right to privacy. Privacy is not mentioned specifically anywhere in the Constitution, but a right to privacy was accepted by the Court in *Griswold v. Connecticut*.[36] Justice Douglas argued that several precedents and five amendments in the Bill of Rights "create zones of privacy," but he admitted that none of these precedents or amendments explicitly mentions a general right to privacy. He concluded by saying, "We deal with a right to privacy older than the Bill of Rights."[37] Here, he seems to admit that the right to privacy rests at least partly on values that are independent of laws or precedents.

Such uses of morality lead to a dilemma. When fundamental rights are at stake, it seems especially important for judges' decisions to be in line with what morality and justice require. Yet it is precisely in such areas that deep controversies arise and there is little consensus about what justice and morality require. When moral values are invoked in such controversial areas, we need to ask, How can judges justify using one moral value instead of another?

One possible source of moral values is tradition. The Court often appeals to tradition, as it did when it characterized fundamental rights as those "deeply rooted in this Nation's history and tradition."[38] The point of relying on tradition, as Justice White wrote in *Bowers*, is for the Court "to assure itself and the public that announcing rights not readily identifiable in the Constitution's text involves much more than the imposition of the Justices' own choice of values on the States and the Federal Government."[39] Values are supposed to be less subjective and objectionable when they have been accepted by many people for a long time.

However, as J. M. Balkin argues in this anthology, judicial value judgments inevitably come into play in determining which traditions are applicable and which rights are "deeply rooted" in "our" tradition. Homosexual relationships have a documented history going back at least to ancient Greece, but Chief Justice Burger wrote in *Bowers* that "[c]ondemnation of those practices is firmly rooted in Judaeo-Christian moral and ethical standards."[40] The choice of Judaeo-Christian standards and traditions over the others that citizens are free to adopt in our pluralistic democracy reflects a value judgment by the Court. Furthermore, since a tradition—like a precedent—can be described at various levels of generality, whether the tradition in question was described as protecting the right of intimate association or as protecting the right to engage in homosexual sodomy also depended on the values of the justices.

In other cases concerning fundamental rights, the Court has sometimes rejected the criterion that the right be "deeply rooted in this Nation's history and tradition." For example, in *Loving v. Virginia*,[41] the Court invalidated Virginia's law prohibiting interracial marriages in spite of the fact that prohibitions against miscegenation were deeply rooted in that state's legal, social, and religious traditions. Some long-standing traditions are morally wrong, and the Court has felt free to invalidate laws based on them. But when the Court bases a decision on whether a tradition is immoral, it is clearly applying its own views about what is immoral and what is not.

Judges might try to avoid imposing their own moral values on the Constitution by relying instead on the current views of the majority of citizens. An immediate problem with this solution is that it would undermine one main purpose of having a Bill of Rights, namely, to protect the rights of unpopular minorities against majoritarian legislation.

Judges have on occasion attempted to protect minorities against prejudices by appealing to a "reasonable person" standard. In *Pope v. Illinois*, for example, Justice White wrote: "The proper inquiry is not whether an ordinary member of any given community would find serious literary, artistic, political or scientific value in allegedly obscene material, but whether a reasonable person would find such value in the material, taken as a whole."[42] The problem with this strategy is that we often disagree about what a "reasonable person" would decide. He— or is it she?—is no more, some would argue, than a rationalization for the imposition of the judges' own moral preferences.

What judges take to be objective positions can be unintentionally biased, if they fail to take into account the different perspectives and circumstances of those unlike themselves. In this anthology, Martha Minow and Patricia Williams emphasize the importance of understanding different perspectives, especially those of traditionally marginalized groups. It is easy to mistake one's partial view of the law for the truth if one is ignorant of how it looks to those in different contexts. As Minow shows, supposedly objective notions of what equality requires can lead to laws that disadvantage groups of people who are in important respects different from the supposed norm. Providing equal opportunity for persons with disabilities, for example, can require treating them *un*equally, since they need special facilities or services to be able to participate fully in an educational or an employment setting. But unless one is able to view the world from the perspective of a person with a disability, one may not notice these needs and may continue to think that equality means that everyone should be treated the same.

Williams and other critical race theorists have employed first-person narratives about their own and others' experiences of racial discrimination and harassment in order to expand the partial vision of those who are not members of targeted racial minorities. Such stories are intended to provide imaginative access to others' experiences and can serve as correctives to uninformed or biased value judgments by judges who usually do not come from such marginalized groups.

A different way to correct judicial value judgments is by appealing to moral theory. Some might claim that judges should directly apply a moral theory in order to determine which decision is morally correct. A less direct application of moral theory is advocated by Ronald Dworkin in this anthology. In Dworkin's view, constitutional interpretation involves surveying our legal history and discerning those principles inherent in it that make it "the best it can be" from the standpoint of a theory of political morality.

The question that immediately arises from an appeal to moral theory is, Which moral theory? Some might suppose that we should focus on the moral precepts of Christianity, since this religion has been dominant in our country. However, there are many variations and even conflicts within Christian moral precepts. Furthermore, appeals to religion are not persuasive to those who do not accept the dominant religion. And even people who do share religious beliefs often recognize the inappropriateness of using them to interpret the Constitution, especially in light of the First Amendment prohibition against a governmental establishment of religion.

Another suggestion is that judges should choose interpretations that bring the greatest benefit to society in the long run. According to this utilitarian theory, for example, the Court should interpret the First Amendment so as to allow legislation banning pornography if and only if such interpretations or legislation would maximize social utility in the long run. Many object that utilitarianism allows the majority to legislate away minority rights, but social utility still might be one of the factors that should guide judicial decisions. This view is shared by pragmatists like Richard Posner in this anthology, who argues that judges should base their interpretations at least partly on social consequences as determined by various sciences, especially economics.

Dworkin denies that judges should base their interpretations on policy considerations designed to further social utility. In his view, although legislators may base their decisions on policies, judges should decide solely on the basis of principles, which specify rights. Rights in his account function as trumps over considerations of social utility. Even if a community would be better off banning pornography, for example, judges should rule such legislation unconstitutional if that policy would violate the rights of pornography producers or users.

But which moral rights do people have? Dworkin has his own theory,[43] partly based on John Rawls's *A Theory of Justice*.[44] But some judges might prefer a different moral theory, for example, that in Robert Nozick's *Anarchy, State, and Utopia*.[45] John Hart Ely parodied Dworkin's approach by imagining a scenario in which judges argued "'We like Rawls, you like Nozick. We win, 6-3.'"[46] Ely argued that if judges rely on moral theory "there will be a systematic bias in judicial choice of fundamental values, unsurprisingly in favor of the values of the upper-middle, professional class from which most lawyers and judges, and for that matter most philosophers, are drawn."[47]

In order to respond to such a charge, Dworkin needs to show that his theory is correct or at least preferable to its competitors. Proving that superiority will not be easy. Moral philosophers have developed a number of sophisticated methods for deciding among moral theories, but there is little consensus on the right method or even on which theory is favored by which method.

One way to seek greater agreement is to focus on some special subset of moral theory.[48] For example, in a series of recent articles, John Rawls has attempted to define a political conception of the right by "identifying a partial similarity in the structure of citizens' permissible conceptions of the good once they are regarded as free and equal persons."[49] This political conception of the right might provide a justifiable basis for constitutional interpretation, even if more comprehensive theories of the good cannot do so. However, it is still not clear exactly what would be included in this conception of the right or why it is more justifiable to base constitutional interpretation on it. It is also not clear why one's political conception of the right should take priority over one's comprehensive conception of the good when the two conflict.

Given the difficulties of justifying moral judgments on the basis of tradition, contemporary opinion, and moral theory, it seems inevitable that judges sometimes base their interpretations on their own personal moral opinions or intuitions. This is upsetting to those who fear that judges are likely to get things wrong. Even those who share judges' convictions often deny that unelected judges have the authority to impose their values on the majority. And if judges vary widely in their value judgments, chaos and instability will result from allowing judges to base their interpretations on their personal moral beliefs.

On the other side, there are also costs if judges are *not* allowed to use their value judgments about the case at hand. Judges will not be able to avoid clear disasters that they can now see in a particular case, but that the legislators did not foresee when they wrote the general law. And as Mark Tushnet suggests in his contribution to this anthology, a proper judicial selection process that pays sufficient attention to judges' character and experience can reduce the dangers of judicial reliance on moral intuition.

The basic issue is, again, who should be trusted with power. Those who trust judges and think that legislators will often make mistakes that judges should correct will be inclined to give judges more leeway in using their moral convictions. Those who believe strongly in some moral theory will be inclined to allow judges to base their decisions on that moral theory. And those who distrust both judges and moral theories might want to restrict judges to those value judgments that have the support of popular opinion or tradition.

Almost everyone agrees, though, that the Constitution is a morally justifiable document and that interpretations of it must be in accord with morality. This assumption helps to explain the purpose of having a constitution in the first place. If we did not think that justice required that certain individual rights be safeguarded, for example, it would be hard to explain the point of having a Bill of Rights. In controversial cases involving fundamental liberties or equal protection, we consider it especially important that the Constitution be interpreted in a morally justifiable way. Conservatives may argue that judges should let the majority rule in controversial cases, while liberals may argue that judges should interpret the Constitution so as to limit majoritarian decision making in such cases. But both sides assume that the true Constitution is in line with their moral values. This assumption is questioned by Robin West in her contribution to this anthology. West argues that we need to give up this assumption in order to notice certain aspects of the Constitution that may not be morally justifiable.

Conclusions

We have seen that constitutional interpretations can be based on many different kinds of reasons: meanings, intentions, precedents, and moral values. Each of these reasons is complex in itself, and even more complexities are introduced by the multiplicity of factors and their interactions. It is hard to bring all of these factors together into a coherent overall theory.

One might hope to pick one kind of reason and claim that all constitutional interpretations should be based on that kind of reason alone. The problem is that each of these kinds of reasons seems to produce unacceptable results in some cases when used alone.

A more complex form of theory ranks several different kinds of reasons. A lexical ordering, for example, might claim that meaning must always be considered first, but one can turn to intention when meaning is indeterminate and to precedent when both meaning and intention are indeterminate. Or one might claim that each factor has a certain weight, and the correct interpretation is determined by somehow adding together all of the relevant weights. However, it is hard to see how to formulate and justify any single ordering or system of weights that will yield plausible results in all cases. One might say simply that judges should consider all of the relevant factors in some kind of holistic judgment, but this advice will not provide any guidance to judges or to those who want to evaluate judicial decisions.

If no single reason, ordering, or weighting can cover all cases uniformly like a blanket, then one might turn to a patchwork quilt theory in which different kinds of reasons have different weights in different courts and in different areas of the law. It seems plausible to claim, for example, that precedents should have more weight in lower courts than in the Supreme Court. Although Chief Justice Rehnquist wants the Supreme Court to overturn several important precedents, he wrote, "[U]nless we wish anarchy to prevail within the federal judicial system, a precedent of this [Supreme] Court must be followed by the lower federal courts no matter how misguided the judges of those courts may think it to be."[50] Even within the Supreme Court, one might put more weight on meaning in areas of law where people base their decisions on reading the words of the Constitution, more weight on precedent in areas of law where stability is more important, and more weight on judicial value judgments in areas where stability and notice are less important and where judges are authorized by the very language of the Constitution to use their values. Whether this kind of theory can be worked out in detail remains to be seen, but at least we should not assume that each factor has the same weight throughout all of the different occasions of interpretation.[51]

Notes

1. Respectively, *Planned Parenthood of Southeastern Pennsylvania v. Casey,* 120 L. Ed. 2d 674 (1992), *Lee v. Weisman,* 120 L. Ed. 2d 305 (1992), *R.A.V. v. St. Paul,* 120 L. Ed. 2d 467 (1992), *International Society for Krishna Consciousness, Inc. v. Lee,* 120 L. Ed. 2d 541 (1992), and *Lucas v. South Carolina Coastal Council,* 120 L. Ed. 2d 798 (1992).

2. This focus on judges is questioned by Frederick Schauer in his contribution to this anthology, but our goal here is to introduce the traditional debate.

3. The term "interpretation" is sometimes restricted to tests that are controversial (see Schauer, below, pp. 36-39), but we will focus on the more general notion.

4. Schauer develops this claim below, pp. 29-36.

5. It is also possible to base interpretations on the present meanings of words when these deviate from their original meanings, but most theorists focus on original meaning, and so will we.

6. *In re Winship,* 397 U.S. 358 at 378 (1970) (Black, J., dissenting).

7. Bork, below, pp. 50-51.

8. If a judge takes incorrect standards to be correct and finds a punishment cruel when it is not, then the judge did not really obey the Constitution on this interpretation. Nonetheless, the only way for a judge to *try* to obey the Constitution is to use his or her own best judgment of the correct standards of cruelty.

9. This view is often associated with realist theories of meaning, such as in Michael Moore, "A Natural Law Theory of Interpretation," *Southern California Law Review,* vol. 58 (1985), pp. 277-398; and David Brink, "Legal Theory, Legal Interpretation, and Judicial Review," *Philosophy and Public Affairs,* vol. 17, no. 2 (Spring 1988), pp. 105-48. However, nonrealists can also distinguish word meaning from standards or criteria. See R. M. Hare, *The Language of Morals* (Oxford: Clarendon Press, 1952), ch. 6.

10. *Wallace v. Jaffree*, 478 U.S. 38 at 113 (1984).

11. Robert Bork, "Neutral Principles and Some First Amendment Problems," *Indiana Law Journal*, vol. 47, no. 1 (Fall 1971), p. 17.

12. This was the position of Justice Felix Frankfurter according to Tushnet, below, pp. 220-21.

13. In *Essays on Actions and Events* (New York: Oxford University Press, 1980), Donald Davidson analyzes an intention roughly as a desire plus a belief about how to fulfill the desire. More recently, in *Intention, Plans, and Practical Reason* (Cambridge: Harvard University Press, 1987), Michael Bratman argues that intentions involve choice or planning. Different theories of intention might affect interpretations based on original intentions, but we will not explore these complications here.

14. See Posner's discussion of legislative deals, below, p. 108.

15. Intent theorists can reduce indeterminacy by constructing intentions out of incomplete or conflicting records, much as scientists construct lines through the middle of discordant experimental results. However, intent theorists will need to justify one method of construction as opposed to another, and that will require reasons independent of the intentions themselves.

16. The higher levels of intentions are sometimes called "purposes," but they still lie on the same continuum of levels of generality.

17. Pace Bork, below, pp. 55-56.

18. See Posner's criticisms of imaginative reconstruction, below, pp. 106-8.

19. As is emphasized by John Hart Ely, *Democracy and Distrust* (Cambridge: Harvard University Press, 1980), and Charles Black, *Structure and Relationship in Constitutional Law* (Woodbridge, Conn.: Ox Bow Press, 1969).

20. *Planned Parenthood of Southeastern Pennsylvania v. Casey*, 120 L. Ed. 2d 674 at 699-700 (1992) (citations omitted).

21. 410 U.S. 113 (1973).

22. Some commentators refer to analogies only when the new decision extends the law in controversial ways, but the same basic form of argument is used even when the similarities are obvious to all.

23. In Epstein's version, the chain of analogies begins in paradigm cases determined by common meaning, but similar methods could start either with cases intended by the ratifiers or with precedents that are not grounded in meaning or intention. It is not clear how these different starting points would affect the defensibility or the ultimate results of the method of analogy.

24. 403 U.S. 602 at 612-13 (1971).

25. This problem is similar to Nelson Goodman's "New Riddle of Induction" in *Fact, Fiction, and Forecast* (Indianapolis: Hackett, 1969) and also to Ludwig Wittgenstein's views on following a rule in *Philosophical Investigations*, translated by G.E.M. Anscombe (New York: Macmillan, 1958).

26. In such arguments, the term "precedent" refers to the court's opinion rather than to the facts of the case or the court's decision.

27. For example, cases about school prayer (*Wallace v. Jaffree*, 478 U.S. 38 [1984]) and creationism (*McLean v. The Arkansas Board of Education*, 529 F. Supp. 1255 [1982]).

28. *Abrams v. United States,* 250 U.S. 616 at 630 (1919). Holmes is giving the purpose of the right to free speech rather than a specific test for applying the first amendment, but statements of purpose like this one can greatly influence future decisions.

29. *Chaplinsky v. New Hampshire,* 315 U.S. 568 at 571-72 (1942).

30. 304 U.S. 144 at 152-53 n.4 (1938) (citations omitted).

31. See, for example, *Minersville School District v. Gobitis,* 310 U.S. 586 at 606 (1940) and *Regents of the University of California v. Bakke,* 438 U.S. 265 at 288 and 290 (1978).

32. *Korematsu v. United States,* 323 U.S. 214 at 216 (1944) quoted at *Regents of the University of California v. Bakke,* 438 U.S. 265 at 291 (1978).

33. *Bowers v. Hardwick,* 478 U.S. 186 at 199 (1986).

34. See Bork, below, pp. 61-62, for a list of some important precedents that were overturned.

35. *Schenck v. United States,* 249 U.S. 47 at 52 (1919).

36. 381 U.S. 479 (1965).

37. 381 U.S. 479 at 486 (1965).

38. *Moore v. East Cleveland,* 431 U.S. 494 at 503 (1977).

39. *Bowers v. Hardwick,* 478 U.S. 186 at 191 (1986).

40. *Bowers v. Hardwick,* 478 U.S. 186 at 196 (1986).

41. 388 U.S. 1 (1967).

42. *Pope v. Illinois,* 481 U.S. 497 at 500-01 (1987).

43. See Ronald Dworkin, "What is Equality? Part 1: Equality of Welfare,"*Philosophy and Public Affairs,* vol. 10, no. 3 (1981), pp. 185-246; "What is Equality? Part 2: Equality of Resources," *Philosophy and Public Affairs,* vol. 10, no. 4 (1981), pp. 283-345; "What is Equality? Part 3: The Place of Liberty," *Iowa Law Review,* vol. 73 (1988), pp. 1-54; "What is Equality? Part 4: Political Equality," *University of San Francisco Law Review,* vol. 22 (1988), pp. 1-54; and "Equality, Democracy, and Constitution: We the People in Court," *Alberta Law Review,* vol. 28 (1990), pp. 324-46.

44. Cambridge: Harvard University Press, 1971.

45. New York: Basic Books, 1974.

46. *Democracy and Distrust,* p. 58.

47. *Ibid.,* p. 59.

48. This general kind of move is also made by Dworkin when he restricts judges to principles instead of policies, and by Ely in *Democracy and Distrust* when he argues that judges should appeal only to procedural and not to substantive values.

49. "The Priority of Right and Ideas of the Good," *Philosophy and Public Affairs,* vol. 17, no. 4 (Fall 1988), p. 257. See also John Rawls, "The Idea of an Overlapping Consensus," *Oxford Journal of Legal Studies,* vol. 7, no. 1 (1987), pp. 1-25; John Rawls, "Justice as Fairness: Political not Metaphysical," *Philosophy and Public Affairs,* vol. 14, no. 3 (Summer 1985), pp. 223-51.

50. *Hutto v. Davis,* 454 U.S. 370 at 375 (1982).

51. For helpful comments on this introduction, we would like to thank Ted Brader, Bill Fischel, Bob Fogelin, Natalie Stoljar, and Joan Vogel.

1

THE NATURE OF CONSTITUTIONAL INTERPRETATION

What is constitutional interpretation? It might seem that this question must have a single answer if different theories of constitutional interpretation are to be about a single topic. However, in this volume, Frederick Schauer argues that what counts as an interpretation—and even what counts as the Constitution—will vary from theory to theory, depending on which kinds of reasons are recognized by the theory and which cases are hard cases according to the theory.

Schauer argues that there is also no single answer to the question, How should the Constitution be interpreted? Instead of advocating a single method of constitutional interpretation, Schauer suggests that different methods are appropriate on different occasions. The Constitution is interpreted not only by Supreme Court justices but also by lower court judges, by attorneys-general who decide which cases to prosecute, by police officers who decide when to give Miranda warnings, and by town clerks who decide whether to issue parade permits. These different interpreters face different pressures, possess different information, undergo different training, and have different political views. Consequently, Schauer argues, the best results will be reached more often if different methods are used at different times by different people. As he puts it, constitutional theory should be "interpreter-relative."

Schauer is not saying that interpreters should use whichever method seems right to them at the time. Instead, there is supposed to be an underlying rationale that determines which methods are appropriate in which contexts. This general criterion of adequacy needs to be spelled

*out precisely and justified fully in order to be useful in resolving
controversies, but the formulation and defense of such a criterion will be
a very difficult task. However this fundamental problem is solved in
the end, Schauer's approach teaches us that we need to look closely at
the details of the contexts in which the Constitution is interpreted.*

W. S-A.

The Occasions of
Constitutional Interpretation

Frederick Schauer

At first glance the various theories of constitutional interpretation appear quite distinct. Some assert that the Constitution should be interpreted to reflect the original intentions of the framers, while others
contend that such intentions are largely irrelevant. Some insist that
majoritarian democracy should be the guiding principle of constitutional interpretation, while others reject any pre-occupation with the
"counter-majoritarian difficulty." Some view the task of constitutional
interpretation as almost at one with moral philosophy, while others
believe that the words of the text are the recurring constraint.

Spanning the diversity among the various theories, however, some
constants appear. And among the most constant of these constants is a
preoccupation with the United States Supreme Court. For the past several generations, the voice of constitutional theory has focused on urging a majority of the members of the Supreme Court to adopt some
particular interpretive methodology. This focus is by no means inappropriate; indeed, it remains appropriate despite the unlikelihood that
current or foreseeable Justices of the Supreme Court will adopt the prescriptions offered by academic constitutional theorists. If the enterprise
of academic constitutional law in general—and constitutional theory in
particular—serves as a shadow Supreme Court,[1] then any disjunction
between what constitutional theorists offer and what the Supreme
Court is likely to accept is largely irrelevant.

Even within the voice of constitutional prescription, however, there
remains an odd preoccupation with the Supreme Court. As long as *all*

judges and *all* officials take an oath to support the Constitution,[2] there is every reason to believe that such officials also confront interpretive problems. Are these problems the same, however, when the domain of interpretation shifts from the Supreme Court to other venues of constitutional interpretation? If interpretation is an exercise in ideal theory, pursuant to which there is one best interpretation for any interpretive problem, then the answer is "yes." But constitutional interpretation differs from many other interpretive exercises, with the difference flowing from the fact that constitutional interpretation necessarily implicates the very questions of power allocation that much of ideal theory routinely ignores. And because one of these institutions whose power is at issue is the judiciary, a court interpreting the Constitution is necessarily claiming its own interpretive authority and simultaneously engaging in substantive interpretations pursuant to that authority.[3] Because of this interpreter-dependent presupposition in any act of constitutional interpretation, it is mistaken to assume that Supreme Court-centered accounts of the principles of constitutional interpretation are necessarily transferable to the interpretive tasks of other officials.

One of the inquiries falling under the heading of "the occasions of constitutional interpretation," therefore, is an inquiry into the appropriate principles of constitutional interpretation for officials other than Supreme Court Justices. I will spend some time with that issue here. I will also attend to a second and closely related inquiry, one faced by all constitutional interpreters from Supreme Court Justices to the cop on the beat—and one logically prior to any question of *how* the Constitution should be interpreted—of determining just when a situation requires an act of interpretation at all. As I will show, different interpretive theories generate different interpretive occasions. The interpretive occasions to which interpretive theories are designed to respond are accordingly themselves dependent upon the selection of one interpretive theory rather than another. Theories of interpretation, therefore, including theories of constitutional interpretation, purport not only to give us the answers to interpretive questions, but also to tell us when we have an interpretive question in the first place.

I.

Must constitutional theories be indifferent to the identity of the decision-maker? Traditionally the answer to this question has been "yes," for little else could explain the virtual exclusivity with which constitutional theorists have focused on the Supreme Court. So let us distinguish between two types of constitutional theory, the *interpreter-indifferent* and the *interpreter-relative*.

According to interpreter-indifference there is, in theory, a correct interpretive method, and, consequentially, correct interpretive outcomes. The interpreter, therefore, must locate the correct interpretive method and then employ it to generate the correct answer. Now this description of interpreter-indifference is simply a construct, which of course does not presuppose that all people will agree on a correct interpretive method or even on the results generated by methods on which they do agree.[4] For my purposes, however, the importance of the construct lies in what it does *not* include. Specifically, it does not make reference to the identity of the interpreter or to the role the interpreter occupies. If, for example, *New York Times Co. v. United States*,[5] the case of the *Pentagon Papers*, is a correct interpretation of the First Amendment, then the lower court judges in that case should have reached the same result even before the Supreme Court decided the case. Additionally, if the correctness of the result was ontologically antecedent to the Supreme Court decision, then the United States Attorney who prosecuted the case and the Attorney General (and President) who authorized the prosecution acted unconstitutionally as well.[6] Moreover, and central to my inquiry, interpreter-indifference dictates that the same account of and instructions for constitutional interpretation apply to all of these officials. If I am asked to "give" a theory of constitutional interpretation, I need not ask "Who wants to know?" Similarly, an official need not revise her constitutional theory as she changes positions or roles. The task of the municipal official determining whether the First Amendment requires her to issue a parade permit which she would not otherwise issue is no different, in theory, from the task of the Supreme Court in determining whether the official acted unconstitutionally in denying the permit.

Interpreter-indifference meshes well with the traditions of many domains of philosophical inquiry. Most philosophers treat questions of epistemology, metaphysics, and logic as questions that have, in theory, objective answers not varying with the identity or role of the philosopher. Whatever the answer to a question of metaphysics or logic, those who offer it presuppose that it does not depend on the identity or role of the particular individual who poses or confronts the question.[7]

Turning from epistemology, metaphysics, and logic to ethics, however, the presuppositions of interpreter-indifference become more problematic, for it is not self-evident that the demands of morality are independent of identity or role. We may, for example, have special moral obligations to those closest to us. The answer to the question, "Should Joan relieve Bob's distress or Ann's distress, if Joan can only relieve the distress of one of them?" may not turn on some universal distress-relieving potential that happens at the moment to be borne by Joan. The answer, rather, may depend on whether Joan has some special *relation-*

ship with either Ann or Bob. According to one philosophical tradition, therefore, ethics requires partiality, such that the answers to moral questions vary with the particular relationships of the individuals involved.[8] Similarly, while the issues remain deeply contested, the demands of morality may also vary with the *role* the decision-maker occupies. If some roles impose obligations not imposed by others, while different roles preclude their occupiers from taking into account everything taken into account by others, then the question of what to do depends in part on who it is who is doing the doing.[9]

Although interpreter-relativity bears some relationship to positions of agent-partiality and role-relativity, and interpreter-indifference bears an affinity with their negations, my goal here is not to resolve, nor even directly to address, broad questions about agent-relativity and role-morality in ethical theory. Rather, having identified the issues, I will discuss them in the context of interpretive problems, particularly the interpretive problems that confront constitutional decision-makers.

How does a constitutional decision differ from a decision *simpliciter*? Although constitutions do many things, one thing that all of them do is decide who makes what decisions. If the all-things-considered rightness of an act were a sufficient condition for its constitutionality, and if the all-things-considered wrongness of an act were a sufficient condition for its unconstitutionality, then constitutionality would be redundant, and there would be little point in having notions of constitutionality and unconstitutionality at all. A non-redundant conception of constitutionality, therefore, presupposes the possibility of decisions that are all-things-considered right but unconstitutional, and decisions that are all-things-considered wrong but still constitutional. Constitutionalism thus presupposes the existence of second-order reasons for not doing what we would otherwise have good first-order reasons to do, and vice versa.[10]

Within the class of second-order reasons, the subclass of constitutional reasons is uniquely related to questions of separation of powers, in the non-constitutional and non-technical sense of that term. This relationship is most obviously demonstrated by those acts whose constitutionality depends on the identity of the actor. Congress may coin money and grant letters of marque and reprisal,[11] but the states may not.[12] The federal government may enter into treaties with foreign nations,[13] but the states may not.[14] Congress may create distinctions between intrastate and interstate commerce[15] but, again, the states may not.[16] Only Congress may declare war,[17] while only the President commands the troops.[18] The states may dispense with juries for all civil trials,[19] but Congress may not.[20] The state action principle "allows" private actors to take actions that governmental actors may not.[21] And so on. Although arguments might be marshalled against a role-centered conception of morality, anything other than a role-centered conception of constitutionality thus conflicts with the central features of constitutionalism itself. Whether some political act is or is not constitutional necessarily depends on the identity of the actor.

What does this tell us about constitutional interpretation? As a start, it tells us that constitutional interpretation necessarily involves questions of allocation of power. An official confronting a constitutional question is also confronting a second-order question about her own power, and a third-order question about who should decide questions about her own power.[22] And although there may be good reasons to suppose that people are not the best judges of the limits of their own authority, the accuracy of this perspective may vary depending on the reasons for allocating the authority in the first instance.

I want to distinguish two arguments for limiting the power of a political decision-maker. One argument rests on considerations of ideal political theory, such as the desire to limit the power of courts in recognition of majoritarianism, or to limit the power of Congress in recognition of individual civil liberties. Here the concern is not about which institution will, as an empirical matter, better protect certain rights or interests, but about whether certain institutions have the "right" or the authority to decide certain kinds of questions.

Apart from such questions of ideal theory, however, stand empirical questions about which decision-making institutions are better at making certain kinds of decisions. Often such allocative decisions are premised in part on conceptions of distrust. Regardless of whether that distrust is based on perceptions of bias or well-meaning error, trusting one institution to make certain kinds of decisions necessarily implies distrusting other institutions to make such decisions. Consequently, many of the power-limiting aspects of the United States Constitution are based on a distrust of the ability of certain governmental decision-makers to take, or refrain from taking, certain kinds of actions. For example, the First Amendment's protections of freedom of speech and press are premised, in part, on the view that imperfections in the marketplace of ideas are less threatening than the imperfections of governmental decision-makers,[23] and the Fourth Amendment's warrant requirement establishes an institutional structure to compensate for the expected excessive zeal of governmental criminal investigators.[24]

How is this posture of distrust relevant to the contrast between interpreter-relativity and interpreter-indifference? If substantive constitutional principles are indeed premised on distrust of decision-makers, then a decision-maker confronting a question of constitutional interpretation must realize that her own possible bias or mistake is likely the very rationale for the principle whose scope she now seeks to interpret. And if so, then awareness of the heightened possibility of error in her own interpretive endeavor ought, ideally, to factor into the act of interpretation.

The perspective of distrust, however, suggests that the interpreter is also likely to under-assess the possibility of her own error. Indeed, this possibility is of considerable importance when we focus less on how the act of interpretation appears to the interpreter and more on prescribing interpretive principles for constitutional interpreters. In that context, those who prescribe interpretive principles to such officials might plausibly take into account and compensate for a decision-maker's likely tendency to over-assess her own decision-making capabilities.

Take as an example the rule in *Miranda v. Arizona*,[25] which, like all rules, is actually or potentially over-inclusive vis-à-vis its background justification.[26] Consequently, there may be circumstances under which the canonically formulated rule requires that a police officer give a *Miranda* warning even though the background justification for the rule indicates otherwise. Moreover, like virtually all constitutional rules, this rule has been subsequently qualified, refined, and elaborated such that there are now a panoply of caveats, qualifications, and exceptions indicating circumstances in which a *Miranda* warning need not be given.[27] Against this legal background, we know that police officers will routinely face questions of constitutional interpretation in deciding whether and when to give a *Miranda* warning. So what interpretive advice should we give police officers? More concretely, how should the task of constitutional interpretation in general, and *Miranda* interpretation in particular, be described in the police officer's manual?

Consider some of the more widely-held constitutional theories. Consistent with a central theme of American legal theory, background purpose typically trumps inconsistent plain meaning.[28] Consequently, one principle of constitutional interpretation dictates that even the plain meaning of a constitutional provision is not dispositive when it produces a result inconsistent with its background purpose.[29] Another principle of interpretation, one most associated with Ronald Dworkin, considers the text of the Constitution, the reported cases of the Supreme Court, and other political acts not necessarily emanating from the courts, as raw data from which the interpreter constructs interpretations of the Constitution satisfying a minimal standard of fit. And from among the interpretations satisfying this standard, the interpreter then selects the one that is morally best.[30] Other theorists focus on original intent, even to the extent of subordinating the text when contrary to the actual intentions of its drafters.[31] And still others make moral theory the pre-eminent focus of constitutional decision-making.[32]

One would suppose that even those advocating such divergent theories would be reluctant to put the prescriptions entailed by those theories into the police officer's manual. Insofar as *Miranda* exists precisely because of the perception that police officers have tendencies to concentrate more on securing convictions than on safeguarding constitutional rights, an increase in officers' interpretive freedom would likely result in lax rather than vigorous enforcement of *Miranda*'s central themes.

Or consider the First Amendment. Under current First Amendment interpretations, standards for the issuance of licenses or permits for speech-related activities must be substantially more specific than the First Amendment itself.[33] In other words, the Supreme Court appears to hold the view that the task it performs in interpreting the First Amendment is not a task that the First Amendment allows to be performed by police officers or other municipal officials.

Some may not find these examples persuasive. They may believe, not implausibly, that the task before the police officer or municipal official is no different from the task before the Justices of the Supreme Court. Each must apply the best interpretive theory in order to discern the proper meaning of the Constitution, and then apply that interpretive theory to particular cases. If there exists, in theory, an objectively correct interpretation, then the identity of the agent searching for it becomes irrelevant (interpreter-indifference). If, on the other hand, no objectively correct interpretations exist—only answers chosen by political bodies within broad textual constraints—then any particular interpretation will likely turn on the identity of the interpreter (interpreter-relativity).

But even if there are, in theory, correct interpretive methods, and consequently correct objective interpretations, it does not follow that the responsibility for locating them falls upon all officials in all circumstances. Because an interpretive method is applied to a variety of situations, it should be possible to assess the proportion of correct interpretations that any interpretive method may yield. Thus, the use of some seemingly non-ideal interpretive methods may actually yield a higher proportion of correct interpretations, in certain circumstances, than would the use of theoretically correct or optimal interpretive methods. Suppose, for example, that an official who provides interpretive instructions to other officials subscribes to a basically Dworkinian interpretive strategy. Suppose she also believes that over the course of one hundred cases, she will reach the correct result ninety-eight times if she applies the "correct" method herself. Finally, suppose she believes that someone else will reach the same result eighty-seven times using the same interpretive strategy, but ninety-two times using an inferior interpretive strategy, such as one more constrained by literal word meanings. Under these circumstances, it appears as if the instruction-giver ought to give instructions for constitutional interpretation that diverge from the methods that she herself would apply to the same set of cases.[34]

Two further complications now present themselves. First, we must consider whether the interpretive authority of the recipient of the instructions has independent value. Just as substantive rights, like the right to privacy, grant value to decision-making independent of the value of the decision actually made, so too may the independent value of the certain officials' decision-making authority justify allocating decision-making authority to these officials even when such an allocation will not produce the highest number of correct decisions. Consequently, the allocator of decision-making authority might allocate such authority to an official who would produce the right result on ninety-six out of one hundred occasions, even though an allocation of less authority would produce the right result on ninety-eight occasions, if decision-making authority was thought "worth" the cost of two fewer correct decisions.

The second complication arises from the sense that instructing an official to use an interpretive method that the giver herself would not use is simply deceitful. Suppose that a newly appointed Justice of the Supreme Court asks for my advice on how to interpret the Constitution. Furthermore, suppose that I believe there are arguments from text, precedent, tradition, and commentary that can be arrayed on both sides of any issue that winds up before the Supreme Court. As a result, the Justices can, without embarrassment, make decisions as a matter of policy or principle substantially unconstrained by "legal" materials in the narrow positivist sense of that term.[35] Finally, suppose I believe that this Justice, whose values I often disagree with, will likely make more decisions I would find unacceptable under *my* methodology than she would make under a more constraining methodology that I myself would not apply.

Under these circumstances, am I "lying" if I advise the Justice to adopt the more constraining methodology? In other words, am I behaving dishonestly by not assuming that my inquirer is me? I think not, in part due to the literal distinction between "What would I do?" and "What would I have you do?" Apart from this literal distinction, however, the act of intentionally distorting or over-simplifying a situation is simply part of what rules do all the time, although a full treatment of this issue would take into account the difference between intentional over-simplification and intentional falsehood, as well as the very morality of lying and truth-telling. Still, just as we might tell a small child that Santa Claus exists even though we know otherwise, or that she should *never* cross the street alone, even though we can imagine circumstances in which we would want her to do so, intentional over-simplification—telling the addressee of instructions to ignore factors the teller herself would take into account—cannot be dismissed out of hand.

Neither Supreme Court Justices, nor police officers, nor municipal officials are children, however. Accordingly, an inevitable tension arises between the desire to minimize interpretive mistakes by offering intentionally over-simplified interpretive principles and the need to respect the decision-making abilities and autonomy of others. The extent of this tension, however, and the principles for its management, themselves depend upon the interpretive theory at issue. Insofar as ideal interpretive theories are neither overly complex nor dependent on specialized knowledge, the gap between what the offeror of an interpretive principle would do and what that offeror would tell others to do will be the smallest, and the arguments in favor of interpreter-indifference will be strongest. Conversely, a complex, technical, or indeterminate interpretive methodology makes arguments for interpreter-relativity more compelling.[36] As a result, although it is possible to identify the distinction between interpreter-relativity and interpreter-indifference, and possible to present some of the arguments about the virtues of each, it is impossible to go any further without addressing questions of substantive interpretive methodology.

II.

What does it mean to *interpret* in the first place? In one important sense, all *applications* of the Constitution are interpretations. When people decide not to run for President, for the Senate, or for the House of Representatives because they are under the age designated in the text of the Constitution, they are interpreting the Constitution as prohibiting their holding the relevant office. Whenever a police officer gives a *Miranda* warning based on her perception that the Constitution (as authoritatively interpreted) requires it, or whenever a criminal defendant claims a jury trial, or whenever a vetoed bill is not treated as law, the Constitution is being interpreted.

Although it may seem odd to regard such mechanical applications of the Constitution as "interpretations," characterizing them in this manner demonstrates that even routine applications are premised on conventions that could have been—and yet may be—otherwise. There is a difference between the routine and the inevitable, and characterizing routine applications as interpretations serves to highlight that the things we all do, even reflexively, could have been different under different social understandings.

It is somewhat more common, however, to limit the word "interpretation" to those instances in which someone confronting a text encounters a difficulty, a problem, or a quandary.[37] Although this conception risks excessively downplaying the extent to which apparently non-problematic situations may still rest on contingent social understandings, it has the advantage of treating simple reading and application as different from those occasions on which we self-consciously grapple with difficult questions.

Even if we limit "interpretation" to the problematic, however, the issues remain complex. Principally, we must address—and reject—the widely-held view that an act of interpretation only occurs when the text is unclear. According to this view, legal and constitutional texts are sometimes clear and sometimes not. When they are clear, it is unnecessary to consider difficult questions of interpretive theory, but when, and only when, they are unclear must we address questions of where to look for interpretive guidance. Thus, judges and others who apply constitutional rules engage in interpretive tasks when they try to decide which actions of the state deny "equal protection" or "due process," or which punishments are "cruel and unusual," or which searches and seizures are "unreasonable," but not when they decide that Presidents cannot serve for three terms,[38] or that ratification by three-fourths of the states is a necessary prerequisite for constitutional amendment.[39]

Similarly, under this view there is a pre-theoretical notion of what distinguishes a hard case from an easy one, with interpretive theory only being necessary for the hard cases. Thus, we confront the full range of questions about interpretive theory when we determine how much bail is "excessive,"[40] what activities count as "commerce,"[41] and what is within the scope of the "executive power."[42] Conversely, interpretive theory may safely be set aside when we decide whether a defendant suing for twenty dollars in federal court may demand trial by jury,[43] whether the Vice-President becomes President upon the resignation of the President,[44] and whether a state may enter into a contract with another state without the consent of Congress.[45]

This view of what makes an easy case easy is premised on the view that a result plainly indicated by the text has a lexical primacy over a result indicated by any other interpretive source. And there are, in fact, legal and constitutional regimes in which plain meaning is dispositive in just this way. It is equally possible, however, for different legal and constitutional regimes to exist. Suppose, for example, that unmistakable original intent had the same interpretive status as unmistakable textual meaning.[46] Further, suppose there is concrete evidence that the framers plainly intended for the dollar amount specified in the Seventh Amendment to be adjusted to account for inflation. If a defendant who was sued for one hundred dollars then demanded a jury trial, the two interpretive methods would point in opposite directions. What would be an easy case, were the text to have lexical priority, now becomes a hard case, demanding interpretation.

Other interpretive methodologies may similarly generate interpretive quandaries that would not arise under different methodologies. For example, if constitutional interpretation is based in part on moral theory, then an interpretive quandary arises whenever the text points in one direction and moral theory in another. If the purpose—which is not the same as intent—of a provision is as important as the plain meaning of the text, interpretive occasions arise for all cases in which the purpose might indicate a result different from that indicated by a literal reading of the text. If moral theory and underlying purpose are both permissible interpretive guides, then a case involving unclear text and divergent moral theory and underlying purpose would require interpretation, although a case with the same unclear text but congruent moral theory and underlying purpose would not. If moral theory were relevant in interpreting the Constitution, and if it were not lexically inferior to text, intent, or purpose, then an interpreter of the Three-Fifths Clause,[47] even immediately after its ratification, would face an interpretive quandary. But if moral theory were not a permissible interpretive method, or if it were lexically inferior to text, purpose, and intent, however, then the Three-Fifths Clause would present no interpretive difficulty at or shortly after its adoption.[48]

The identification of an occasion for interpretation is thus dependent on, rather than antecedent to, selection of an interpretive method. Once we accept that there are interpretive sources other than the text of the Constitution, and that such sources are not necessarily secondary to the text, then it is clear that occasions for interpretation arise whenever these interpretive sources are in conflict. If interpretive methods dictate what evidence is relevant in answering an interpretive question, then the indications of such evidence—whether consistent or equivocal—dictate whether there is an interpretive occasion in the first instance.

Thus, interpretive theories not only generate hard cases, they generate easy ones as well. Suppose it is universally agreed that the first line of interpretive recourse in the case of linguistically indeterminate text is the intention of the Congress that proposed the relevant amendment. Furthermore, suppose that there exists a case in which all agree that the text is indeterminate and that the congressional intent concerning how the provision should be interpreted is unmistakable.[49] In such a situation there would be no question about the outcome—congressional intent would prevail. Thus, what appeared to be a case requiring interpretation in the "quandary" sense turned out to be an easy case needing no such interpretation. If we assume, for example, that the Equal Protection Clause is primarily concerned with race discrimination, even though it does not specify race, then any interpretation rests not only on background empirical knowledge regarding the adoption of the Fourteenth Amendment, but also on background interpretive presuppositions that make such empirical knowledge relevant.

So it turns out that we cannot identify interpretive occasions unless we first identify and order the potential interpretive sources. If a lexical hierarchy of interpretive sources exists, such that we do not descend the hierarchy unless we discover an indeterminate source at some level, then interpretive occasions will exist only when those higher order sources provide no clear answer. But if, as is likely the case in American constitutional law, there are multiple legitimate, unordered sources,[50] then interpretive occasions arise whenever the indications of such sources are in conflict.

III.

By determining which cases warrant interpretation, interpretive theory also predetermines which cases will be litigated. As interpretive theory identifies permissible sources of law, it necessarily identifies those events in which all of the permissible sources point in the same direction. And when all permissible sources point in one direction, only a foolhardy litigant would litigate the contrary position.[51] Accordingly, litigants are likely to pursue only those cases in which plausible arguments from permissible interpretive sources point in opposite directions, thus determining the composition of the set of cases that wind up in court.

Consider *Hans v. Louisiana*[52] and *Monaco v. Mississippi*.[53] In both cases, the Supreme Court held that, because of the Eleventh Amendment, a citizen could not bring suit in federal court against that citizen's *own* state, despite the fact that the Eleventh Amendment's prohibition is expressly limited to suits brought against a state by citizens "of another State."[54] Yet if the plain and ordinary meaning of the constitutional text had conclusive force, the defendants in those cases would not have suspected that an Eleventh Amendment defense would succeed, or even be taken seriously, and thus would be unlikely to have raised such a defense in the first instance. The existence of a principle of interpretation pursuant to which the purpose of a constitutional provision is deemed relevant even when that purpose contradicts the plain meaning of the text, however, gave the defendants reason to raise a defense that they would not otherwise have raised.

This analysis applies to the force of precedent as well as to the force of other interpretive sources. Unlike pre-1966 British practice,[55] the Supreme Court may overrule its own decisions.[56] Consequently, a litigant faced with unavoidable, unfavorable precedent can still argue that the precedent should be overruled, and can still non-frivolously pursue the litigation.[57] But, if the Supreme Court could not overrule its previous decisions, many cases that are now litigated would not even be considered.

Of course, the interpretive factors I am describing in dichotomous terms are, in fact, scalar. Different interpretive cultures assign different weights to various interpretive factors, rather than completely accepting or completely denying the relevance of such factors.[58] And so, just as the choice among plain meaning, original intent, underlying purpose, political policy, economic efficiency, moral theory, or any other interpretive source will determine what issues are pursued, so too will the relative weight of the interpretive factors have, in variable degree, the same effect.

Interpretive theory, therefore, answers rather than follows the question of which cases are easy and which are hard, largely determining which cases are disputed and which are not. The question of constitutional interpretation is thus intriguingly circular. If we have a hard case, we use interpretive theory to resolve it. The same interpretive theory, however, dictates whether we have a hard case in the first instance.

IV.

I have avoided two questions that many people may consider larger and more important than the ones I have confronted. First is what interpretive principles should we adopt. With respect to constitutional interpretation, the answer to that question will likely be in some ways similar to—and in other ways different from—the interpretive principles that prevail in our legal culture generally. Sociologically and politically—even if not legally—we require that our constitutional judges be lawyers. Moreover, the absence of a constitutional court[59] requires the same judges to decide constitutional cases under the Equal Protection Clause and statutory cases under the Longshoremen and Harbor Workers Compensation Act. Under such a system, a merging of interpretive methodologies is likely, if not inevitable. At the same time, however, the special place of constitutional decision-making is likely to prevent that merger from being total. As long as there is some merger, then determining—descriptively or normatively—what our interpretive principles are or should be is a task that implicates not only constitutional interpretation, but the complete realm of legal interpretation as well. I do not deny that much can be said about this topic; indeed, I have on occasion said some of it.[60] Still, I will content myself here with more modest observations about the place of constitutional interpretation rather than its substance.

I have also said nothing about how to resolve the quandaries generated by interpretive theory. Interpretive theories *can* tell us something about how to resolve those cases in which one permissible interpretive source points in one direction and a different source points in another. Principles of ordering among sources are as much a part of interpretive theory as the identification of the permissible sources in the first instance. But once the interpretive sources are identified and ranked, it is likely, especially at the highest appellate levels, that the answer to an interpretive question will also depend on factors that extend beyond the comparative competence of the legal or constitutional theorist. I do have views about what courts should do when the relevant "legal" materials do not generate an answer. It is less important to me, however, to offer those views than it is to emphasize my belief that they do not depend on personal attributes as to which legal training, a faculty position in law school, or publication in a law review gives the offeror any comparative expertise.

I have tried instead to offer an account of the role that interpretive theory plays in constitutional interpretation. Interpretive theory does not only tell the interpreter what to do in hard cases. Interpretive theory also determines what sources are relevant to constitutional interpretation and thus determines which cases are hard cases in the first instance. Only under a view that treats text as exclusive can the actual piece of paper headed "The Constitution of the United States of America" function as the constitution of the United States of America. Under any other interpretive theory, the constitution is either something more or something less than that piece of paper, or perhaps both. In any case, determining what sources are relevant in interpreting the Constitution will tell us just what the Constitution is.

Notes

1. This does not imply that academic constitutional theory serves, or should serve, only this one role.

2. U.S. CONST. art. VI, cl. 3.

3. This point is well made in Charles Fried, *Two Concepts of Interests: Some Reflections on the Supreme Court's Balancing Test*, 76 HARV. L. REV. 755, 760-61 (1963).

4. Here I follow Ronald Dworkin in distinguishing between the concept of a single right answer and the empirical fact of people's agreement about what that right answer is. *See, e.g.*, RONALD DWORKIN, A MATTER OF PRINCIPLE (1986); RONALD DWORKIN, LAW'S EMPIRE (1987).

5. 403 U.S. 713 (1971).

6. The point of this example is not that these actors misinterpreted previous prior restraint cases, such as Freedman v. Maryland, 380 U.S. 51 (1965), and Near v. Minnesota, 283 U.S. 697 (1931). Rather, an interpreter-indifferent account would maintain that the correct result preceded even these cases. Although the result may have been different and harder to find without these cases, there was still, in theory, a correct result to be found.

7. With respect to epistemology, the truth of what I maintain here depends upon the falsity of a subjectivist account of knowledge pursuant to which there can be no object of knowledge that is knower-independent.

8. The role that partiality should play, however, is deeply contested. *See generally Symposium on Impartiality and Ethical Theory*, 101 ETHICS 698 (1991); David O. Brink, *Utilitarian Morality and the Personal Point of View*, 83 J. PHIL. 417, 431-38 (1986).

9. Part of the question is whether a distinction exists between a criterion of rightness for a moral decision and the procedure that agents should use to reach a moral decision. *See* Michael S. Moore, *Three Concepts of Rules*, 14 HARV. J.L. & PUB. POL'Y 771 (1991). Assuming the distinction is sound, my focus here is on the latter, and on the question of whether procedures for constitutional decisions should vary with the identity and role of the decision-maker.

10. On the distinction between first-order and second-order reasons, *see* JOSEPH RAZ, PRACTICAL REASON AND NORMS 36-37 (1975); JOSEPH RAZ, THE MORALITY OF FREEDOM 33 (1986). The distinction, however, is not without controversy. *See, e.g.,* Chaim Gans, *Mandatory Rules and Exclusionary Reasons*, 15 PHILOSOPHIA 373, 381-96 (1986); Michael Moore, *Authority, Law, and Razian Reasons*, 62 S. CAL. L. REV. 827, 849-96 (1989).

11. U.S. CONST. art. I, § 8, cls. 5, 11.

12. *Id.* § 10, cl. 1.

13. *Id.* art. II, § 2, cl. 2.

14. *Id.* art. I, § 10, cl. 1.

15. *See, e.g.,* Quill Corp. v. North Dakota, 112 S. Ct. 1904, 1916 (1992); Northwest Cent. Pipeline Corp. v. State Corp. Comm'n, 489 U.S. 493, 524 (1989); Prudential Ins. Co. v. Benjamin, 328 U.S. 408, 427 (1946).

16. *See, e.g.,* Chemical Waste Management, Inc. v. Hunt, 112 S. Ct. 2009, 2012-17 (1992); Hughes v. Oklahoma, 441 U.S. 322, 335-38 (1979).

17. U.S. CONST. art I, § 8, cl. 11.

18. *Id.* art. II, § 2, cl. 1.

19. *See* Melancon v. McKeithen, 345 F. Supp. 1025, 1048 (E.D. La. 1972), *aff'd,* 409 U.S. 943 (1973).

20. U.S. CONST. amend. VII.

21. Jackson v. Metropolitan Edison Co., 419 U.S. 345, 349 (1974); Moose Lodge No. 107 v. Irvis, 407 U.S. 163, 172 (1972).

22. If the first-order question is what should happen, and the second-order question is who should decide what happens, then the third-order question is who should decide who decides what happens. This is not simply the "meta" question that can be appended to any other question; rather, questions of constitutional law typically involve this type of third-order question. For example, in Cruzan v. Director, Missouri Department of Health, 497 U.S. 261 (1990), the first-order question was whether Nancy Cruzan should die, the second-order question was

whether Nancy Cruzan, Nancy Cruzan's parents, a medical committee, or the state should decide whether Nancy Cruzan should die, and the third-order question, the one actually decided by the Supreme Court, was whether the Missouri legislature or the Supreme Court of the United States should decide the second-order question.

23. *See* Abrams v. United States, 250 U.S. 616, 630 (1919) (Holmes, J., dissenting).

24. U.S. CONST. amend. IV.

25. 384 U.S. 436 (1966).

26. *See* FREDERICK SCHAUER, PLAYING BY THE RULES: A PHILOSOPHICAL EXAMINATION OF RULE-BASED DECISION-MAKING IN LAW AND IN LIFE 32 (1991).

27. *See, e.g.*, People v. Rucker, 605 P.2d 843, 854 (Cal. 1980). *See generally* 3 WAYNE LAFAVE, SEARCH AND SEIZURE: A TREATISE ON THE FOURTH AMENDMENT § 8 (2d ed. 1987).

28. *See* P.S. ATIYAH & ROBERT S. SUMMERS, FORM AND SUBSTANCE IN ANGLO-AMERICAN LAW: A COMPARATIVE STUDY IN LEGAL REASONING, LEGAL THEORY, AND LEGAL INSTITUTIONS 100 (1987); *see also* GUIDO CALABRESI, A COMMON LAW FOR THE AGE OF STATUTES (1982); Lon L. Fuller, *Positivism and Fidelity to Law*, 71 HARV. L. REV. 630, 667 (1958).

29. *See, e.g.*, Keystone Bituminous Coal Ass'n v. DeBenedictis, 480 U.S. 470, 502-03 (1987); Monaco v. Mississippi, 292 U.S. 313, 322 (1934); Hans v. Louisiana, 134 U.S. 1, 14-15 (1890).

30. RONALD DWORKIN, LAW'S EMPIRE 355-413 (1986). Dworkin is criticized on this score in Lawrence Alexander & Michael Bayles, *Hercules or Proteus? The Many Theses of Ronald Dworkin*, 5 SOC. THEORY & PRAC. 267, 276-78 (1980).

31. *See, e.g.*, RAOUL BERGER, GOVERNMENT BY JUDICIARY: THE TRANSFORMATION OF THE FOURTEENTH AMENDMENT 363-72 (1977).

32. *See, e.g.*, MICHAEL PERRY, THE CONSTITUTION, THE COURTS AND HUMAN RIGHTS 91-145 (1982) ; DAVID A.J. RICHARDS, TOLERATION AND THE CONSTITUTION 304 (1986).

33. *See, e.g.*, Lakewood v. Plain Dealer Publishing Co., 486 U.S. 750, 772 (1988); Kunz v. New York, 340 U.S. 290, 295 (1951); *see also* Vincent Blasi, *Prior Restraints on Demonstrations*, 68 MICH. L. REV. 1481, 1572 (1970).

34. For the jurisprudential underpinnings of the view that agents may at times enforce rules that they would not follow themselves, see Larry Alexander, *Law and Exclusionary Reasons*, 18 PHIL. TOPICS 5 (1990), and Larry Alexander, *The Gap*, 14 HARV. J.L. & PUB. POL'Y 695 (1991). *See also* SCHAUER, *supra* note 26, at 128-34; Frederick Schauer, *Rules and the Rule of Law*, 14 HARV. J.L. & PUB. POL'Y 645, 691-94 (1991).

35. For a more extended discussion of this point, see Frederick Schauer, *Judging in a Corner of the Law*, 61 S. CAL. L. REV. 1717, 1726-27 (1988).

36. If there are social values that favor interpreter-indifference, such as the values of having publicly accessible constitutional principles, then such values may also favor simpler principles of constitutional interpretation, even though the answers generated by such simpler principles may be inferior to the answers that the best interpreters could achieve using the best interpretive principles.

37. *See* COLIN MCGINN, WITTGENSTEIN ON MEANING: AN INTERPRETATION AND EVALUATION 15 (1984); Marcelo Dascal & Jerzy Wroblewski, *Transparency and*

Doubt: Understanding and Interpretation in Pragmatics and in Law, 7 L. & PHIL. 203, 204 (1988).

38. U.S. CONST. amend. XXII, § 1.

39. *Id.* art. V.

40. *Id.* amend. VIII.

41. *Id.* art. I, § 8, cl. 3.

42. *Id.* art. II, § 1.

43. *Id.* amend. VII.

44. *Id.* amend. XXV, § 1.

45. *Id.* art. I, § 10, cl. 3.

46. *See* BERGER, *supra* note 31.

47. U.S. CONST. art. I, § 2, cl. 3.

48. I do not mean to suggest, however, that a morally sensitive agent should have followed the dictates of the Three-Fifths Clause. I distinguish here the act of interpreting the law from the question of what an agent to whom the law is addressed should do. This distinction, of course, presupposes some version of legal positivism, pursuant to which the identification of what the law requires is not *necessarily* a moral determination; thus the identification of what the law requires does not *necessarily* suggest what the moral agent should do. On this conception of positivism and its moral advantages, see H.L.A. Hart, *Positivism and the Separation of Law and Morals*, 71 HARV. L. REV. 593 (1958); Neil MacCormick, *A Moralistic Case for A-Moralistic Law?*, 20 VAL. U. L. REV. 1 (1984); Frederick Schauer, *Positivism as Pariah*, *in* THE AUTONOMY OF LAW: ESSAYS ON LEGAL POSITIVISM (Robert L. George ed., forthcoming 1993). *But see* Fuller, *supra* note 28; Philip Soper, *Choosing a Legal Theory on Moral Grounds*, *in* PHILOSOPHY AND LAW 31, 33 (Jules Coleman & Ellen F. Paul eds., 1987).

49. Things are a bit sticky here. The existence of documentary evidence of legislative intent usually presupposes that there is a real question, since saying something in many contexts presupposes the plausibility of its negation. *See* JOHN SEARLE, SPEECH ACTS: AN ESSAY IN THE PHILOSOPHY OF LANGUAGE 143 (1969). It is possible, therefore, that where intent was clearest at the time of enactment, there would have been little cause to write it down, and thus there will be no current evidence or documentation of that intent. Consider the question of whether the First Amendment was intended to prohibit the award of monetary damages for breach of an oral contract, which, after all, involves taking money away from someone based solely on what they have *said*. There is no specific evidence regarding this issue, in large part because such a position would have been absurd to argue in 1791. (I think it equally absurd to argue it now, but that is beside the point.) Specific evidence does, however, exist regarding issues that were then more plausibly debatable, such as the acceptance of seditious libel. *See* LEONARD LEVY, EMERGENCE OF A FREE PRESS 220-81 (1985).

50. *See* PHILIP BOBBITT, CONSTITUTIONAL FATE: THEORY OF THE CONSTITUTION 9-119 (1982).

51. There are obvious exceptions to this general rule, perhaps the most obvious of all being *in forma pauperis* criminal appeals. If litigation involves no financial cost to the litigant, involves no expenditure of time that could otherwise be used for better purposes, and is perhaps even a more enjoyable activity in its own right than the available alternatives (Would you rather do legal research or make

license plates?), then there are no incentives operating against the pursuit of a frivolous claim. Still, there is substantial formal and empirical support for the common sense proposition that willingness to litigate is positively correlated with likelihood of success. *See, e.g.,* George L. Priest & Benjamin Klein, *The Selection of Disputes for Litigation,* 13 J. LEGAL STUD. 1, 15 (1984); Stewart J. Schwab & Theodore Eisenberg, *Explaining Constitutional Tort Litigation: The Influence of the Attorney Fee Statute and the Government as Defendant,* 73 CORNELL L. REV. 719, 742 (1988).

52. 134 U.S. 1 (1890).

53. 292 U.S. 313 (1934).

54. U.S. CONST. amend. XI.

55. *See* London Tramways v. London County Council, [1898] 1 App. Cas. 375, 381 (appeal taken from Eng.); *see also* RUPERT CROSS, PRECEDENT IN ENGLISH LAW 107-13 (3d ed. 1977).

56. I mention the early British practice only to demonstrate the contingency of the American approach. The early British approach reflects a version of legal positivism pursuant to which courts exercise discretion to make law if, and only if, there is no applicable law. But because the law exists once the court makes it, the court's authority to make, remake, or unmake law ends once a decision is in place.

57. *See, e.g.,* Patterson v. McLean Credit Union, 491 U.S. 164, 172 (1990).

58. *See generally* INTERPRETING STATUTES: A COMPARATIVE STUDY (D. Neil MacCormick & Robert S. Summers eds., 1991). There is no reason to suspect that the cross-national variability that exists with respect to statutes is not equally present with respect to constitutions.

59. In contrast to the American legal system, the legal system in the Federal Republic of Germany includes a constitutional court, and the African National Congress has also proposed the establishment of such a court in its draft constitution.

60. Citations omitted in the service of uncharacteristic modesty.

2

ORIGINALISM

Robert Bork is best known as Ronald Reagan's nominee to the Supreme Court in 1987. He was nominated and rejected, because of his conservative political views and also because he is one of the most vocal and extreme defenders of originalism and judicial restraint.

Like other originalists, Bork tells us both what judges should do and what they should not do. Judges should interpret the Constitution by reading the document and its history. In an early article, "Neutral Principles and Some First Amendment Problems," Bork argued that judges must follow the intentions of the framers. In our selection from his recent book The Tempting of America, *Bork says instead that judges should follow the original understanding, which is "what the public of that time would have understood the words to mean." Either way, judges are required to base their interpretations on facts about the time when the amendment was passed.*

What judges should not do is impose their own values. Bork argues that judicial neutrality is necessary in order to escape the Madisonian dilemma: Majority rule in the United States is limited by rights of minorities and individuals, but who determines which rights exist? Majorities have incentives to underestimate these rights, minorities have incentives to overestimate them, and judges cannot be trusted not to take sides in such conflicts. A truly impartial determination is supposed to come only from the document itself. The present majority then gets limited by the past super-majority of ratifiers, but the present majority still should rule whenever the document and its history are not clear.

Bork's opponents counter that his view prevents judges from protecting minority rights against the majority and also that there is no neutral way for judges to discover any original understanding that is precise enough to decide particular, controversial cases. Bork responds

*to these and more objections in the following selection. Whether or not
his responses are finally adequate, his arguments remain so prominent
and powerful that they cannot be ignored.*

W. S-A.

The Original Understanding

Robert H. Bork

The Madisonian Dilemma and
the Need for Constitutional Theory

The central problem for constitutional courts is the resolution of the
"Madisonian dilemma." The United States was founded as a Madisonian system, which means that it contains two opposing principles that
must be continually reconciled. The first principle is self-government,
which means that in wide areas of life majorities are entitled to rule, if
they wish, simply because they are majorities. The second is that there
are nonetheless some things majorities must not do to minorities, some
areas of life in which the individual must be free of majority rule. The
dilemma is that neither majorities nor minorities can be trusted to
define the proper spheres of democratic authority and individual
liberty. To place that power in one or the other would risk either
tyranny by the majority or tyranny by the minority. The Constitution
deals with the problem in three ways: by limiting the powers of the
federal government; by arranging that the President, the senators, and
the representatives would be elected by different constituencies voting
at different times; and by providing a Bill of Rights. The last is the
only solution that directly addresses the specific liberties minorities
are to have. We have placed the function of defining the otherwise
irreconcilable principles of majority power and minority freedom in a
nonpolitical institution, the federal judiciary, and thus, ultimately, in
the Supreme Court of the United States. The task of reconciliation
cannot be accomplished once and for all. The freedom of the majority to
govern and the freedom of the individual not to be governed remain
forever in tension. The resolution of the dilemma must be achieved

anew in every case and is therefore a never ending search for the correct balance.

There is, of course, more to the Court's constitutional function than defining in so direct a fashion the rights of the individual against the state. There is the related task of maintaining the system of government the Constitution creates. The Court must often discern the powers of Congress and those of the President when the claims of each come into conflict, as, it appears, they increasingly do. Similarly, though the Court has largely abandoned the role, there is the job of defining the respective spheres of national and state authority. These questions of governmental structure, competence, and authority are, of course, closely related to the resolution of the Madisonian dilemma and may in fact amount to much the same thing. When the President and Congress come into a conflict requiring resolution by the Court, or when such a dispute arises between the national and a state government, it is usually because the contending bodies would decide an issue in different ways. It matters greatly to the individual, therefore, which arm of government has legitimate authority in a field that affects him. It matters not only in terms of the result that one branch of government ordains but, since different governmental bodies have constituencies of different sizes and compositions, it matters to the citizen's chances of participating in decisionmaking.

The functions assigned the Court impose a need for constitutional theory. How is the Court to reason about the resolution of the disputes brought before it? If we have no firm answer to that question, it will not be possible to know, or even rationally to discuss, whether judicial decisions are within the range of the acceptable. In resolving the Madisonian dilemma, courts must be energetic in protecting the rights of individuals while being equally scrupulous to respect the rights of majorities to govern. Should judges make serious mistakes in either direction, they abet either majority or minority tyranny. Should they make serious mistakes in structural issues, they also alter the balance of freedom and power. Modern debate about constitutional theory, however, is less about structural questions and the allocation of authority between arms of government than it is about the individual's right to be free of democratic governance.

We need a theory of constitutional adjudication, then, that defines the spheres of the majority and the individual in a sense that can be called "correct." If there is no correct solution, there is no dilemma to be resolved; there is no way to assess the work of the courts; there is no way to choose among a constitutional theory that calls for complete majoritarianism, one that demands unlimited power for the judiciary, and a theory that insists upon freedom so extreme that it approaches anarchy. This means that if there is no single correct solution, there must be at least a limited range of outcomes that can be called correct. That, in turn, means that any theory worthy of consideration must both state an acceptable range of judicial results and, in doing that, confine the judge's power over us. It is as important to freedom to confine the judiciary's power to its proper scope as it is to confine that of the President, Congress, or state and local governments. Indeed, it is probably more important, for only courts may not be called to account by the public. For some reason unintelligible to me, Lord Acton's dictum that "Power tends to corrupt and absolute power corrupts absolutely"[1] is rarely raised in connection with judges, who, in our form of government, possess power that comes closer to being absolute than that held by any other actors in our system. The theory must, therefore, enable us to say what is the limit of the judge's legitimate authority. . . .

The Original Understanding

What was once the dominant view of constitutional law—that a judge is to apply the Constitution according to the principles intended by those who ratified the document—is now very much out of favor among the theorists of the field. In the legal academies in particular, the philosophy of original understanding is usually viewed as thoroughly passé, probably reactionary, and certainly—the most dreaded indictment of all—"outside the mainstream." That fact says more about the lamentable state of the intellectual life of the law, however, than it does about the merits of the theory.

In truth, only the approach of original understanding meets the criteria that any theory of constitutional adjudication must meet in order to possess democratic legitimacy. Only that approach is consonant with the design of the American Republic.

The Constitution as Law: Neutral Principles

When we speak of "law," we ordinarily refer to a rule that we have no right to change except through prescribed procedures. That statement assumes that the rule has a meaning independent of our own desires. Otherwise there would be no need to agree on procedures for changing the rule. Statutes, we agree, may be changed by amendment or repeal. The Constitution may be changed by amendment pursuant to the procedures set out in article V. It is a necessary implication of the prescribed procedures that neither statute nor Constitution should be changed by judges. Though that has been done often enough, it is in no sense proper.

What is the meaning of a rule that judges should not change? It is the meaning understood at the time of the law's enactment. Though I have written of the understanding of the ratifiers of the Constitution, since they enacted it and made it law, that is actually a shorthand formulation, because what the ratifiers understood themselves to be enacting must be taken to be what the public of that time would have understood the words to mean. It is important to be clear about this. The search is not for a subjective intention. If someone found a letter from George Washington to Martha telling her that what he meant by the power to lay taxes was not what other people meant, that would not change our reading of the Constitution in the slightest. Nor would the subjective intentions of all the members of a ratifying convention alter anything. When lawmakers use words, the law that results is what those words ordinarily mean. If Congress enacted a statute outlawing the sale of automatic rifles and did so in the Senate by a vote of 51 to 49, no court would overturn a conviction because two senators in the majority testified that they really had intended only to prohibit the *use* of such rifles. They said "sale" and "sale" it is. Thus, the common objection to the philosophy of original understanding—that Madison kept his notes of the convention at Philadelphia secret for many years—is off the mark. He knew that what mattered was public understanding, not subjective intentions. Madison himself said that what mattered was the intention of the ratifying conventions. His notes of the discussions at Philadelphia are merely evidence of what informed public men of the time thought the words of the Constitution meant. Since many of them were also delegates to the various state ratifying conventions, their understanding informed the debates in those conventions. As Professor Henry Monaghan of Columbia has said, what counts is what the public understood.[2] Law is a public act. Secret reservations or intentions count for nothing. All that counts is how the words used in the Constitution would have been understood at the time. The original understanding is thus manifested in the words used and in secondary materials, such as debates at the conventions, public discussion, newspaper articles, dictionaries in use at the time, and the like. Almost no one would deny this; in fact almost everyone would find it obvious to the point of thinking it fatuous to state the matter—except in the case of the Constitution. Why our legal theorists make an exception for the Constitution is worth exploring.

The search for the intent of the lawmaker is the everyday procedure of lawyers and judges when they must apply a statute, a contract, a will, or the opinion of a court. To be sure, there are differences in the way we deal with different legal materials, which was the point of John Marshall's observation in *McCulloch v. Maryland* that "we must never forget, that it is *a constitution* we are expounding."[3] By that he meant that narrow, legalistic reasoning was not applied to the document's broad provisions, a document that could not, by its nature and uses, "partake of the prolixity of a legal code." But he also wrote there that it was intended that a provision receive a "fair and just interpretation," which means that the judge is to interpret what is in the text and not something else. And, it will be recalled, in *Marbury v. Madison* Marshall placed the judge's power to invalidate a legislative act upon the fact that the judge was applying the words of a written document.[4] Thus, questions of breadth of approach or of room for play in the joints aside, lawyers and judges should seek in the Constitution what they seek in other legal texts: the original meaning of the words.[5]

We would at once criticize a judge who undertook to rewrite a statute or the opinion of a superior court, and yet such judicial rewriting is often correctable by the legislature or the superior court, as the Supreme Court's rewriting of the Constitution is not. At first glance, it seems distinctly peculiar that there should be a great many academic theorists who explicitly defend departures from the understanding of those who ratified the Constitution while agreeing, at least in principle, that there should be no departure from the understanding of those who enacted a statute or joined a majority opinion. A moment's reflection suggests, however, that Supreme Court departures from the original meaning of the Constitution are advocated *precisely because* those departures are not correctable democratically. The point of the academic exercise is to be free of democracy in order to impose the values of an elite upon the rest of us.

If the Constitution is law, then presumably its meaning, like that of all other law, is the meaning the lawmakers were understood to have intended. If the Constitution is law, then presumably, like all other law, the meaning the lawmakers intended is as binding upon judges as it is upon legislatures and executives. There is no other sense in which the Constitution can be what article VI proclaims it to be: "Law."[6] It is here that the concept of neutral principles, which Wechsler said were essential if the Supreme Court was not to be a naked power organ, comes into play. Wechsler, it will be recalled, in expressing his difficulties with the decision in *Brown v. Board of Education,*[7] said that courts must choose principles which they are willing to apply neutrally, apply, that is, to all cases that may fairly be said to fall within them. This is a safeguard against political judging. No judge will say openly that any particular group or political position is always entitled to win. He will announce a principle that decides the case at hand, and Wechsler had no difficulty with that if the judge is willing to apply the same principle in the next case, even if it means that a group favored by the first decision is disfavored by the second. That was precisely what Arthur M. Schlesinger, Jr., said that the Black-Douglas wing of the Court was unwilling to do. Instead, it pretended to enunciate principles but in fact warped them to vote for interest groups.[8]

The Court cannot, however, avoid being a naked power organ merely by practicing the neutral application of legal principle. The Court can act as a legal rather than a political institution only if it is neutral as well in the way it derives and defines the principles it applies. If the Court is free to choose any principle that it will subsequently apply neutrally, it is free to legislate just as a political body would. Its purported resolution of the Madisonian dilemma is spurious, because there is no way of saying that the correct spheres of freedom have been assigned to the majority and the minority. Similarly, if the Court is free to define the scope of the principle as it sees fit, it may, by manipulating the principle's breadth, make things come out the way it wishes on grounds that are not contained in the principle it purports to apply. Once again, the Madisonian dilemma is not resolved correctly but only according to the personal preferences of the Justices. The philosophy of original understanding is capable of supplying neutrality in all three respects—in deriving, defining, and applying principle.

Neutrality in the Derivation of Principle

When a judge finds his principle in the Constitution as originally understood, the problem of the neutral derivation of principle is solved. The judge accepts the ratifiers' definition of the appropriate ranges of majority and minority freedom. The Madisonian dilemma is resolved in the way that the founders resolved it, and the judge accepts the fact that he is bound by that resolution as law. He need not, and must not, make unguided value judgments of his own.

This means, of course, that a judge, no matter on what court he sits, may never create new constitutional rights or destroy old ones. Any time he does so, he violates not only the limits to his own authority but, and for that reason, also violates the rights of the legislature and the people. To put the matter another way, suppose that the United States, like the United Kingdom, had no written constitution and, therefore, no law to apply to strike down acts of the legislature. The U.S. judge, like the U.K. judge, could never properly invalidate a statute or an official action as unconstitutional. The very concept of unconstitutionality would be meaningless. The absence of a constitutional provision means the absence of a power of judicial review. But when a U.S. judge is given a set of constitutional provisions, then, as to anything not covered by those provisions, he is in the same position as the U.K. judge. He has no law to apply and is, quite properly, powerless. In the absence of law, a judge is a functionary without a function.

This is not to say, of course, that majorities may not add to minority freedoms by statute, and indeed a great deal of the legislation that comes out of Congress and the state legislatures does just that. The only thing majorities may not do is invade the liberties the Constitution specifies. In this sense, the concept of original understanding builds in a bias toward individual freedom. Thus, the Supreme Court properly decided in Brown that the equal protection clause of the fourteenth amendment forbids racial segregation or discrimination by any arm of government, but, because the Constitution addresses only governmental action, the Court could not address the question of private discrimination. Congress did address it in the Civil Rights Act of 1964 and in subsequent legislation, enlarging minority freedoms beyond those mandated by the Constitution.

Neutrality in the Definition of Principle

The neutral definition of the principle derived from the historic Constitution is also crucial. The Constitution states its principles in majestic generalities that we know cannot be taken as sweepingly as the words alone might suggest. The first amendment states that "Congress shall make no law . . . abridging the freedom of speech,"[9] but no one has ever supposed that Congress could not make some speech unlawful or that it could not make all speech illegal in certain places, at certain times, and under certain circumstances. Justices Hugo Black and William O. Douglas often claimed to be first amendment absolutists, but even they would permit the punishment of speech if they thought it too closely "brigaded" with illegal action. From the beginning of the Republic to this day, no one has ever thought Congress could not forbid the preaching of mutiny on a ship of the Navy or disruptive proclamations in a courtroom.

But the question of neutral definition remains and is obviously closely related to neutral application. Neutral application can be gained by defining a principle so narrowly that it will fit only a few cases. Thus, to return to *Griswold*,[10] we can make neutral application possible by stating the principle to be that government may not prohibit the use of contraceptives by married couples. But that tactic raises doubts as to the definition of the principle. Why does it extend only to married couples? Why, out of all forms of sexual behavior, only to the use of contraceptives? Why, out of all forms of behavior in the home, only to sex? There may be answers, but if there are, they must be given.

Thus, once a principle is derived from the Constitution, its breadth or the level of generality at which it is stated becomes of crucial importance. The judge must not state the principle with so much generality that he transforms it. The difficulty in finding the proper level of generality has led some critics to claim that the application of the original understanding is actually impossible. That sounds fairly abstract, but an example will make clear both the point and the answer to it.

In speaking of my view that the fourteenth amendment's equal protection clause requires black equality, Dean Paul Brest said:

> The very adoption of such a principle, however, demands an arbitrary choice among levels of abstraction. Just what *is* "the general principle of equality that applies to all cases"? Is it the "core idea of *black* equality" that Bork finds in the original understanding (in which case Alan Bakke [a white who sued because a state medical school gave preference in admissions to other races] did not state a constitutionally cognizable claim), or a broader principle of "*racial* equality" (so that, depending on the precise content of the principle, Bakke might have a case after all), or is it a still broader principle of equality that encompasses discrimination on the basis of gender (or sexual orientation) as well? . . .
>
> The fact is that all adjudication requires making choices among the levels of generality on which to articulate principles, and all such choices are inherently non-neutral. No form of constitutional decisionmaking can be salvaged if its legitimacy depends on satisfying Bork's requirements that principles be "neutrally derived, defined and applied."[11]

If Brest's point about the impossibility of choosing the level of generality upon neutral criteria is correct, we must either resign ourselves to a Court that is a "naked power organ" or require the Court to stop making "constitutional" decisions. But Brest's argument seems to me wrong, and I think a judge committed to original understanding can do what Brest says he cannot. We may use Brest's example to demonstrate the point.

The role of a judge committed to the philosophy of original understanding is not to "*choose* a level of abstraction." Rather, it is to find the meaning of a text—a process which includes finding its degree of generality, which is part of its meaning—and to apply that text to a particular situation, which may be difficult if its meaning is unclear. With many if not most textual provisions, the level of generality which is part of their meaning is readily apparent. The problem is most difficult when dealing with the broadly stated provisions of the Bill of Rights. It is to the latter that we confine discussion here. In dealing with such provisions, a judge should state the principle at the level of generality that the text and historical evidence warrant. The equal protection clause was adopted in order to protect the freed slaves, but its language, being general, applies to all persons. As we might expect, and as Justice Miller found in the *Slaughter-House Cases*,[12] the evidence of what the drafters, the Congress that proposed the clause, and the ratifiers understood themselves to be requiring is clearest in the case of race relations. It is there that we may begin in looking for evidence of the level of generality intended. Without meaning to suggest what the historical evidence in fact shows, let us assume we find that the ratifiers intended to guarantee that blacks should be treated by law no worse than whites, but that it is unclear whether whites were intended to be protected from discrimination in favor of blacks. On such evidence, the judge should protect only blacks from discrimination, and Alan Bakke would not have had a case. The reason is that the next higher level of generality above black equality, which is racial equality, is not shown to be a constitutional principle, and therefore there is nothing to be set against a current legislative majority's decision to favor blacks. Democratic choice must be accepted by the judge where the Constitution is silent. The test is the reasonableness of the distinction, and the level of generality chosen by the ratifiers determines that. If the evidence shows the ratifiers understood racial equality to have been the principle they were enacting, Bakke would have a case. In cases concerning gender and sexual orientation, however, interpretation is not additionally assisted by the presence of known intentions. The general language of the clause, however, continues to subject such cases to the test of whether statutory distinctions are reasonable. Sexual differences obviously make some distinctions reasonable while others have no apparent basis. That has, in fact, been the rationale on which the law has developed. Society's treatment of sexual orientation is based upon moral perceptions, so that it would be difficult to say that the various moral balances struck are unreasonable.

Original understanding avoids the problem of the level of generality in equal protection analysis by finding the level of generality that interpretation of the words, structure, and history of the Constitution fairly supports. This is a solution generally applicable to all constitutional provisions as to which historical evidence exists. There is, therefore, a form of constitutional decisionmaking that satisfies the requirement that principles be neutrally defined.

To define a legal proposition or principle involves simultaneously stating its contents and its limits. When you state what is contained within the clause of the first amendment guarantee of the free exercise of religion, you necessarily state what is *not* contained within that clause. Because the first amendment guarantees freedom of speech, judges are required reasonably to define what is speech and what is its freedom. In doing these things, the judge necessarily decides that some things are not speech or are not abridgments of its freedom. As to things outside the proposition, the speech clause gives the Judge no power to do anything. Because it is only the content of a clause that gives the judge any authority, where that content does not apply, he is without authority and is, for that reason, forbidden to act. The elected legislator or executive may act where not forbidden; his delegation of power from the people through an election is his authority. But the judge may act only where authorized and must do so in those cases; his commission is to apply the law. If a judge should say that the freedom of speech clause authorizes him to abolish the death penalty, we would unanimously say that he had exceeded the bounds of his lawful authority. The judge's performance is not improved if, following *Griswold v. Connecticut* he adds four more inapplicable provisions to his list of claimed authorizations and claims that five inapplicable provisions give him the authority one alone did not. Where the law stops, the legislator may move on to create more; but where the law stops, the judge must stop.

Neutrality in the Application of Principle

The neutral or nonpolitical application of principle has been discussed in connection with Wechsler's discussion of the *Brown* decision. It is a requirement, like the others, addressed to the judge's integrity. Having derived and defined the principle to be applied, he must apply it consistently and without regard to his sympathy or lack of sympathy with the parties before him. This does not mean that the judge will never change the principle he has derived and defined. Anybody who has dealt extensively with law knows that a new case may seem to fall within a principle as stated and yet not fall within the rationale underlying it. As new cases present new patterns, the principle will often be restated and redefined. There is nothing wrong with that; it is, in fact, highly desirable. But the judge must be clarifying his own reasoning and verbal formulations and not trimming to arrive at results desired on grounds extraneous to the Constitution. This requires a fair degree of sophistication and self-consciousness on the part of the judge. The only external discipline to which the judge is subject is the scrutiny of professional observers who will be able to tell over a period of time whether he is displaying intellectual integrity.

An example of the nonneutral application of principle in the service of a good cause is provided by *Shelley v. Kraemer*,[13] a 1948 decision of the Supreme Court striking down racially restrictive covenants. Property owners had signed agreements limiting occupancy to white persons. Despite the covenants, some whites sold to blacks, owners of other properties sued to enforce the covenants, and the state courts, applying common law rules, enjoined the blacks from taking possession.

The problem for the Supreme Court was that the Constitution restricts only action by the state, not actions by private individuals. There was no doubt that the racial restrictions would have violated the equal protection clause of the fourteenth amendment had they been enacted by the state legislature. But here state courts were not the source of the racial discrimination, they merely enforced private agreements according to the terms of those agreements. The Supreme Court nonetheless held that "there has been state action in these cases in the full and complete sense of the phrase."[14]

In a 1971 article in the Indiana Law Journal,[15] I pointed out the difficulty with *Shelley*, for which I was severely taken to task in my Senate hearings and elsewhere. That criticism consisted entirely of the observation that I had disapproved of a case that favored blacks and was therefore hostile to civil rights. Both the fact that many commentators had criticized *Shelley* and my approval of other cases that favored blacks were ignored. The implicit position taken by some senators and activist groups was that a judge must always rule for racial minorities. That is a position I reject, because it requires political judging. Members of racial minorities should win when the law, honestly applied, supports their claim and not when it does not. *Shelley v. Kraemer* rested upon a theory that cannot be honestly applied, and, in the event, has not been applied at all.

The Supreme Court in *Shelley* said that the decision of a state court under common law rules constitutes the action of the state and therefore is to be tested by the requirements of the Constitution. The racial discrimination involved was not the policy of the state courts but the desire of private individuals, which the courts enforced pursuant to normal, and neutral, rules of enforcing private agreements. The impossibility of applying the state action ruling of *Shelley* in a neutral fashion may easily be seen. Suppose that a guest in a house becomes abusive about political matters and is ejected by his host. The guest sues the host and the state courts hold that the property owner has a right to remove people from his home. The guest then appeals to the Supreme Court, pointing out that the state, through its courts, has upheld an abridgment of his right of free speech guaranteed by the first amendment and made applicable to the states by the fourteenth. The guest cites *Shelley* to show that this is state action and therefore the case is constitutional. There is no way of escaping that conclusion except by importing into the rule of *Shelley* qualifications and limits that themselves have no foundation in the Constitution or the case. Whichever way it decided, the Supreme Court would have to treat the case as one under the first amendment and displace state law with constitutional law.

It is necessary to remember that absolutely anything, from the significant to the frivolous, can be made the subject of a complaint filed in a state court. Whether the state court dismisses the suit out of hand or proceeds to the merits of the issue does not matter; any decision is, according to *Shelley*, state action and hence subject to constitutional scrutiny. That means that all private conduct may be made state conduct with the result that the Supreme Court will make the rules for all allowable or forbidden behavior by private individuals. That is not only a complete perversion of the Constitution of the United States, it makes the Supreme Court the supreme legislature. The result of the neutral application of the principle of *Shelley v. Kraemer* would be both revolutionary and preposterous. Clearly, it would not be applied neutrally, and it has not been, which means that it fails Wechsler's test.

Shelley was a political decision. As such, it should have been made by a legislature. It is clear that Congress had the power to outlaw racially restrictive covenants. Subsequently, in fact, in a case in which as Solicitor General I filed a brief supporting the result reached, the Supreme Court held that one of the post-Civil War civil rights acts did outlaw racial discrimination in private contracts.[16] That fact does not, however, make *Shelley* a proper constitutional decision, however much its result may be admired on moral grounds.

Judicial adherence to neutral principles, in the three senses just described, is a crucial element of the American doctrine of the separation of powers. Since the Court's invocation of the Constitution is final, the judiciary is the only branch of the government not subject to the ordinary checks and balances that pit the powers of the other branches against each other. If it is to be faithful to the constitutional design, therefore, the Court must check itself.

The Original Understanding of Original Understanding

The judicial role just described corresponds to the original understanding of the place of courts in our republican form of government. The political arrangements of that form of government are complex, its balances of power continually shifting, but one thing our constitutional orthodoxy does not countenance is a judiciary that decides for itself when and how it will make national policy, when and to what extent it will displace executives and legislators as our governors. The orthodoxy of our civil religion, which the Constitution has aptly been called, holds that we govern ourselves democratically, except on those occasions, few in number though crucially important, when the Constitution places a topic beyond the reach of majorities.

The structure of government the Founders of this nation intended most certainly did not give courts a political role. The debates surrounding the Constitution focused much more upon theories of representation than upon the judiciary, which was thought to be a comparatively insignificant branch. There were, however, repeated attempts at the

Constitutional Convention in Philadelphia to give judges a policymaking role. The plan of the Virginia delegation, which, amended and expanded, ultimately became the Constitution of the United States, included a proposal that the new national legislature be controlled by placing a veto power in a Council of Revision consisting of the executive and "a convenient number of the National Judiciary."[17] That proposal was raised four times and defeated each time. Among the reasons, as reported in James Madison's notes, was the objection raised by Elbridge Gerry of Massachusetts that it "was quite foreign from the nature of ye. office to make them judges of policy of public measures."[18] Rufus King, also of Massachusetts, added that judges should "expound the law as it should come before them, free from the bias of having participated in its formation."[19] Judges who create new constitutional rights are judges of the policy of public measures and are biased by having participated in the policy's formation.

The intention of the Convention was accurately described by Alexander Hamilton in The Federalist No. 78: "[T]he judiciary, from the nature of its functions, will always be the least dangerous to the political rights of the Constitution; because it will be least in a capacity to annoy or injure them."[20] The political rights of the Constitution are, of course, the rights that make up democratic self-government. Hamilton obviously did not anticipate a judiciary that would injure those rights by adding to the list of subjects that were removed from democratic control. Thus, he could say that the courts were "beyond comparison the weakest of the three departments of power," and he appended a quotation from the "celebrated Montesquieu": "Of the three powers above mentioned [the others being the legislative and the executive], the JUDICIARY is next to nothing." This is true because judges were, as King said, merely to "expound" law made by others.

Even if evidence of what the founders thought about the judicial role were unavailable, we would have to adopt the rule that judges must stick to the original meaning of the Constitution's words. If that method of interpretation were not common in the law, if James Madison and Justice Joseph Story had never endorsed it, if Chief Justice John Marshall had rejected it, we would have to invent the approach of original understanding in order to save the constitutional design. No other method of constitutional adjudication can confine courts to a defined sphere of authority and thus prevent them from assuming powers whose exercise alters, perhaps radically, the design of the American Republic. The philosophy of original understanding is thus a necessary inference from the structure of government apparent on the face of the Constitution.

The Claims of Precedent
and the Original Understanding

The question of precedent is particularly important because, as Professor Henry Monaghan of Columbia University law school notes, "much of the existing constitutional order is at variance with what we know of the original understanding."[21] Some commentators have argued from this obvious truth that the approach of original understanding is impossible or fatally compromised, since they suppose it would require the Court to declare paper money unconstitutional and overturn the centralization accomplished by abandoning restrictions on congressional powers during the New Deal.[22] There is in these instances a great gap between the original understanding of the constitutional structure and where the nation stands now. But the conclusion does not follow. To suppose that it does is to confuse the descriptive with the normative. To say that prior courts have allowed, or initiated, deformations of the Constitution is not enough to create a warrant for present and future courts to do the same thing.

All serious constitutional theory centers upon the duties of judges, and that comes down to the question: What should the judge decide in the case now before him? Obviously, an originalist judge should not deform the Constitution further. Just as obviously, he should not attempt to undo all mistakes made in the past. Whatever might have been the proper ruling shortly after the Civil War, if a judge today were to decide that paper money is unconstitutional, we would think he ought to be accompanied not by a law clerk but by a guardian. At the center of the philosophy of original understanding, therefore, must stand some idea of when the judge is bound by prior decisions and when he is not.[23]

Many people have the notion that following precedent (sometimes called the doctrine of *stare decisis*) is an ironclad rule. It is not, and never has been.[24] As Justice Felix Frankfurter once explained, "*stare decisis* is a principle of policy and not a mechanical formula of adherence to the latest decision, however recent and questionable, when such adherence involves collision with a prior doctrine more embracing in its scope, intrinsically sounder, and verified by experience."[25] Thus, in Justice Powell's words, "[i]t is . . . not only [the Court's] prerogative but also [its] duty to re-examine a precedent where its reasoning or understanding of the Constitution is fairly called into question."[26] The Supreme Court frequently overrules its own precedent. In 1870, *Hepburn v. Griswold*[27] held it unconstitutional to make paper money legal tender for antecedent debts, but in 1871 Hepburn was overruled in the *Legal Tender Cases*.[28] The New Deal Court swiftly began overruling or ignoring precedent, some of it of fifty years' standing, and often did so by five-to-four votes. Indeed, the Court has overruled important precedent in cases where nobody asked it to do so. *Swift v. Tyson* held in 1842 that federal courts could apply a "general law" independent of the state law that would apply had the suit been brought in a state court sitting nearby.[29] The rule lasted for ninety-six years until *Erie Railroad Co. v. Tompkins* did away with it in 1938.[30] *Plessy v. Ferguson*,[31] and the rule of separate-but-equal in racial matters, lasted fifty-eight years before it was dispatched in *Brown v. Board of Education*.[32] In a period of sixteen years the Court took three different positions with respect to the constitutionality of federal power to impose wage and price regulations on states and localities as employers.[33] Indeed, Justice Blackmun explained recently in the last of these decisions that prior cases, even of fairly recent vintage, should be reconsidered if they "disserve[] principles of democratic self-governance."[34] Every year the Court overrules a number of its own precedents. As the examples given show, both recent and ancient precedents are vulnerable.

The practice of overruling precedent is particularly common in constitutional law, the rationale being that it is extremely difficult for an incorrect constitutional ruling to be corrected through the amendment process. Almost all Justices have agreed with Felix Frankfurter's observation that "the ultimate touchstone of constitutionality is the Constitution itself and not what we have said about it."[35] But that, of course, is only a partial truth. It is clear, in the first place, that Frankfurter was talking about the Supreme Court's obligations with respect to its own prior decisions. Lower courts are not free to ignore what the Supreme Court has said about the Constitution, for that would introduce chaos into the legal system as courts of appeal refused to follow Supreme Court rulings and district courts disobeyed their appellate courts' orders. Secondly, what "the Constitution itself" says may, as in the case of paper money, be irretrievable, not simply because of "what [the Justices] have said about it," but because of what the nation has done or become on the strength of what the Court said.

It is arguable that the text of the Constitution counsels some ambivalence about precedent. Article VI states: "This Constitution, and the Laws of the United States which shall be made in Pursuance thereof" are to be "the supreme Law of the Land."[36] That could be taken to mean that recourse is continually to be had to the text of the Constitution and statutes without regard to prior judicial decisions since the latter are not given the status of supreme law. But article III vests the "judicial Power" in the Supreme Court and lower federal courts.[37] At the time of the ratification, judicial power was known to be to some degree confined by an obligation to respect precedent. Whatever may be made of that, it has been commonly understood that a judge looking at an issue for the second time is, or should be, less free than one who looks at it for the first time. In constitutional law, as in all law, there is great virtue in stability. Governments need to know their powers, and citizens need to know their rights; expectations about either should not lightly be upset.

The law currently has no very firm theory of when precedent should be followed and when it may be ignored or overruled. It is an important subject nonetheless, and it is particularly so to a judge who abides by the original understanding, because, as Monaghan said, so much of our constitutional order today does not conform to the original design of the Constitution. If we do not possess anything worthy of being called a theory of precedent, it is possible at least to suggest some of the factors that should be considered when facing a question of following or over-ruling a prior decision.

No question arises, of course, unless the judge concludes that the prior constitutional decision, which is urged as controlling his present deci-sion, was wrong. In making that determination, particular respect is due to precedents set by courts within a few decades of a provision's ratifi-cation since the judges of that time presumably had a superior knowl-edge of the original meaning of the Constitution. Similarly, precedents that reflect a good-faith attempt to discern the original understanding deserve far more respect than those that do not. Here, there are not only the claims of stability and continuity in the law, but respect for the knowledge and intelligence of those who have gone before. Today's judge should reflect that if the prior court has been wrong, he too may fall into error.

But if the judge concludes that a prior decision was wrong, he faces additional considerations. The previous decision on the subject may be clearly incorrect but nevertheless have become so embedded in the life of the nation, so accepted by the society, so fundamental to the private and public expectations of individuals and institutions, that the result should not be changed now. This is a judgment addressed to the prudence of a court, but it is not the less valid for that. Judging is not mechanical. Many rules are framed according to predictions of their likely effects, and it is entirely proper for a decision to overrule or not to overrule to be affected by a prediction of the effects likely to flow from that. Thus, it is too late to overrule not only the decision legalizing paper money but also those decisions validating certain New Deal and Great Society programs pursuant to the congressional powers over commerce, taxation, and spending. To overturn these would be to overturn most of modern government and plunge us into chaos. No judge would dream of doing it. It was never too late to overrule the line of cases represented by *Lochner*, because they were unjustifiable restrictions on governmental power, and allowing additional regulation of economic matters did not produce any great disruption of institutional arrangements. Similarly, it will probably never be too late to overrule the right of privacy cases, including *Roe v. Wade*, because they remain unaccepted and unaccept-able to large segments of the body politic, and judicial regulation could at once be replaced by restored legislative regulation of the subject.

To say that a decision is so thoroughly embedded in our national life that it should not be overruled, even though clearly wrong, is not neces-sarily to say that its principle should be followed in the future. Thus, the expansion of Congress's commerce, taxing, and spending powers has reached a point where it is not possible to state that, as a matter of ar-ticulated doctrine, there are any limits left. That does not mean, how-ever, that the Court must necessarily repeat its mistake as congres-sional legislation attempts to reach new subject areas. Cases now on the books would seem to mean that Congress could, for example, displace state law on such subjects as marriage and divorce, thus ending such fed-eralism as remains. But the Court could refuse to extend the commerce power so far without overruling its prior decisions, thus leaving exist-ing legislation in place but not giving generative power to the faulty principle by which that legislation was originally upheld. It will be said that this is a lawless approach, but that is not at all clear. The past decisions are beyond reach, but there remains a constitutional prin-ciple of federalism that should be regarded as law more profound than the implications of the past decisions. They cannot be overruled, but they can be confined to the subject areas they concern. Similarly, there may be no real point in overturning the decision in *Griswold v. Connecticut*. It was unimportant in its immediate consequences since no jurisdiction wants to enforce a law against the use of contraceptives by married couples. But that does not mean that *Roe v. Wade* should not be overruled or that the spurious right of privacy that *Griswold* created should ever be used to invalidate a statute again. *Griswold* has had generative power, spawning a series of wrong decisions, and will cer-tainly bring a series of new and unjustifiable claims before the federal courts. But should it become apparent that the Court will not apply it again, the stream of claims will dwindle and ultimately dry up. A case like *Shelley v. Kraemer* has generated no subsequent decisions and is most unlikely to. The Supreme Court has refused to follow its rationale, and there would be no point in overruling the decision. There are times when we cannot recover the transgressions of the past, when the best we can do is say to the Court, "Go and sin no more."[38]

Finally, it should be said that those who adhere to a philosophy of original understanding are more likely to respect precedent than those who do not. As Justice Scalia has said, if revisionists can ignore "the most solemnly and democratically adopted text of the Constitution and its Amendments . . . on the basis of current values, what possible basis could there be for enforced adherence to a legal decision of the Supreme Court?"[39] Indeed, it is apparent from our recent history that the Justices most inclined to rewrite the Constitution have the least patience with precedent that stands in their way. If you do not care about stability, if today's result is all-important, there is no occasion to respect either the constitutional text or the decisions of your predecessors.

*   *   *

The interpretation of the Constitution according to the original under-standing, then, is the only method that can preserve the Constitution, the separation of powers, and the liberties of the people. Only that approach can lead to what Felix Frankfurter called the "fulfillment of one of the greatest duties of a judge, the duty not to enlarge his author-ity. That the Court is not the maker of policy but is concerned solely with questions of ultimate power, is a tenet to which all Justices have subscribed. But the extent to which they have translated faith into works probably marks the deepest cleavage among the men who have sat on the Supreme Bench. . . . The conception of significant achieve-ment on the Supreme Court has been too much identified with largeness of utterance, and too little governed by inquiry into the extent to which judges have fulfilled their professed role in the American constitu-tional system."[40]

Without adherence to the original understanding, even the actual Bill of Rights could be pared or eliminated. It is asserted nonetheless, and sometimes on high authority, that the judicial philosophy of orig-inal understanding is fatally defective in any number of respects. If that were so, if the Constitution cannot be law that binds judges, there would remain only one democratically legitimate solution: judicial supremacy, the power of courts to invalidate statutes and executive ac-tions in the name of the Constitution, would have to be abandoned. For the choice would then be either rule by judges according to their own de-sires or rule by the people according to theirs. Under our form of gov-ernment, under the entire history of the American people, the choice between an authoritarian judicial oligarchy and a representative democracy can have only one outcome. But this is a false statement of alternatives, for judicial interpretation of the Constitution according to its original understanding is entirely possible. When that course is fol-lowed, judges are not a dictatorial oligarchy but the guardians of our liberties. . . .

Notes

1. Letter from Lord Acton to Bishop Mandell Creighton (Apr. 5, 1887), *quoted in* G. Himmelfarb, *Lord Acton: A Study in Conscience and Politics* 160-161 (1952).

2. Monaghan, *Stare Decisis and Constitutional Adjudication*, 88 Colum. L. Rev. 723, 725-27 (1988) ("The relevant inquiry must focus on the *public* understanding of the language when the Constitution was developed. Hamilton put it well: 'Whatever may have been the intention of the framers of a constitution, or of a law, that intention is to be sought for in the instrument itself, according to the usual & established rules of construction.'" [emphasis in original; footnotes omitted]).

3. 17 U.S. (4 Wheat.) 316, 407 (1819).

4. 5 U.S. (1 Cranch) 137, 177-79 (1803).

5. *See also* Scalia, *Originalism: The Lesser Evil*, 57 U. Cin. L. Rev. 849, 853 (1989) (It is a canard to interpret Marshall's observation in *McCulloch* as implying that our interpretation of the Constitution must change from age to age. "The real implication was quite the opposite: Marshall was saying that the Constitution had to be interpreted generously because the powers conferred upon Congress under it had to be broad enough to serve not only the needs of the federal government originally discerned but also the needs that might arise in the future. If constitutional interpretation could be adjusted as changing circumstances required, a broad initial interpretation would have been unnecessary.")

6. U.S. CONST. art. VI.

7. 347 U.S. 483 (1954).

8. Schlesinger, *The Supreme Court: 1947*, Fortune, vol. 35, Jan. 1947, at 73, 201–02.

9. U.S. CONST. amend. I.

10. *Griswold v. Connecticut*, 381 U.S. 479 (1965).

11. Brest, *The Fundamental Rights Controversy: The Essential Contradictions of Normative Constitutional Scholarship*, 90 Yale L.J. 1063, 1091–92 (1981) (footnotes omitted).

12. *Slaughter-House Cases*, 83 U.S. (16 Wall.) 36 (1873).

13. 334 U.S. 1 (1948).

14. *Id.* at 19.

15. Bork, *Neutral Principles and Some First Amendment Problems*, 47 Ind. L.J. 1 (1971).

16. *Runyon v. McCrary*, 427 U.S. 160 (1976).

17. P. Bator, P. Mishkin, D. Meltzer & D. Shapiro, *Hart and Wechsler's The Federal Courts and the Federal System* 7 (3d ed. 1988) quoting 1 Farrand, *The Records of the Federal Convention* 21 (May 29) (1911).

18. *Ibid.*, quoting 1 Farrand, *The Records of the Federal Convention* 97–98, 109 (June 4) (1911).

19. *Ibid.*

20. *The Federalist No. 78*, at 465–66 (A. Hamilton) (C. Rossiter ed. 1961).

21. Monaghan, *supra* note 2, at 727.

22. *Id.; see also* Bittker, *The Bicentennial of the Jurisprudence of Original Intent: The Recent Past*, 77 Calif. L. Rev. 235 (1989).

23. *See* Scalia, *supra* note 5, at 861-65.

24. Monaghan, *supra* note 2, at 741-43; Maltz, *Some Thoughts on the Death of Stare Decisis in Constitutional Law*, 1980 Wis. L. Rev. 467, 494–96 ("It seems fair

to say that if a majority of the Warren or Burger Court has considered a case wrongly decided, no constitutional precedent—new or old—has been safe.").

25. *Helvering v. Hallock*, 309 U.S. 106, 119 (1940).

26. *Mitchell v. W. T. Grant Co.*, 416 U.S. 600, 627–28 (1974) (Powell, J., concurring).

27. 75 U.S. (8 Wall.) 603 (1870).

28. 79 U.S. (12 Wall.) 457 (1871).

29. 41 U.S. (16 Pet.) 1 (1842).

30. 304 U.S. 64 (1938).

31. 163 U.S. 537 (1896).

32. 347 U.S. 483 (1954).

33. *Compare Maryland v. Wirtz*, 392 U.S. 183 (1968); *National League of Cities v. Usery*, 426 U.S. 833 (1976); *Garcia v. San Antonio Metropolitan Transit Authority*, 469 U.S. 528 (1985).

34. 469 U.S. 528, 547 (1985).

35. *Graves v. New York*, 306 U.S. 466, 491–92 (1939) (Frankfurter, J., concurring).

36. U.S. CONST. art. VI, cl. 2.

37. U.S. CONST. art. III, § 1.

38. *See* R. Berger, *Death Penalties* 82-83 n. 29 (1982) (Berger makes this statement while referring to a Supreme Court decision that in my judgment is unquestionably correct. His misapplication of the biblical command in this context, however, does not detract from his general point about *stare decisis*—that past errors in particular cases should not be expanded and elaborated simply because they cannot be undone.)

39. Scalia, *supra* note 5, at 861.

40. F. Frankfurter, *The Commerce Clause* 80-81 (1937).

3

COMMON LAW METHOD

Like Bork, Richard Epstein thinks that judges should not impose their personal values but instead should follow the words in the Constitution. In his book Takings, *Epstein wrote, "If the power of the judges is to be legitimated, . . . they must be able to provide authoritative interpretations of the constitutional text that are not simply manifestations of their own private beliefs about what legislation should accomplish." To accomplish this feat, "The dominant loyalty is to the text as written and not to the framers' views of the consequences it entailed." However, this theory runs into a problem: How can judges interpret the Constitution when its words are not clear? The present selection can be seen as a response to that question.*

Epstein describes and endorses a method of interpretation that derives from Roman law. This method has three basic steps. First, the common meanings of the words in a law are used to pick out certain cases as paradigms. Second, the judge extends the words to cover new cases that are analogous or "so similar to [the paradigms] that they should be treated in the same fashion." Third, the judge determines which behaviors among the paradigms and analogies are justified or should not be forbidden. This method is supposed to enable judges to adapt the Constitution to new cases while remaining tied to its original words.

Epstein also hopes that by using his method, "persons of radically different political and intellectual points of view should be able to reach agreement as to the proper disposition of a case under the constitutional provision." Critics might doubt that there will be this much agreement on which cases are paradigmatic, analogous, and justified. In any case, Epstein's approach teaches us that traditional methods of interpretation have more flexibility than critics often suppose.

W. S-A.

69

A Common Lawyer Looks at Constitutional Interpretation

Richard A. Epstein

A High Stakes Game

The question of interpretation now enjoys the distinction of being the single most debated issue of constitutional law, surpassing the once dominant debate over the legitimacy of judicial review. The stakes involved in this interpretive venture are enormous, given the possible range of outcomes in any particular constitutional dispute. Take one view of interpretation, and affirmative action is forbidden; take another, and it is required; take a third, and it is allowed. Similarly, to take one view of the Takings Clause—mine—stops the New Deal in its tracks;[1] on a second view—the Court's—the clause is a bystander to the transformation to the welfare state, and of importance only for the resolution of individual grievances of single landowners or at most small groups of landowners.[2] A similar range of positions may be detected on abortion,[3] the scope of the exclusionary rule,[4] the scope of the Commerce Clause,[5] the doctrines of intergovernmental immunity, self-incrimination, right to counsel,[6] and the like.

Such a fundamental issue inevitably engenders countless theories. Some argue that we should simply follow the plain meaning of the text and the ordinary sensibilities of competent speakers of the English language.[7] Others regard so straightforward an approach as the sure sign of linguistic and philosophical naivete.[8] Professor Richard Fallon has identified five separate strands of interpretive thought taken into account by responsible judges:

> Arguments from the plain, necessary, or historical meaning of the constitutional text; arguments about the intent of the framers; arguments of constitutional theory that reason from the hypothesized purposes that best explain either particular constitutional provisions or the constitutional text as a whole; arguments based on judicial precedent; and value arguments that assert claims about justice and social policy.[9]

The order in which Fallon places these approaches to interpretation was not chosen by mere happenstance. Quite consciously, he moved from the more restrictive to the more expansive views of interpretation. In particular, it is the open-ended appeal to arguments about justice and social policy that create the greatest sense of unease. Arguments of this sort proceed on a very high level of generality and often are invoked not to explicate a text, but to demolish it. Exotic theories of interpretation increase the levels of judicial freedom, and thus shift the power to make decisions away from the original drafters of the Constitution to its contemporary expositors.[10]

There is something deeply disturbing about this modern interpretive tradition. One obvious concern with it is that the tradition almost always works in the negative. When Paul Brest describes at length the difficulties of interpretivism, he explains why text is insufficient without an understanding of intention, and intention is insufficient because of its inability to identify whose intention counts, and because of its insufficient appreciation of changed circumstances.[11] His catalog of objections to the process of interpretation is so comprehensive and so formidable that it is a wonder that he thinks anyone could understand his own arguments as to why sensible textual interpretation is impossible. The proof of the pudding, however, is in the eating. If the usual devices of text and intention—or, with a deserved nod to Herbert Wechsler, neutral principles[12]—do not advance the cause of responsible interpretation, then what does? It is here that the well starts to run dry. Consider the response of Brest:

> Having abandoned both consent and fidelity to the text and original understanding as the touchstones of constitutional decisionmaking, let me propose a designedly vague criterion: How well, compared to possible alternatives, does the practice contribute to the well-being of our society—or more narrowly, to the ends of constitutional government? Among other things, the practice should (1) foster democratic government; (2) protect individuals against arbitrary, unfair, and intrusive official action; (3) conduce to a political order that is relatively stable but which also responds to changing conditions, values, and needs; (4) not readily lend itself to arbitrary decisions or abuses; and (5) be acceptable to the populace.[13]

Oh? It is difficult to imagine that so freewheeling an inquiry is suitable for the interpretation of any set text, whether we deal with a constitution, statute, regulation, or even a humble commercial contract. Brest has not given us a tool for constitutional interpretation. He has provided us with an agenda for a constitutional convention—one that is consistent with a wide range of constitutional solutions. No one can figure out exactly what each of these five factors uniquely requires: are indirect elections consistent with the electoral college? If they are not, do we read those provisions out of the Constitution? Do we think that a strong or weak institution of private property is necessary to protect against unfair and arbitrary government power? Or is it sufficient to have procedural protections that deal with hearing and notice, and nothing more? Do we have an institution of judicial review, or one of legislative supremacy, or some intermediate position that requires supermajority votes to override limitations on individual freedoms, assuming these could be defined? The list of questions can be multiplied at length until the line between constitutional interpretation and constitutional nullification vanishes into a list of multiple factors of indeterminate weight.

The rich profusion of constitutional materials, and for that matter constitutional theories, is too often regarded as a strength when, in truth, it should be understood as a weakness. The proliferation of interpretive approaches does nothing to bind the responsible judge. Rather, it gives that judge freedom to reach virtually any result by stressing that single factor that points most clearly to the outcome that the judge desires. Claims supported by "justice and social policy," without more, give full reign to judicial imagination across the political spectrum. The most difficult task of interpretation is keeping separate and distinct our views about what the law is and what the law ought to be. The latter is a free ranging inquiry that allows individuals to develop and apply a constitutional theory most congenial to their political or moral views; it allows persons to use various consequentialist arguments to justify the retention or elimination of particular clauses from the Constitution. In *Takings*, for example, I advance many arguments to show that allocative inefficiencies are likely if the state is not required to pay compensation when it takes private property for public use.[14]

Although these arguments might explain why a takings clause is necessary, they do not interpret it. Rather, the interpretive task accepts the clause as a given, and asks only how it should be applied. If the interpreter succeeds, then persons of radically different political or intellectual points of view should agree on the proper disposition of a case under the constitutional provision.[15] Supporters of the underlying textual provision should be satisfied that the interpretation yields their desired conclusion in the case at hand; opponents of the constitutional provision should take some modest comfort in knowing that the unsound outcome follows logically from an unsound major premise. In the ideal interpretive world, the Marxist and the market economist should agree on the interpretation of the Takings Clause, as written, even if the former would repeal it tomorrow, and the latter would afford it pride of place in his constitutional hierarchy.

The critical point is that theories of constitutional interpretation are not theories of substantive transformation. No one should be able to win through interpretation what was lost in the initial drafting. I suspect that many of these novel theories of interpretation are attempts to do just that. No one would need, for example, an elaborate theory of interpretation to explain why "commerce" does not include manufacture and agriculture; however, such an elaborate theory is sorely needed to explain why it does include those activities and not coincidentally to justify the enormous expansion of federal jurisdiction since 1937.[16]

The basic task, then, is to develop a framework for constitutional interpretation that avoids the pitfall mentioned above. To discharge this project, I looked to the interpretive methods used by common lawyers. This approach might seem, at first, to be odd, given that common law principles have been so often rejected on substantive grounds as guides to constitutional decisionmaking.[17] Nonetheless, I hope to show by elaboration that the distinctive way in which private lawyers construed the central propositions of common law, and the statutes that were so much a part of private law as to blend into the common law, provides the best clue of how to engage in the business of constitutional interpretation.

The stakes of course are far lower if the question of construction concerns a common law rule, subject to overruling or qualification, or even a statute, subject to revision and amendment. I am well aware of Chief Justice Marshall's famous observation in *McCulloch v. Maryland*[18] that "it is *a constitution* we are expounding." So it is, but that makes it more imperative to ensure that it is correctly expounded. Higher stakes do not guarantee that different interpretive principles are required from those applicable to more mundane issues. The opposite might be true, and the rules that serve us well in private law may be best suited for dealing with these issues.

What is critical is a comprehensive understanding of the legal subject matter. There is a strong affinity between the general propositions of private law and the set of constitutional norms. Both stand in opposition to the highly reticulated statutes that mark, say, a tax code, or an air pollution statute. In general, the proper approach to linguistic meaning depends less on the era of the document that is involved and more on the level of detail and specificity that it contains. The new sophistication that constitutional lawyers have injected into the debate might be the unintended source of our intellectual downfall. Meanwhile, older principles drawn from a different era might continue to serve us well.

By examining the past with a somewhat critical eye, we are no longer forced to make a fateful choice between the claims of modernity on the one hand and dogmatic fidelity to the past on the other. Rather, age-old methods of interpretation afford us unappreciated resources for coping with the problems of the present. In sum, I hope to show that the methods of "ordinary language" interpretation to which I am habitually drawn are neither simple nor simple minded, but require an enormous level of patience and sophistication and might afford us the best method of constitutional interpretation.

To see how the common law system works, I will examine one statute that has been subject to an enormous amount of common law elaboration: not the common law of our own system, but the common law as it developed casuistically in Rome, where the rules of tort law were remarkably similar to our own. The historical remoteness of the Roman law system is, for these purposes, a point in favor of making the comparison. If the approach of Roman lawyers can survive the enormous transitions of space, time, and circumstance, as the Roman rules of tort have done, then there might be less than meets the eye to the frequent assertion that our common law rules of interpretation are short term matters of convenience, unlike lasting constitutional principles.

Ironically, constitutional norms, ostensibly written for the ages, have a far shorter half-life because of the greater political pressures that they face. It is no accident that constitutional interpretation goes into overdrive when Supreme Court decisions are attacked on textual grounds: such was the case with the broad construction of "commerce" in the 1930s,[19] the requirements of desegregation under *Brown v. Board of Education*[20] in the 1950s, and the creation of abortion rights under *Roe v. Wade*[21] in the 1970s. The construction of private law statutes has been largely immune from these pressures. The stability of much of the law of tort may give us an insight as to how to construe the broad substantive guarantees that are contained in the Constitution, even though it will not lead us all the way through the maze.

The *Lex Aquilia*

The text I shall address is the *Lex Aquilia*,[22] the Roman statute that codifies much of the tort law of ancient Rome. I concentrate on the first section of the statute, which has the virtue of being both comprehensive and short. "If any one kills unlawfully a slave of either sex belonging to another or a four-footed animal of the kind called *pecudes*, let him be ordered to pay the owner whatever was the highest value of the victim in that year."[23]

A text of this generality is a peculiar mixture of old and new. Like many Roman statutes, it deals with the question of slavery, and says nothing about the protection that free individuals have in their own person.[24] Yet, by the same token, its comprehensive coverage gives it a surprisingly modern ring. Because it was a statute of major importance, it was subject to a great deal of gloss by judges who knew that they were unable, by simple judicial decree or interpretation, to alter the outcome dictated by the text. These judges also knew that the principle that lay behind the statute was in some serious sense incomplete, and the question that they had to address was stunningly similar to that of our constitutional scholars, namely, is there a way to caress and interpret the text so as to avoid any outrages and anomalies, without moving so far as to repeal or amend the statute in the same breath? Thus, the sense of the need to move beyond what language must strictly require, and yet to recognize that the constraint of language is a problem that was faced in the early Roman context just as it is faced in ours. Indeed, because the evidence suggests that the *Lex Aquilia* was engraved in stone,[25] it was as hard to change as our Constitution is to amend. Thus, the parallels in ambition and position between the Roman statute and the American Constitution are quite close.

Given the constraints faced by early Roman lawyers, the interpretation of this statute was a genuine analytical success. Wholly apart from any precedential force it might contain, it offers us useful guidelines for addressing similar problems in our own constitutional order. In particular, the statute addresses two fundamental tasks that have to be undertaken as part of the general system of statutory interpretation. The first is deciding what the statute reaches by way of *analogical extension*. The second is determining what *implicit justifications* arise under the statute.[26] The existence of these two distinct interpretive processes (which could apply as well to ancient or modern commands, such as "thou shalt not kill," or "murder is the unlawful killing of person with malice aforethought") is important because it allows for a clear demarcation between a complete interpretive system of a basic statute and a more simple minded theory of plain meaning.

The task of analogical extension requires that a textual command be taken beyond its plain meaning to encompass those behaviors that are beyond the scope of the statute but are so similar to it that they should be treated in the same fashion. Implicit justifications require that there be a comprehensive theory of what circumstances "make right" actions that are prima facie unlawful.[27] Again, that task presupposes that semantic meaning (and its extensions) have already been established, and thus requires not an interpretation of the words presented, but the articulation of a general theory drawn from an understanding of the basic prohibition that explains with equal force the permissible exceptions (and their qualifications) to it.

As these two components demonstrate, the full interpretive system does not depend solely upon a simple comparison of dictionary meaning with substantive command. Rather, it seeks to use the specific command as the lodestar for a more comprehensive view of the subject that it covers. In so doing, it tries to steer a path through the uneasy middle ground between literal interpretation and freewheeling revision of the substantive law. To see how this process works, it is important to look at both parts of it with sufficient concreteness. An abstract claim that this middle ground is tenable counts for naught, without a practical demonstration of how it might be done.

Analogical Extension

The first issue relates to the scope of the statute. *Occidere* in Latin, loosely translated as "to kill," is something of a term of art, because its origins, associated with *caedere*, to cut, suggest that the killing had to take place by the use of direct force against the person of the slave, or the covered animal. The question is whether the statute reached beyond the case that was clearly set out in the text, whose clarity in Latin is somewhat greater than the English translation would allow. The early answer to the question was, first with some hesitation, and then with great conviction, yes.

The interpretive development took place in several stages. First, the easy case was given, in which the use of a sword or stick to strike the blow did not defeat the charge of the killing act, which did not have to be done with bare hands.[28] Second, there were a host of intermediate cases in which it is not clear that the actor was responsible for the killing although he was responsible for an act, perhaps a negligent act, which increased the risk of death. The third *Digest* case goes one step further: a man who slips and crushes the slave with his burden. The slipping need not be regarded as an act, but culpability attaches because there was discretion in carrying so heavy a load in the first instance.[29] In the first case, there was the clear use of force. In the next case, there was no intentional use of force, but death was brought about by circumstances for which the actor himself was culpable. Only in the third case do we reach the situation in which the defendant has not acted at all, but was held responsible solely for the prior decision on what to carry or where to go. All these cases were brought within the definition of *occidere* in the struggle to reach some larger conception of responsibility without going beyond the language of the act. They extend the scope of the statute while seeking to avoid express application of the principle of analogical extension.

Similarly, when one is thrown into a river only to die of exhaustion, there the blow has not killed, but the case is nonetheless brought under the statute "just as if someone had dashed a boy against a stone."[30] This last clause points to conscious use of analogical extension. The thrashing about of the doomed victim, the act with the most direct causal link to the death, should not insulate the defendant from causal responsibility, because death could be linked to the wrongful act of the defendant. The progression made by Roman jurists is clear. One starts with death on impact, a clear case, and moves to the case of instant drowning, where an intentional or negligent blow is the only action involved, and then moves to the case of exhaustion, where the plaintiff is in a position to prevent the loss but fails to succeed. The effort to cabin cases within the literal language becomes more uneasy because *occidere* is a dominant instance, but not the complete story, of the theory of causation.

Hence, when Celsus makes the critical distinction: "it makes a great deal of difference whether a person kills or furnishes a cause of death, seeing that one who furnishes a cause of death is liable, not to the *Aquilian* action but to an action *in factum*,"[31] the dynamics of the situation change markedly, and the interpretation of the *Lex Aquilia* bursts forth from its limited confines within the language of *occidere*. It is thus appropriate to acknowledge, even at this late date, how bold a step the Roman jurists took when faced with their statute engraved in stone. Why did the jurists make such a leap? Initially the leap is analogical, but the analogy only opens a wedge into a larger theory of causation. For example, there are cases in which the defendant did *not* kill by a blow, and yet the moral responsibility for the action is so great that it is difficult to find a relevant distinction of principle that separates that case from others. The judges and scholars, therefore, could have argued that one could go outside the text, create the *actio in factum*, or what we would call the action on the case,[32] to deal with a situation that the *occidere* did not cover because the actor had the same relevant moral standard of responsibility. Thus, *occidere* could yield to a more general theory of causation by implication, as good in our own time as in Roman days.

The stakes in this shift in approach are of course very high. Romans, as readers of Robert Graves's *I, Claudius*[33] would attest, seem to have had an inordinate fondness for killing by poisoning. In the crude cases, the poison was forced down the throat of the hapless victim. That was solemnly held to be a case of *occidere*, even though no cutting and tugging occurred.[34] In many cases, however, the poisoning took place by means more subtle and effective. The perpetrators deceived the victim who ingested the poison believing it to be medicine. Because no case of *occidere* occurred here, the *in factum* mode allowed the action. One can only reach that conclusion by inserting an implicit premise, done by way of interpretation, that acts of the plaintiff induced by the defendant's deception should be regarded as equivalent in law to actions that the defendant himself performed *corpore corpori*, by the body and to the body.

The need for interpretation required the Romans to develop an elaborate theory of responsibility. There are cases of intervening acts that do not sever causal connection. Here, the defendant coerces or deceives the victim or some third party into doing the act that results in physical harm. The first order wrong results when the force or fraud is applied directly against the victim. The analogous wrong results when the defendant's conduct misleads or coerces an innocent actor into doing an act that causes harm. The Romans, therefore, started with no theory of causation, but they quickly developed one, even though they never articulated the general principles on which it rested. Their process of analogical extension, however, did not continue without end. For example, the entire theory of responsibility collapsed if the victim *knew* that she would ingest poison and still chose to take it. Here, the harm resulted from her own act. Even though a fraud or deception had been attempted, the victim had ingested the poison with full knowledge of its fatal properties.

This process captures both ancient and modern strains of thought. The emphasis on force and misrepresentation recalls the conditions that Aristotle identified for voluntary actions in the *Nicomachean Ethics*.[35] There, Aristotle did not offer an affirmative account of what constituted voluntary action but instead identified two conditions— mistake and coercion—that negated voluntariness.[36] These two elements, when imposed on one actor by another, allow us to impute responsibility for the later act to the prior actor who is responsible because of the constraint on voluntary behavior. In a more modern vein, force and fraud have a place in basic libertarian theory, which holds that the central office of the law is to constrain their use. What better way to do this than to hold those who practice these techniques responsible for the actions undertaken by their victims? The generality of the results achieved by analogical reasoning to general principles is an impressive accomplishment. The humble task of interpretation, conducted by Roman commentators who had no political agenda to advance, required them to leap from one core case of causation to a more general theory of the subject—no modest enterprise, and no modest achievement.

Justification

The level of interpretation, however, did not end with the articulation of analogous causation cases that subjected a defendant to liability. The command of the *Lex Aquilia*, like the command of many of our most elusive constitutional provisions, reads as though it were an absolute. If one's actions result in the *occidere* or, by extension, the furnishing of a cause of death, then liability follows. Yet, the actual development of the law is far more complex than this because of the unanticipated consequences that attach to the word *iniuria*, not lawful, that is also found in the text. The Romans had an odd exposition of the subject because the *Lex Aquilia* considered the question of justification before it undertook to examine the issue of causation.[37] As a matter of principle, that sequence seems out of order because justifications for a prima facie wrong are discussed before the scope of the initial wrong is determined. The puzzle is resolved not by some deep theory of constitutional interpretation but through an observation of the word order in this sentence, which following the usual practice places the verb at the end of the relevant clause. Accordingly, *iniuria* comes before *occidere* and thus, in the remorseless dissection of the provision, it is the first term to be explicated.

Our concern, however, is not with the oddities of the Roman sequence in exposition, but with the universal necessity to deal with the question of justification under a statute that gives only the barest hint that this exercise must be undertaken at all. The simple issue is whether to treat the word "unlawful" as idle and redundant in the grand scheme of things, so that all killing is unlawful—"thou shalt not kill" is a perfectly serviceable commandment in non-Roman traditions as well. Because of the heavy weight that moral theory has over the structure of doctrinal interpretation, legal doctrine does not treat killing in such a manner. To insist that all killings are unlawful is to treat a legal prohibition like a stiff tree exposed to a strong wind. It will topple because it cannot bend.

A dramatic hypothetical shows that this interpretation is wrong. If a person is set upon by an ambush and finds himself compelled to use force in self-defense, he is nonetheless liable to his aggressor, just as if he had been in the wrong. It does not take great sophistication to realize that unless self-defense is allowed, then all persons will find themselves possessed of a perfect legal remedy only after they are maimed or dead, leaving scant deterrent against the use of aggression. The wrongdoer—wrong by the very standards of the *Lex Aquilia*—will therefore be able to profit from his own wrongs. The introduction of a self-defense justification stems from the correct belief that the articulation of the basic rule of liability is not meant to be complete, for the word "wrongful" can be taken as an invitation to explore the circumstances by which that wrong is made right.

Once self-defense is introduced into the system, a host of related questions follow. Who is entitled to self-defense? Can force be used in defense of property or in the discipline of slaves or family? What are the risks of excessive or deadly force if there is no danger of life and limb? The statute does not answer such questions. Self-defense cannot afford an absolute justification any more than killing can be an absolute wrong. Further qualifications have to be introduced into the system.

The point is well recognized in both the Roman and the common law, for each adopts a system of pleading that allows each party to introduce new matter until the parties choose to join an issue on a matter of law or fact.[38] In essence, one must resort to a theory, even an inchoate theory, to decide what should be done in these cases. I believe it is possible to formalize these intuitions into a single theory.[39] Here, the central task is to ensure that persons who are victims of aggression are permitted to stand their ground, at least when their lives or safety are threatened. Yet, it is necessary to see that an attack, once repulsed, does not become a pretext to allow greater mayhem on the other side. These issues are with us today in the interpretation of the defense of self-defense under both the modern criminal and tort law, and they are unavoidable once the prohibition against the use of force is regarded as one of the linchpins of the social order.

The question of justification under the statute is still more complex than this, for if the defense of self-defense is to be allowed, then what is to be made of the kindred defense of necessity when the injuries sustained by the plaintiff occurred because the defendant had no other choice but to inflict the harm in question? The modern debates on this subject show that there is a sharp division over the question of whether the privilege to damage property (for which slaves and animals could qualify) was conditional on the payment of damages, or whether that privilege was absolute, thus affording protection against suits for compensation.[40] There exists a division of opinion in the Roman texts as well.[41] The Romans, like the common lawyers many centuries later, always tried to work with an assumption of individual autonomy and self-control but found themselves unable to universalize that assumption to all the cases before them.

The question of justification also extends to the issue of consent. If one can bind himself by promise, then why cannot one release a cause of action that otherwise would be available? Here, the Roman law comes up a bit short, as there is no explicit discussion of consent in connection with killing, only the hint of the defense in connection with the killing that takes place in a boxing match.[42] There is, however, a clear explanation for this omission. Roman law did not recognize slaves as free individuals. Thus, they did not have the capacity to consent any more than they had the capacity to contract. Let the action for killing be extended to the killing of a free person, however, and the consent defense fairly invites inclusion in the system. If consent is a way that persons can bind themselves to perform affirmative actions, then it is a way that they can bind themselves to surrender a cause of action that they might otherwise have. As with self-defense, the question of consent cannot function as an absolute defense, but is subject to caveats such as duress, misrepresentation, nondisclosure, mistake, incapacity, and the like.

The list is not over, for there are still other defenses that might be made against the use of force.[43] Discipline invoked by a teacher or parent is yet another illustration. It is of potentially great relevance because it gives the discipliner a kind of sovereign power, which may be exerted even without the special warrant provided by consent or self-defense. The connection between private master and public sovereign is one that cannot be ignored even in modern constitutional law.

The purpose of this essay is not to work out all the details in either the Roman or American contexts, but to show how the logic of interpretation is sufficient to allow, nay require, that we forge an entire system of substantive law from materials that might be thought too meagre for the task. It is first necessary to figure out the provision that animates the core prohibition of the statute—here, the control of the use of force. It is then necessary to cover those cases that are analogous to it. Finally, it is critical to deal with justifications for the use of force— self-defense—subject to suitable limitations. So by degrees we stumble into a general theory that works quite well over the entire constellation of rules that govern the killing of individuals.

The Constitutional Payoff

One may ask what connection this has with constitutional interpretation. The answer is that there had better be some, or else we find that we have looked in vain. Fortunately, for our purposes, most of the great provisions of the Constitution are drafted with the same type of generality found in the *Lex Aquilia* so that it becomes necessary to flesh out the broad outlines of constitutional provisions by reference to similar ideas of analogy (on coverage) and justifications (for covered acts) as are found in the Roman texts. This method will not work (nor will it be needed) to interpret clear provisions such as the minimum age requirements for both representatives[44] and senators.[45] The method will be relevant for those clauses on which the interpretive demands are greatest.

Analogical Extension

The first question that must be faced in dealing with various constitutional provisions is the scope of the coverage that they afford. Like the *Lex Aquilia*, these are often written in grand and general language, without any thought to the details of their coverage. Indeed, the brief elegance associated with many constitutional provisions did not happen by accident and happenstance, but was often engineered by design, as the framers likely knew that foresight in drafting was always imperfect and that some interpretation would be required to make difficult texts clear. Toward that end, it is instructive to consider several examples of analogical extension that arise quite naturally in the constitutional context.

Searches and Seizures. The first clause of the Fourth Amendment provides that "[t]he right of the people to be secure in their persons, houses, papers, and effects, against unreasonable searches and seizures, shall not be violated."[46] What is the scope of the constitutional protection against searches and seizures? Here, the obvious point is that any entrance onto the property of a private person will normally constitute a search of the property in question, although any effort to physically occupy land or to take a chattel will count as a seizure. In this area, the Constitution tracks the idea of the wrongs that one private party can commit against another, and uses them to define the wrongs that the state can commit against any person through its agents. The linkage between the private and public law narrows because the law of trespass to land and to chattels gives content to the constitutional provision.

One major issue under the Fourth Amendment, however, concerns those actions taken by the police or other public officers that do not amount to a trespass in the sense of either an entrance onto land or a seizure of chattels. The question is whether these cases are covered by the Fourth Amendment even though, as a literal textual matter, they fall outside its limits. The early constitutional authority questioned analogical extensions and read the Fourth Amendment with a strictness that would have astonished the Roman interpreters of the *Lex Aquilia*.[47] The courts ruled that Fourth Amendment violations did not occur in the absence of a physical entrance on property or a taking of a chattel. Even the class of cases that could have amounted to serious incursions on the privacy interests of the parties against which the early forms of constitutional theory developed could not provide any form of relief.

The private law response to the same problem reveals the error of this restrictive view. The normal protection afforded individuals against the entrance of strangers on their property serves important interests. It creates an exclusive zone in which each person can control his or her own destiny, and it is an important instrument for the protection of individual privacy, the right to be let alone. The sense that private property is not an end in itself but a means to achieve other ends has important consequences for the way in which the common law construed the scope of its protection. At one level, limitations could be made on the absolute right to exclude—persons could enter private property under circumstances of necessity to save themselves from imminent peril. Additionally, individuals tolerate low level nuisances, reciprocal between neighbors, under a live and let live doctrine that gives each side greater freedom of action. Similarly, landowners are normally under a duty to supply lateral support to a neighbor, even though the removal of that support (by digging on one side of the line) does not constitute a physical invasion of the neighbor's land.[48] Even on matters that have little or nothing to do with privacy, the structure of ownership at common law treated the physical invasion test as a rough proxy for the sound relationships between neighbors. It did not treat it as an absolute litmus test in either direction: there are invasions that may be privileged or excused; likewise, there are *noninvasions* of property that may nonetheless be actionable. Both sets of exceptions aimed, to the extent that imperfect institutions can achieve such ends, to improve the position of both owners in their interactions with each other.

The same logic of noninvasive harms extends to the privacy interest related to real property. Thus, even though each of two neighbors might be able to erect a wall that prevents the other from hearing private conversations, the wall will have other undesirable effects, such as blocking views and cutting off light. A social convention, backed by the force of the state, that says that each neighbor will not overhear the conversation of the other goes a long way to enhance the general value of the property that each has. Noninvasive forms of snooping can therefore be avoided by private custom, and these customs can eventually harden into legal commands. In *Roach v. Harper*,[49] the plaintiff, a tenant of the defendant living in the defendant's downstairs apartment, brought an action for trespass against tenant landlord for using a device to overhear the plaintiff's "confidential and private conversations."[50] The landlord installed the hearing device not in the premises of the plaintiff, which would have supported a claim of physical invasion, but in the landlord's own apartment, where that claim could not be supported. Nonetheless that court had no difficulty in reaching the conclusion that this invasion of privacy (chosen in strict analogy to the trespass actions) enabled a valid suit.[51] Even if the landlord had physically invaded the tenant's apartment, this invasion would not have been the source of the injury sustained. The information gleaned by the hearing device, not its location, constituted the threat to the tenant's interests, and it is against that threat that remedies, whether by way of injunction or damages, should lie. The analogical method thus overcomes the dominant physical motif.

The treatment of the noninvasion cases under the tort law foreshadowed their principled resolution under the Search and Seizure Clause of the Fourth Amendment. The key case in this regard is still *Katz v.*

United States,[52] where the government tapped a public telephone booth in which the accused made a phone call. The government argued that the tap did not constitute a search and seizure because it did not "penetrate" the walls of the booth.[53] The Supreme Court denied that contention and held that the accused had a "reasonable expectation of privacy" in the use of the booth that entitled him to constitutional protection.[54] The use of the "reasonable expectation" language has caused difficulty because of the obvious charge of circularity: if there is no legal protection against the noninvasive search, then what is the source of the reasonable expectation that privacy is observed? Once the citizen knows of the law, then he has assumed the risk of being overheard. Yet, if the protection is extended against this sort of phone taps, then why is there any need to resort to the language of reasonable privacy at all? The phrase, therefore, often has been regarded as question-begging, even by those who regard the result as sound and correct.[55]

The result looks far less dramatic to those schooled in the Roman tradition, in which the doctrine of analogous extension seems to apply. Here, the question about the reasonableness of the expectations is in turn answered by a two stage inquiry. The first question is whether there should be an action for trespass if the conduct undertaken by the government were undertaken by a private party. The decision in *Roach*, handed down nine years before *Katz* and consistent with a number of earlier decisions,[56] indicates that the private right of action should be available against a private defendant. The second question is whether that private right of action can be allowed without running into the same circularity about reasonable expectations that plagues the decision in *Katz*. Again, the answer is yes. The relaxation of the invasion requirement created an alternative rights structure (no overhearing) that left both sides better off than the strict no physical invasion rules of a more primitive system of entitlements. The expectations are reasonable because they represent a configuration of rights that works to the mutual advantage of both parties in the vast run of ordinary cases. Because these extended rights have that desirable characteristic, it is reasonable to adopt them, and hence reasonable for individuals to form expectations that rest upon them. It is therefore possible to forge a closer connection between expectation and entitlement than is evident in *Katz*. The mistake made by the Supreme Court in articulating the *Katz* rule is a familiar one. The same elusive connection between expectation and entitlement was, in a sense, evident to Jeremy Bentham over two hundred years ago: "[p]roperty is nothing but a basis of expectation; the expectation of deriving certain advantages from a thing which we are said to possess, in consequence of the relation in which we stand towards it."[57] This passage, like *Katz*, recognizes the role of expectations in formulating rights, but it offers no clue to indicate which expectations ripen into rights and which do not. What is missing from Bentham is also missing from *Katz*—the way in which the superior set of social returns indicate which set of rights best fulfills the set of desired social expectations. It is possible to meet that higher standard and give to *Katz* a stronger and more persuasive answer than it received in the case law.

The approach that I have taken to Fourth Amendment interpretation has been adopted by writers who, although unaware of the Roman methods of textual interpretations, have championed the principles that they adopted. For example, Albert Alschuler has stressed that reading the term "search" to cover more than a visual inspection is not a linguistic invention of recent origin, but a well-established interpretive practice.[58] He refers to passages from Chaucer, the *King James Bible*, Shakespeare, Milton, Locke, and *Webster's Dictionary*.[59]

This display of erudition assists in understanding the issues at hand. Alschuler considers the case where a husband is forced to reveal confidences that he has received from his wife concerning property located in their household, which the police could not enter and directly inspect themselves. "If the fourth amendment were to block one route to Sandra's [the wife's] dresser but leave the other open, the law would be an ass."[60] Sure enough, the insistence on the method of analogical extension gives rise to the conclusion advanced above: namely, that if the definition of a search as visual inspection "is rejected, no stopping point short of construing the term to encompass all privacy-invading criminal investigations seems apparent."[61] All roads in this case, then, do lead to Rome. The class of cases that are covered by analogy under Alschuler's formulation consists of those in which X is forced to reveal the results of a visual search to the state, which is little different from a case in which A makes B kill C, covered by the *Lex Aquilia*.

Takings. The question of analogical extension is also of great importance in connection with the Takings Clause of the Fifth Amendment: "nor shall private property be taken for public use, without just compensation."[62] The threshold question under the clause is, what kinds of activities undertaken by the government constitute a taking? Under present law, that issue receives a restricted answer. Those cases in which there is physical dispossession of the private owner and physical occupation by the government constitute a straight transfer of the "property" from private to public hands. Once that case is identified, the rest remain shrouded in mystery, at least if one believes current law. One source of the confusion is the inveterate tendency of the Court to lump together the question of prima facie taking with the justifications that might be offered for those takings,[63] a strategy no more likely to produce clarity in public constitutional law than in Roman tort law. So, in this section, I shall concentrate on the initial issue of the taking simpliciter, leaving the matter of justification for the discussion that follows.

The key question here is the extent to which the principle of analogical extension allows one to figure out the reach of the Takings Clause. There are two separate issues worthy of discussion: first, the relationship between the taking and destruction of property; and second, the relationship between physical and regulatory taking. Turning to the first, it has sometimes been argued that the term "taking" should be treated as a term of limitation, and read in opposition to the word "destruction". The argument has a narrow linguistic base in the sense that some state constitutions offer protection against government action that "takes or damages" property, and it may, therefore, be argued that the term "taking" cannot be read as including the very phrase against which it is read in opposition. Nonetheless, that approach leads to an exceedingly crabbed view of interpretation.

Suppose, first, that the state decides that it will blow up a building and then condemn the land. Is there a taking of the land only, or of the land plus the building? The case is no different from one where the government first buys the land and building at market value, and then proceeds to rip down the building to put the land to some other use. It would be odd indeed if the government could reduce its own financial obligations by reversing the sequence of events. Just as with the *Lex Aquilia*, where the prohibition against killing led to an analogous protection against furnishing a cause of death, so too here, the prohibition against takings leads to an analogous prohibition against the destruction of property by the state. The great fear that drives the Takings Clause is that the government, by the use of its coercive power, will be able to internalize all the gain from its operation, while forcing other persons (whose property has been taken) to bear the costs. The risk (like the risk of causation of harm) remains the same whether the strategy adopted by the state is one of take, then destroy or destroy, then take. Indeed the risk goes further, to cases where the government destroys without taking at all, as with sonic booms.

It is arguments like these that initially led the Supreme Court to take the view that both the destruction of private property and the taking of that property are covered by the same constitutional provision.[64] Yet, its adherence to this position has been less than consistent. Oddly enough, the sonic boom case a century later resulted in no compensation at all.[65] In many cases the question is what should be done with business good will, attachable to some particular site, which is destroyed when the government takes the underlying land? As a matter of private law, the recognition of good will as a species of property that can be destroyed has long been understood: the businessman who cannot serve his customers because others defame his name, or harass his customers, has an action for the loss of good will, even if no one lays a finger on his premises. Yet, the destruction of good will receives scant constitutional protection, as the Supreme Court in this context gives property a physical interpretation so narrow as to mock the comprehensive nature of the institution.[66]

A similarly narrow view of causation is taken in other cases where a dispossessed landowner brings an action for consequential damages. In *Community Redevelopment Agency v. Abrams,*[67] the issue was whether the Redevelopment Agency had to pay compensation to a pharmacist, whose premises it had condemned, for the loss of his prescription drugs. State law required that these drugs be reopened and reinspected before they could be sold to another pharmacist, a process that cost more than the drugs' worth. The issue is the same one of remoteness of damages that troubled the Roman lawyers under the *Lex Aquilia.* Only here, the California Supreme Court denied the claim for compensation for these losses on the grounds that the Redevelopment Agency did not "take" the drugs. Yet, so long as the initial condemnation compelled the reinspection of the drugs, the causal connection between public action and private loss seems clear. The required loss of use value is tantamount to the destruction of drugs, which, for the reasons developed above, should be treated as a taking. The older Roman precedents contain better intuitions than our modern takings jurisprudence.

Other complications arise in connection with the analysis of regulatory takings, that is, those government actions that leave a private owner in possession of property, but nonetheless limit the use and disposition of the property above and beyond what would be allowed at common law. The question here is why does a prohibition against taking without compensation not include a prohibition against a *partial* taking without compensation? The risk that the government will keep all of the benefits while forcing others to bear all of the costs is every bit as great with regulation as it is with taking outright possession. It seems odd indeed that the Supreme Court should decree that compensation should be provided when a landowner has to endure the presence of a small cable television box on her property, at no real inconvenience,[68] but is often unwilling to lift a finger against the far greater losses inflicted by regulations.[69] Again, the ability to move cautiously from one case to the other, and to link the results by a general theory, seems a standard part of analogical reasoning. In this corner of the law at least, however, the Court strives to take a narrow and literal interpretation of a great constitutional guarantee. Although it is a constitution that we are expounding, in an age of dubious constitutional sophistication, literalism has its strange constitutional bedfellows.

Justification

The second great issue that arises in dealing with any constitutional text is justification. Just as the *Lex Aquilia* sets out a presumptive right that the private owner has against the state, so too the Constitution sets out a presumptive right that the citizen enjoys against the state. Of course, the protections that are given could be absolutes if they were so drafted: "nor shall private property be taken for public use, without just compensation, no matter what" is a rather different clause than the one that we now must interpret. The usual view on this subject is that a constitutional command is the first stage in a larger inquiry that allows justifications to be asserted for the limitations that are imposed. Here, as with the *Lex Aquilia*, the search for suitable justifications is not a semantic inquiry solved by reference to plain meaning, or indeed any more complicated set of linguistic tests. Rather, it is a substantive inquiry, which asks what justifications are congruent, as a matter of theory, with the admitted forms of protection afforded by the constitutional clause. One vast area of constitutional interpretation is a search for these justifications. Historically, scholars conducted the inquiry under the rubric of the police power, for although these terms are nowhere to be found in the Constitution, entire treatises of great eminence have been written on its scope.[70] In modern times, the police power language has tended to give way to a more complex terminology, which speaks of the level of scrutiny that is given to a state limitation on a constitutional right, and which may well vary from clause to clause. Thus, in some instances, it is said that the state must have a "compelling" interest to justify the limitation of a private constitutional right. In others, it might be said that some intermediate level of scrutiny should be required. In still others, it is said that any rational (read incorrect and unsound) basis may justify the state limitation on the protected interest in question. As the constitutional text affords no neat hierarchical classification of interests, enormous energies are used to explain why some constitutional rights, e.g. speech, are more important than others, e.g. property, and why shifting levels of justification are appropriate as we move from class to class.

These issues of justification are similar to those faced under the *Lex Aquilia*, and should be resolved in large measure by the same kinds of considerations. The first step is to identify the type of interest that is protected from government misconduct. The next is to find the general principle that animates the selection of that substantive provision. The third is to find the exceptions that are congruent with the basic theory. In the *Lex Aquilia*, for example, the major concern was with the control of private force, which was why self-defense was let in as a justification for harming other individuals.

A similar argument applies across the board in constitutional areas. When the question is the First Amendment, and the protection of freedom of speech, its limitations can divide into two large categories driven by a concern for individual freedom in all its manifestations. First, freedom is not so large a category as to allow the use of force. As a matter of good libertarian theory, a threat of the use of force is actionable as between private parties on the theory of assault. If the threat is so imminent that escape is not possible, then it may be met by the use of force in self-defense. The long line of cases on subversive advocacy, starting with *Schenck v. United States*,[71] *Abrams v. United States*,[72] *Dennis v. United States*,[73] and *Brandenburg v. Ohio*,[74] illustrates the proposition that the state may use force to prevent the overthrow of the government and, on occasions, speech that threatens that overthrow, consistent with First Amendment protections. Accordingly, the interpretive constitutional question is, what form of anticipatory self-defense is available to the state? The same considerations that arise in the ordinary law of self-defense thus come into play. Were lesser means available? What was the level of the danger imposed? How close was the plan to its fruition? Who should bear the risk of uncertainty? Although this essay does not purport to solve these questions, the critical point is that we should expect even a strict theory of constitutional construction to range over the same class of issues that give rise to difficult problems in the private law of tort.

The justifications for the limitations on speech are not restricted to the control of force, because there is also the risk of fraud or misrepresentation. No one, I take it, thinks that the First Amendment renders unconstitutional all laws against fraud, and the same result should be true with respect to defamation, which consists in some cases at least, as deliberate fraud on large portions of the population for private advantage. Again, both deceit and defamation are extensive and complex categories of liability at common law, which, like constitutional law, also starts from a presumption of individual freedom. The common law limitations on the freedom to speak are complex in their complete elaboration, and we cannot expect the constitutional rules to escape that complexity.

Justification also arises in other contexts. Earlier, I examined the scope of the phrase "search and seizure" and its relationship to the right of privacy.[75] Even if searches are construed to protect against all invasions of privacy, the justification for a search and seizure is fairly raised by the term "unreasonable" in the Fourth Amendment. Thus, the state may justifiably seize property that is likely to be removed or destroyed if not taken from the custody of a person suspected of a serious crime. There may also be a justification to search and to seize evidence that is necessary to prevent the commission of a crime. No amount of textual elaboration of what the words "search and seizure" mean will answer these questions of justification. As with the speech cases considered above, the problem requires a separate inquiry, with an irreducible component of judicial judgment in making and setting the rules.

The Eminent Domain Clause also presents a similar issue of justification for admitted takings. For example, assume a landowner wants to store large quantities of explosives on private property in an urban setting. It is surely a restriction on the use of that property, and hence a partial taking thereof, if the government imposes any restrictions on that activity. Yet, there is surely a justification for the restriction, if only because the damage remedy that might be available after the harm is caused will not restore either life or limb, even on the happy assumption that the defendant is solvent and willing to answer for his wrongs. Similarly, as between private landowners, the abatement of a nuisance is surely a justification for taking, at least on a temporary basis, someone else's property: so too it should be a justification in this constitutional setting. As with speech and search and seizure, the Constitution, properly understood, commands us to address a set of difficult questions to which it does not supply any answers. It is only an evasion of the interpretive process to assume that no independent inquiries should be made about matters fairly raised by the text, even if not answered by them.

Again, a note of caution. Although the class of justifications for the restriction of property may be broad, it is not unlimited. Thus, suppose that the state claims that it is entitled to prevent the development of real estate because it wants to preserve the scenic beauty of a region known for its tourism.[76] Here, one is hard pressed to find any nuisance-like wrong that a landowner makes in the ordinary use of her property. Therefore, it is not sufficient to claim that others are benefitted by the restrictions on freedom that the law imposes. There must be some distinction among different kinds of benefits. If the state does not seek to control (by way of defense of its citizens) the aggressive behavior of its citizens, then the police power justifications are not available. The taking is to provide some general public benefit, indistinguishable from using private land for a post office. If payments are required for the outright dispossession of land, then they should be required for restrictions in its use. The class of justifications for admitted takings is not infinitely elastic, but the same principles that cover dispossession also extend to regulation.

A similar form of logic applies to the constitutional protection of the free exercise of religion. If a set of religious beliefs involves the sacrifice of strangers, or of children, or if it requires the commission of fraud on persons not part of the faith, then surely some justification lies for the restrictions that are admittedly imposed. Yet, here as with the other cases, the basis for the restrictions should be the threat that religious activities impose on the like freedoms of others. When religious persons wish to practice polygamous marriages, it should be no one's concern but their own.[77] If they wish to stay out of the social security system, both as payors and recipients, that wish should be respected against a claim of justification that the public needs their participation to preserve its own welfare system.[78] Here, the principal justification has always been the prevention of a common law wrong against another person. Religious practices that honor that division should, therefore, be protected against state intervention.

The theory of individual liberty that drives the Free Exercise Clause cannot by interpretation be construed to allow collective justifications that are themselves the antithesis of a belief in individual liberty. Even in a world in which the strong protection of property rights is rejected as a constitutional imperative, it is possible to make sense out of the narrower domain of religious freedom, and the correlative domain of the Establishment Clause. The class of justifications consistent with a general theory of freedom are the same limited class as those that are found in private law theories: combatting aggression and misrepresentation, consent, and imposing duties for which just compensation, in cash or kind, has been provided.

The guarantees of individual rights under the Constitution are not limited to those clauses that call for the protection of enumerated individual rights. Thus, consider the distinct constitutional guarantee under the Fourteenth Amendment that no person shall be deprived of equal protection of the laws. Like the specific substantive guarantees, this clause has spawned an enormous interpretive literature. Nonetheless, on the question of justification, it bears a close similarity to the class of justifications that are available in the clauses that guarantee individual rights. The initial question is whether there is some classification that calls for special government scrutiny. The most obvious of these cases is race, but the matter has been extended to classifications by sex, and in principle could be extended further to deal with questions of age, alienage, and the like. Once it is decided whether the classification is prima facie suspect, the next issue asks what type of public justification can be put forward for the distinction in question. Even with questions of race, the prohibition on racial classifications is not absolute. If a prison warden had to separate individuals by race (or national origin) to prevent gang warfare and to maintain the peace, a court might look very closely at the purported justification, but it would not rule it out of bounds as a matter of course. If it insisted on a per se rule, its argument could not be that these distinctions are in principle never justified, but rather the more modest one that the potential level of abuse is sufficiently great that a per se rule is necessary to control government officials.

The theory that underlies these potential justifications for violation of the equal protection norm is identical to those previously considered: to combat force, to combat fraud, or to advance the interests of both groups that receive separate treatment, when in each case the potential for abuse sets the measure of scrutiny that should be given the proffered justification. The institution of Jim Crow in the South could not be justified by elaborate efforts to show the importance of the purity of the races, or by far-fetched arguments that it was necessary to control violence, given the other means to achieve that last end.[79] Similarly, the reason why there is a larger class of justifications for classifications by sex than there is for classifications by race is that sex classifications are often rightly perceived as working for the mutual advantage of both groups, but racial classifications on the same matter are not. Think of the role of separate but equal in athletics, when sex classifications have vastly different connotations than racial ones.[80]

Certainly, the differences that arise in these cases are hard to make good and require a close evaluation of the way in which these various government schemes work in practice. There is no substitute for hard work: thus, the failure to draw a distinction in some cases amounts to an unacceptable burden on one class or the other. To give but one example, the Supreme Court in *Craig v. Boren*[81] got it wrong when it held that Oklahoma could not have a twenty year minimum age for drinking 3.2% beer for men and an eighteen year age for women. The prohibition in both cases sought to minimize the likelihood of vehicular accidents caused by drinking. If the risks for men and women are different, and in this case teenage men were ten times more likely to drive drunk than women,[82] then it is appropriate for a statute to reflect those differences. If the risk for eighteen-year-old men is greater than that for sixteen-year-old women, then the need to control for external harms suggests, if anything, that younger women should be able to drive when older men cannot. The conclusion holds, moreover, no matter what the reason for the sex-linked differences, be they biological or sociological, or, as seems more likely, some combination of the two. The statute is surely permissible insofar as it cuts off, or at least reduces, an implicit subsidy for men that might otherwise exist given the differential accident rates.

Oddly enough, on this view the hard question is the converse: does a state violate equal protection when it uses the *same* drinking limits for both men and women? Here, the received answer is surely no, especially for courts that regard the different age statutes as fatally defective. Even if the control of differential external harms is a critical issue, the uniform age limit seems sufficiently attractive to withstand constitutional attack. There are other sanctions to keep male drivers under control: thus the higher accident rate may be correlated with higher insurance premiums, and more frequent and higher tort judgments, more frequent tickets, fines, and license suspension than women. Therefore, the differential age limitation on drinking alcohol should not be strictly required, although it should surely be allowed. It is, therefore, on this view a clear violation of the Takings Clause if insurers are required, as is increasingly common today, to underwrite certain risks at a net loss by ignoring the relevant actuarial computations to provide a subsidy for some persons at the expense of others. Again, the class of justifications available under the Equal Protection Clause, like those available anywhere else, is not unlimited.

Conclusion

In dealing with the raw stuff of constitutional adjudication, I have sought to develop a theory of interpretation that relies on two strategies that are appropriate for private law adjudication: extension by way of analogy, and justification for admitted wrongs. In both cases, one searches for the implicit theory that underlies the basic textual norm, and then proceeds to answer these two inquiries in light of that norm. When individual liberty and private property, religious freedom, or for that matter, equal protection are at stake, the group of analogous cases, and the class of admitted justifications, are not endless but rather well-defined: the control of force, fraud, and consent, and just compensation more or less complete the list. The method may appear modest, but it does generate comprehensive and systematic results better than any of its rivals.

Finally, I want to stress a point that should have been implicit throughout: the allegiance that I have is to the common law method, and not necessarily to the common law results that were reached by that method.[83] In most of these cases, the two will converge, and there is a certain prudence in judges' following common law principles, especially when they are unsure of the direction that they should pursue under an independent inquiry. There are cases in which the common law and the theory diverge, and in those cases the theory should prevail. One example should illustrate the point. In common law defamation actions, the issue of truth is normally raised as a justification for the prima facie wrong, which is said to consist in words spoken or written that are harmful to reputation. The greater the truth, the greater the libel, it was sometimes said.[84] This use of truth as a justification, unlike that of self-defense, is said to be absolute in character. That last assertion should be sufficient to tip off the defect in the reasoning of the common law, for it clashes with its usual insistence on presumptive defenses just as it has with presumptive causes of action.

The question of truth arises not only in the private law, but also under the Constitution in connection with statements about public officials and public figures. If the common law rules prevailed, then the burden of proof should be on the defendant to establish the truth of the statement made. That result is wrong as a matter of general theory, however, and it was rejected when the question came before the Supreme Court.[85] Defamation is part of a law that is designed to control the use of force and misrepresentation. To that end, it should be understood as a tort in which the defendant makes a false statement about the plaintiff to a third party who then acts on that misstatement to the plaintiff's detriment. True statements about the plaintiff are normally not those that need any special justification at all, but are instead the outgrowth of speaking one's own mind. Once the false statement is made, there are questions of whether it can be justified in self-defense, consent, or by way of some privilege. Until there is a falsehood, however, there is no occasion for justification at all.

The implications for the case law are clear. When the Supreme Court held that in suits against public officials and public figures, the plaintiff had the burden of proof on the question of falsehood, it adhered to the underlying normative theory of speech under the First Amendment even though its result deviated from the common law. It may be that this decision is wrong, but if so, it is only for a very different reason—namely, that the plaintiff should not be subject to any additional burdens given the current law under *New York Times v. Sullivan*.[86] This last argument is not part of the pure theory of interpretation, but only asks the question of what should be done with problem two, given that there is an error in the solution to problem one? The question of offsetting mistakes gives rise to a set of second best problems that cannot be answered in a wholly satisfactory fashion, and it deserves an extended treatment far beyond the scope of this paper. No matter how subtle the theories of second-best interpretation, they will always be found wanting. It is best, therefore, to adopt sound theories of interpretation in the first instance to avoid facing the really interesting cases.

Notes

1. *See* RICHARD A. EPSTEIN, TAKINGS: PRIVATE PROPERTY AND THE POWER OF EMINENT DOMAIN 281 (1985) [hereinafter EPSTEIN, TAKINGS].

2. *See, e.g.*, Penn Cent. v. New York City, 438 U.S. 104 (1978); Village of Euclid v. Ambler Realty Co., 276 U.S. 365, 397 (1926).

3. Here, the range of positions runs from treating abortion as a fundamental right to treating it as a criminal offense, all under the same constitutional text.

4. *Compare* Wolf v. Colorado, 338 U.S. 25, 33 (1949) *with* Mapp v. Ohio, 367 U.S. 643, 655-57 (1961).

5. *See, e.g.,* Wickard v. Filburn, 317 U.S. 111, 118-29 (1942).

6. *See* Gideon v. Wainwright, 372 U.S. 335, 336-45 (1963).

7. *See* Oliver W. Holmes, *The Theory of Legal Interpretation,* 12 HARV. L. REV. 417, 417 (1899). Its current champion is Justice Scalia. *See, e.g.,* Chisom v. Roemer, 111 S. Ct. 2354, 2369 (1991) (Scalia, J., dissenting). Ordinary meaning, however, is sometimes more complicated than normally supposed.

8. *See, e.g.,* RICHARD A. POSNER, THE PROBLEMS OF JURISPRUDENCE 269 (1990); Cass R. Sunstein, *Interpreting Statutes in the Regulatory State,* 103 HARV. L. REV. 405, 504 (1989).

9. Richard H. Fallon Jr., *A Constructivist Coherence Theory of Constitutional Interpretation,* 100 HARV. L. REV. 1189, 1189-90 (1987).

10. *See, e.g.,* Paul Brest, *The Misconceived Quest for the Original Under-standing,* 60 B.U. L. REV. 204 (1980); Lawrence Lessig, *The Fidelity in Translation,* 71 TEX. L. REV. (forthcoming April 1993); Michael J. Perry, *The Authority of Text, Tradition, and Reason: A Theory of Constitutional "Interpretation,"* 58 S. CAL. L. REV. 551 (1985); Mark V. Tushnet, *Following the Rules Laid Down: A Critique of Interpretivism and Neutral Principles,* 96 HARV. L. REV. 781 (1983).

11. *See* Brest, *supra* note 10, *passim.*

12. *See* Herbert Wechsler, *Toward Neutral Principles of Constitutional Law,* 73 HARV. L. REV. 1 (1959). Mark Tushnet has vigorously attacked Wechsler's theory. *See* Tushnet, *supra* note 10, at 806-24. The difficulties that he points out, the aggregation of preferences of different judges with different personal agendas, the difficulty of applying two or more inconsistent principles to a hard case, the difficulties in working a system of precedent, and the inability of professional craft to solve principled questions, are difficulties that face any theory of interpretation. When there is a document or provision that contains fundamental inconsistency, no doctrine of interpretation can avoid embarrassment, for the choices are no longer semantic, but instead turn on deciding which compromise causes the least disruption to the overall system—the sort of question that no logician could answer about a system that contains a formal contradiction in its axioms.

13. Brest, *supra* note 10, at 226.

14. The inquiry ranges over the choice of the applicable norm for social welfare, the holdout problems that arise when takings are not allowed at all, and the excessive level of government expenditure when they are allowed without compensation. *See, e.g.,* EPSTEIN, TAKINGS, *supra* note 1, at 202-09.

15. Indeed, I take odd comfort from Laurence Tribe and Michael Dorf's use of Lockean notions of private property in structuring the proper interpretation of the Takings Clause. LAURENCE H. TRIBE & MICHAEL C. DORF, ON READING THE CONSTITUTION 70-71 (1991). Although this view undergirds my attack in TAKINGS on the crabbed readings of the Takings Clause, Tribe and Dorf fail to spell out the systematic implications of their position and are content to dismiss mine because of its "false unitary vision" of the Constitution. *Id.* at 28. They also neglect to

explain how the Takings Clause, as interpreted through a Lockean prism, can be reconciled with the New Deal.

16. *See, e.g.,* NLRB v. Jones & Laughlin Steel Corp., 301 U.S. 1 (1937). For my criticism of the Court's Commerce Clause jurisprudence, see Richard A. Epstein, *The Proper Scope of the Commerce Power,* 73 VA. L. REV. 1387 (1987).

17. *See, e.g.,* Cass R. Sunstein, *Lochner's Legacy,* 87 COLUM. L. REV. 873 (1987). His reading of *Lochner* is incorrect, largely because the case did not go far enough into making constitutional imperatives out of common law baselines. It is sufficient to note, however, that the acceptance of extensive regulation of health and safety, notwithstanding contractual agreements to the contrary, is an important deviation from the common law principle of assumption of risk, at least as it was construed during the nineteenth century.

18. 17 U.S. (4 Wheat.) 316, 407 (1819).

19. *See supra* note 16 and accompanying text.

20. 347 U.S. 483 (1954).

21. 410 U.S. 113 (1973). The case has been the subject of a plethora of literature. *See, e.g.,* MARY A. GLENDON, ABORTION AND DIVORCE IN WESTERN LAW (1987); John H. Ely, *The Wages of Crying Wolf: A Comment on* Roe v. Wade, 82 YALE L.J. 920 (1973).

22. *See* DIG. 9.2. The *Lex Aquilia* is reproduced in full in F.H. LAWSON, NEGLIGENCE IN THE CIVIL LAW 80-137 (1950). I have used Lawson's translations.

23. DIG. 9.2.2.

24. The *actio iniuriarum,* an all-purpose statute dealing with insult as well as physical injury, contains the limited protection afforded free men in the codes. Because the *actio iniuriarum* began as a remedy for intentional insult, the statute only protects free men from intentional physical harm, although the *Lex Aquilia* provides remedies for both intentional and unintentional physical harm to slaves. *See generally* W. W. BUCKLAND, A TEXT-BOOK OF ROMAN LAW 584-88 (Wm. W. Gaunt & Sons, Inc. 1990) (1921).

25. *See* David Daube, *On the Third Chapter of the Lex Aquilia,* 52 LAW Q. REV. 253, 268 (1936).

26. The question of personal excuses, however, is not important in public law because the state can always hire someone competent enough to discharge the public task. Excuses differ from justifications because they concede the wrongfulness of the act, but indicate that some personal weakness of the defendant requires that blame not be attached to the individual who has performed that act. To illustrate the difference, consider the case of a battered wife. If she kills her husband, she can plead her condition as an excuse or a justification. If she hired a third person to do the killing for her, then that person could prevail only if a justification is shown.

27. Indeed, this is a literal translation of the Latin that combines *jus* with *facere* into justification.

28. "Now we must take killing to mean whether someone hit him with a sword or even a stick or other weapon or the hands (if, for instance, he strangled him) or kicked or butted or in any way whatever. But if one who is overloaded throws down his burden and kills a slave, the Aquilian action lies; for it was in his discretion not to burden himself so. For even if a man slips and crushes another's slave with his burden, Pegasus says that he is liable under the *Lex Aquilia,*

provided that he loaded himself unduly or carelessly walked through a slippery place." DIG. 9.2.7.1-9.2.7.2. As a telltale sign of the conceptual difficulty in this last case, the result is assigned to a particular authority, Pegasus, which suggests that those of more literal inclinations had disagreed with him on this case.

29. *Id.* 9.2.7.2.

30. "But if a man throws someone off a bridge, Celsus says that, whether he dies from the impact or is at once drowned, or is overcome by the force of the current and dies from exhaustion, the offender is liable under the *Lex Aquilia,* just as if someone had dashed a boy against a stone."*Id.* 9.2.7.7.

31. *Id.* 9.2.7.5.

32. *See* S.F.C. MILSOM, HISTORICAL FOUNDATIONS OF THE COMMON LAW, ch. 11 (2d ed. 1981). Within the common law the verbal grounds of distinction are between harms that are immediate and direct and those that are simply consequential. Behind this verbal distinction, however, lies the same set of concerns faced by the Romans. Those cases in which force was used could not be distinguished in principle from cases in which the injury occurred from an indirect act. This is illustrated in the English cases by the rider who is struck by a falling beam and the rider who trips over a beam that lies in the roadway. Note that the question of plaintiff's conduct is relevant here, just as it is in the Roman poison cases discussed in the text.

33. ROBERT GRAVES, I, CLAUDIUS (1982).

34. "Again if a midwife gives a woman a drug from which she dies, Labeo draws this distinction, that if she administered it with her own hands, she is held to have killed: but if she gave it to the woman for her to take it herself, an action *in factum* must be given; and this opinion is correct, for she furnished a cause of death rather than killed." DIG. 9.2.9.

35. ARISTOTLE, NICOMACHEAN ETHICS, bk. V, ch. 8 (Martin Ostwald trans., 1962).

36. *Id.*

37. *See* DIG. 9.2.3-9.2.5.

38. For the Roman materials, see G. INST. 4.35-4.60; BARRY NICHOLAS, AN INTRODUCTION TO ROMAN LAW 23-27 (1962). For a discussion of the common law rules, see RALPH SUTTON, PERSONAL ACTIONS AT COMMON LAW, ch. 4 (1929).

39. *See* Richard A. Epstein, *Pleadings and Presumptions,* 40 U. CHI. L. REV. 556 (1973). For an application of that system to tort law, see Richard A. Epstein, *A Theory of Strict Liability,* 2 J. LEGAL STUD. 151 (1973); Richard A. Epstein, *Defenses and Subsequent Pleas in a System of Strict Liability,* 3 J. LEGAL STUD. 165 (1974); Richard A. Epstein, *Intentional Harms,* 4 J. LEGAL STUD. 391 (1975).

40. *See, e.g.,* Vincent v. Lake Erie Trans. Co., 124 N.W. 221 (Minn. 1910); Ploof v. Putnam, 71 A. 188 (Vt. 1908).

41. DIG. 9.2.45.4 (requiring payment notwithstanding necessity); *id.* 9.2.41.1 (allowing the defense of necessity, in case of fire).

42. *Id.* 9.2.7.4.

43. *Id.* 9.2.5.3-9.2.7.

44. U.S. CONST. art. I, § 2, cl. 2.

45. *Id.* § 3, cl. 3.

46. *Id.* amend. IV, § 1.

47. *See, e.g.,* Olmstead v. United States, 277 U.S. 438, 466 (1928).

48. For a discussion of these doctrines, see Richard A. Epstein, *Nuisance Law: Corrective Justice and its Utilitarian Constraints*, 8 J. LEGAL STUD. 51, 82-98 (1979).

49. 105 S.E.2d 564 (W. Va. 1958).

50. *Id.* at 565.

51. *Id.* at 568.

52. 389 U.S. 347 (1967).

53. *Id.* at 352.

54. *Id.* at 353.

55. Lucas v. South Carolina Coastal Council, 112 S. Ct. 2886, 2903 (1992) (Kennedy, J., concurring).

56. *See, e.g.*, McDaniel v. Atlanta Coca-Cola Bottling Co., 2 S.E.2d 810, 816 (Ga. Ct. App. 1939); Rhodes v. Graham, 37 S.W.2d 46, 47 (Ky. 1931).

57. JEREMY BENTHAM, THE THEORY OF LEGISLATION 111-12 (C. K. Ogden ed. & Richard Hildreth trans., Routledge & Kegan Paul Ltd. 1950) (1931).

58. Albert W. Alschuler, *Interpersonal Privacy and the Fourth Amendment*, 4 N. ILL. U. L. REV. 1, 41-42 (1983).

59. Alschuler writes: "Chaucer said that no man could sufficiently comprehend nor search the Lord God; the King James version of the bible included the psalm, 'O Lord, thou hast searched me and known me'; Shakespeare inquired 'if zealous love should go in search of virtue'; Milton proclaimed, 'Now clear I understand what oft my steadiest thoughts have searched in vain'; and John Locke spoke of those 'who seriously search after . . . truth.' Noah Webster's first dictionary, published in 1828, defined the word search in part as 'to inquire, to seek for. [A] quest [or] pursuit.' Samuel Johnson's earlier, pre-fourth-amendment work had used almost identical language. Without contending that the fourth amendment governs all searches for truth and virtue, one may recognize that it encompasses more than visual inspections."*Id.* at 42 (footnotes omitted).

60. *Id.* at 43.

61. *Id.* at 43-44.

62. U.S. CONST. amend. V, cl. 3.

63. *See, e.g.*, Yee v. City of Escondido, 112 S. Ct. 1522, 1526 (1992).

64. *See* Pumpelly v. Green Bay Co., 80 U.S. (13 Wall.) 166, 180 (1871).

65. *See* Laird v. Nelms, 406 U.S. 797, 802-03 (1972).

66. *See* EPSTEIN, TAKINGS, *supra* note 1, at 80-86 (1985).

67. 543 P.2d 905, 920 (Cal.), *cert. denied*, 429 U.S. 869 (1975).

68. *See* Loretto v. Teleprompter Manhattan CATV Corp., 458 U.S. 419, 438-40 (1982).

69. Yee v. City of Escondido, 112 S. Ct. 1522 (1992). One manifest irony that pervades this area is that the line between physical invasion and nontrespassory account has been properly scrapped in Fourth Amendment jurisprudence, but receives inordinate sanctification in takings jurisprudence. For criticism of *Yee*, see Richard A. Epstein, Yee v. City of Escondido: *The Supreme Court Strikes Out Again*, 26 LOY. L.A. L. REV. (forthcoming November 1992).

70. *See generally* ERNST FREUND, THE POLICE POWER, PUBLIC POLICY & CONSTITUTIONAL RIGHTS (1904); CHRISTOPHER G. TIEDEMAN, A TREATISE ON THE LIMITATIONS OF POLICE POWER IN THE UNITED STATES (Da Capo Press 1971) (1886). There is also an extensive discussion of the police power in 2 THOMAS M. COOLEY, A TREATISE ON THE CONSTITUTIONAL LIMITATIONS, ch. 16 (1927).

71. 249 U.S. 47, 51-52 (1919).

72. 250 U.S. 616, 624 (1919).

73. 341 U.S. 494, 517 (1951).

74. 395 U.S. 444, 447 (1969).

75. *See supra* notes 46-61 and accompanying text.

76. *See, e.g.,* Lucas v. South Carolina Coastal Council, 404 S.E.2d 895, 896 (1991), *rev'd,* 112 S. Ct. 2886 (1992).

77. *But see* Reynolds v. United States, 98 U.S. 145, 168 (1878).

78. *But see* United States v. Lee, 455 U.S. 252, 259-60 (1982).

79. *See* RICHARD A. EPSTEIN, FORBIDDEN GROUNDS: THE CASE AGAINST EMPLOY-MENT DISCRIMINATION LAWS, ch. 6 (1992).

80. The same could be said about explicit classifications for the military or for many pension and insurance programs as well.

81. 429 U.S. 190 (1976).

82. *Id.* at 200-01.

83. Fred Schauer pressed this issue on me at the initial presentation of my lecture at Dartmouth.

84. The historical explanation for the maxim had, it appears, less to do with the structure of pleading and more to do with the content of the substantive law. The concern was with the mix of truth and falsity in statements made about the Crown (to whom the maxim was confined in any event). Where those statements were manifestly false in all particulars, there was little risk that they could lead to civil disorder or revolution. They would be dismissed by the public as the ravings of a lunatic fringe. But where the false statements were craftily mixed in with true statements, they would gain credibility and hence pose a greater threat to sovereign power because of their enhanced capacity to persuade. The maxim did not mean that wholly truthful statements are the most wrongful. It was an effort to get at concealed half truths. *See, e.g.,* WILFRED A. BUTTON, PRINCIPLES OF LIBEL AND SLANDER 16 (1935); 2 JAMES FITZJAMES STEPHEN, A HISTORY OF THE CRIMINAL LAW OF ENGLAND 307 (1883). For the observation on the historical point, my thanks to Boris Bittker who pointed them out and who supplied some historical references.

85. Philadelphia Newspapers v. Hepps, 475 U.S. 767, 776 (1986).

86. 376 U.S. 254, 279-80 (1964).

4

PRAGMATISM

Pragmatism is an extremely diverse philosophical movement that began in the nineteenth century with Charles Sanders Pierce and was continued by William James, John Dewey, and many others. Today pragmatism is espoused by philosophers and legal scholars whose political views vary from the far left to the far right and whose backgrounds vary from literary theory to economics.

Our representative of pragmatism is Richard Posner, who is not only a prolific author but also a judge on the United States Court of Appeals for the Seventh Circuit. In a recent article, "What has Pragmatism to Offer Law?" Posner defines pragmatism in terms of three "essential elements": "The first is a distrust of metaphysical entities ('reality,' 'truth,' 'nature,' etc.) viewed as warrants for certitude whether in epistemology, ethics, or politics. The second is an insistence that propositions be tested by their consequences, by the difference they make—and if they make none, set aside. The third is an insistence on judging our projects, whether scientific, ethical, political, or legal, by their conformity to social or other human needs rather than to 'objective,' 'impersonal' criteria."

All three of these themes are displayed in the following selection from Posner's recent book, The Problems of Jurisprudence. *Posner attacks the metaphysical notions of plain meaning and legislative intention or purpose. He argues instead that legal interpretations should be tested by their consequences for society. He also claims that judges should look not just at supposedly objective principles but at all human needs, including economic needs. (Posner is one of the leading figures in the "law and economics" movement, which claims that law does and should seek to maximize society's wealth.) In these ways, Posner's theory contrasts sharply with Dworkin's claims that judges should base their decisions on principles rather than policies and should be constrained by past precedents.*

The most common criticism of pragmatism in constitutional interpretation is that it gives judges too much power, because it leaves them free to overlook traditional legal materials and impose their own controversial judgments about the comparative value of the consequences of their decisions. In our selection, Posner responds to these criticisms by pointing out the practical constraints on judicial decisions and the risks of judicial blindness to the concrete consequences of decisions.

W. S-A.

Interpretation Revisited

Richard A. Posner

The Plain-Meaning Fallacy

Interpreting a text is not deduction . . . , but maybe it is something almost as straightforward—a matter of reading carefully and letting the plain meaning of the words dictate the interpretation of the text. Holmes offered an influential version of the plain-meaning approach: "We ask, not what [the author] meant, but what those words would mean in the mouth of a normal speaker of English, using them in the circumstances in which they were used."[1] Adherent to a referential theory of language that he was, Holmes did not consider interpretation of the written word problematic. And, antimentalist that he was, he did not want judges to waste their time trying to peer into people's minds. Apart from the philosophical and evidentiary problems of doing so, there is the distinct possibility that the effort will be fruitless simply because the author meant nothing so far as the case at hand is concerned.[2] A question of interpretation that arose and was addressed in the legislative proceedings may be readily answerable, provided the proceedings are recorded and the question was not divisive. But since there will be no mental state to recover if the question did not arise, a Pentothal theory of statutory interpretation will have at best a limited domain.

Holmes's theory is not much better, however. If, as the quoted passage seems to imply, the meaning of words depends on what the text's authors understood by them, weird discontinuities in reference arise, akin to the suggestion that Democritus and Bohr were not referring to the same thing when they said "atom." The Fourth Amendment on this view could not reach wiretapping or other electronic eavesdropping, because no user of the English language in 1789 could have understood the words "searches and seizures" to refer to wiretapping. The "press" to which the First Amendment refers could not mean a television network. If the government subsidized religious broadcasters, this could not be an establishment of religion. Congress's power to create an army and a navy would not authorize the creation of an air force.

Holmes's "normal English speaker" test designates one of several possible linguistic communities (America 1789, in the case of the Bill of Rights) as authoritative and forbids translation between it and any other such community, including America 1989. Whether the authors' linguistic community is the right one to use to fix statutory meaning is not, as Holmes seems to have thought, self-evident. A statute imposes a duty on imported vegetables but not on imported fruits, and the question arises whether the duty applies to tomatoes.[3] To the botanist, a tomato is a fruit, but so are peas and beans, and to ordinary folk these are all vegetables because they are not eaten for dessert. Which is the relevant interpretive community? Suppose it were known somehow that all the legislators who voted for the statute had thought it exempted tomatoes; what weight if any should their understanding have? Or suppose that although in 1883, when the statute was passed, everyone classified tomatoes as fruits, today everyone classifies them as vegetables, and the statute has not been repealed. Should today's meaning govern here, as most lawyers would think it should govern in the constitutional examples I gave in the preceding paragraph, or should the original meaning? Whatever the answers, Holmes's formulation begs the questions.

The inadequacy of that formulation can be further shown by distinguishing between internal (or semantic) ambiguity and external ambiguity, a distinction corresponding to the contract lawyer's distinction between intrinsic and extrinsic ambiguity. Internal ambiguity is present when a person who reads a sentence and knows the language that it is written in, but nothing about the circumstances in which it was written, finds it unclear. Either there is an internal contradiction, or the grammar and syntax of the sentence fail to disambiguate a word or phrase that has more than one meaning, for example, "due process" in the Fifth and Fourteenth Amendments or "equal" in the equal protection clause of the Fourteenth Amendment. External ambiguity is present, and with the same consequence, when the sentence, though clear to a normal English speaker ignorant of its background, is unclear, garbled, or means something different from what the normal English speaker thinks to someone who *does* know the background. An example is the word "press" in the First Amendment, which to the normal English speaker refers to print media only but, so limited, seems incongruous in light of modern methods of disseminating news and opinion. Another example is the inheritance statute in *Riggs v. Palmer* [where Elmer Palmer was denied inheritance from his grandfather whom he had murdered].[4] The statute said that a bequest in a will complying with specified formalities was enforceable. There was no ambiguity until one brought in from outside the fact that the person named in the bequest had murdered the author of the will. Holmes's plain-meaning approach rules out arguments of external ambiguity, and by doing so artificially truncates the interpretive process. One can understand the appeal of such an approach to a formalist, because it treats meaning as an affair purely of words, unaffected by the things to which the words might be taken to refer. But Holmes was not a formalist, and his approach looks good only in comparison with a plain-meaning approach that by completely ignoring the author's linguistic community puts itself at the mercy of semantic drift.

We can begin to sense the *variety* of interpretive methods that compete for the law's attention. But more important to the quest for interpretive objectivity than flexing our taxonomic muscles is developing a sense of what kind of text a statute is. If we think it is like a work of literature, we might as well throw up our hands, because the prospects for finding agreed-upon meaning in such works are at present dim; the interpretive community in literature has become so fragmented that the meanings of the great literary texts cannot be fixed. The differences between legal and literary texts are so great that the lawyer should not be troubled by the disarray in the literary community, but at the same time he cannot expect much help from the methods of literary interpretation.[5] I think a statute is better understood not as a literary work but as a command, so that Holmes was on the right track when he suggested (but not when he promptly retracted the suggestion, without explanation, in favor of the plain-meaning approach) that "in the case of a statute . . . it would be possible to say that as we are dealing with the commands of the sovereign the only thing to do is to find out what the sovereign wants."[6] . . .

The Quest for Interpretive Theory

Characterizing a statute as a command makes it natural to think of interpretation in terms of ascertaining the drafters' wants, to which their words are only a clue. A lieutenant, commanding the lead platoon in an attack, finds his way blocked by an unexpected enemy pillbox. He has two choices (other than to break off the attack): to go straight ahead at the pillbox or to try to bypass it on the left. He radios his company commander for instructions. The commander replies "Go—" but before he can say anything more the radio goes dead. If the platoon commander decides that, not having received an intelligible command, he should do nothing until communications are restored, his decision will be wrong. The part of the message that was received indicates that his commander wanted him to continue with the attack, and almost certainly the commander would have preferred the lieutenant, as the man on the spot, to make his own decision on how to do this than to do nothing and let the attack fail. For the lieutenant to take the position that he should do nothing because he lacks a clear order would be an irresponsible "interpretation" of his captain's command.

Notice the forward-looking character of the interpretive method illustrated by my military example, compared with the backward-looking character of the truth-serum, or mental-excavation, and plain-meaning approaches. There is a difference, if only in tone or attitude— but such differences can be important—between an interpretive approach that emphasizes fidelity to the past and one that emphasizes adaptation to the future (what is to be *done?*).[7] It is the difference between a traditionalist and a pragmatic approach to law. The pragmatist will recognize the aptness to statutory interpretation of W. H. Auden's description (in his poem "In Memory of W. B. Yeats") of the interpretation of a poem: "The words of a dead man / Are modified in the guts of the living." The plain-meaning approach to statutory interpretation excludes consideration of present-day conditions; the pragmatic approach views a statute as a resource for coping with the problems of the present, which is to say the statute's future. It makes no difference on the pragmatic account whether the text is superficially clear (that is, clear without regard to the world); unclear; or, as in the military example, patently incomplete (a particularly transparent form of unclarity).

American judges are frequently in the position of the platoon commander in my example. The legislature's commands are unclear and the judges cannot ask the legislators for clarification.[8] In that situation the judges should not think of themselves as failed archaeologists or antiquarians. They are part of a living enterprise—the enterprise of governing the United States—and when the orders of their superiors are unclear this does not absolve them from responsibility for helping to make the enterprise succeed. The responsible platoon commander will ask himself what his captain would have wanted him to do if communications should fail, and similarly judges should ask themselves, when the message imparted by a statute is unclear, what the legislature would have wanted them to do in such a case of failed communication. The answer may be "nothing"; or there may be no answer; but the question ought to be asked. . . .

The basic point of the military analogy . . . is that even in a system more hierarchical and homogeneous than the judicial, interpretation is creative rather than mechanical. It is an effort to make sense of a situation (compare the interpretation of dreams), not just of a text or other communication. When confronting unclear statutes, judges, like junior officers confronting unclear commands, have to summon all their powers of imagination and empathy, in an effort—doomed to frequent failure—to place themselves in the position of the legislators who enacted the statute that they are being asked to interpret. They cannot only study plain meanings; they must try to understand the problem that the legislators faced. This is the method of "imaginative reconstruction". . . .

Imaginative reconstruction so conceived sometimes works, especially when the judge is dealing with public interest legislation such as the wills statute in *Riggs*. Its abiding weakness is its patness. There is no trick to putting yourself in Homer's shoes in an effort to understand the *Iliad* (one of Vico's examples of imaginative reconstruction), *if* Homer was just another reasonable guy, like you and me. It is no great trick to put yourself in the shoes of the framers of the Constitution if the framers differ from us only in that we know more, having the benefit of an additional two centuries of history and a knowledge of today that they of course lacked. But suppose we are realistic and acknowledge that the framers were different from us, had different training, upbringing, and experiences and therefore different values. Then we have the impossible task of imagining how they would decide a question arising today if they knew what we know. It is impossible not only in practice but in theory. People are what they are, have the values they have, and so forth not only because of temperament but also because of what they know through experience and study; they are historically situated. If the framers had known what we know, they might have had different values from those they in fact had. Clones of Hamilton, Madison, and the other framers, if living today, might think better or worse of federalism, fundamental rights, religion, and sexual license than their originals did.

Here is a homely illustration of the limitations of imaginative reconstruction. I have invited a friend for dinner at 7:30, and I want to know whether he will be on time. It's unlikely that I will try, or would succeed if I did try, to imagine myself him; instead I will use induction from his record of promptness or tardiness on other occasions to estimate whether he will be early or late (and if so by how much) this time.[9] Induction is full of pitfalls, but imaginative reconstruction has even more. The situation is much the same when statutory interpretation is viewed as a problem in predicting how the legislators would have responded to the interpretive question presented by the case at hand. Usually it will be infeasible for the judge to imagine himself the legislator (in part, of course, because he would have to imagine himself the whole legislature), and he will be remitted to induction. But this will be induction from the past behavior not of friends but of legislators— people the judge probably does not know personally or even know much about—and will be a daunting task.

Statutes passed at a time when women were not eligible to vote often provided that jurors were to be selected from lists of persons eligible to vote. When women get the vote, do they become eligible for jury duty?[10] The legislators who voted for these statutes probably did not think that women should serve on juries. If we say that were they living today they would have a different view, we are changing them into different people—ourselves—and this is always a danger with imaginative reconstruction. We could take the following tack: the apparent *purpose* of the statutes was to tie juror eligibility to voter eligibility, thus ensuring minimum qualifications without the bother of establishing and enforcing separate criteria for jurors. As criteria for voting eligibility change, the criteria for jury eligibility change automatically. The legislators' streamlined approach to determining eligibility for jury duty would be thwarted if every change in the criteria for voting eligibility drove a wedge between those criteria and the criteria for jury eligibility. But if we are to be faithful to legislative purpose, we would have to consider how strongly the legislators opposed the idea of women's serving on juries. Did they feel so strongly on this subject—in enacting a statute not directed at the issue of women on juries at all—as to want to project their feelings into a future era in which the social role of women had changed? That seems unlikely. But perhaps this sort of counterfactual speculation is bootless, and should be avoided altogether.

Against purposive interpretation it can be further argued that statutes are often the result of a compromise between contending factions or interest groups,[11] and purposive interpretation can easily undo a compromise. Suppose the legislature has enacted a statute forbidding some form of securities fraud but has failed to authorize persons injured by a violation of the statute to bring damages suits against violators; and suppose it is demonstrable that there would be greater compliance with the statute if such suits were possible. Should we say that the purpose of the statute would be served by interpreting the statute to authorize them? The omission of any statutory reference to damages suits may have been the price the statute's supporters had to pay in order to assemble a majority in the face of doubts about the statute's wisdom, pressures from securities firms, or whatever. If so, the purposive interpretation would give one of the contending factions a benefit it had been unable to win in the legislative arena. We must also consider what the legislators knew about how courts treat statutes that do not mention damages actions. Suppose they had no idea, maybe because courts were not consistent in their treatment. This would imply that rather than striking a compromise on whether damages actions would be allowed, the legislators had left the question to the courts.

The alternative to purposive interpretation is to attempt to ascertain the deal embodied in the statute and enforce that deal. But since the deal is likely to be under the table, how is the court to determine its terms? Contracts are deals, too, but they set on foot a cooperative activity, and often it is apparent what interpretation is necessary to protect or promote that activity. A legislative deal may simply be a wealth transfer to an interest group, and it may be impossible to discover by the methods available to judges whether the transfer seems incomplete because that was as far as the deal went or because the legislators merely failed, through lack of foresight, to provide for the contingency that has arisen. It does not seem that *all* legislation is of this character, but it is exceptionally difficult for courts to determine whether they are dealing with an unprincipled deal that has no spirit to guide interpretation, with a statute that was passed in the public interest and ought to receive a generous, a purposive, interpretation, or finally with a statute that was passed in the public interest but contains limitations included at the behest of powerful interest groups—limitations that were the price of getting the statute passed.[12] Judges are tempted to ignore such limitations, but if they do, this may make it difficult for such statutes to get passed in the future. And judges would cause an uproar if they refused to enforce a statute whose purpose was clearly discernible on the ground that the statute, though constitutional, reflected an unprincipled deal with some special-interest group and therefore was unworthy of being enforced.

The "deals" approach can be tucked into the purposive approach by noting that the relevant purpose is not that of the faction that was pushing the legislation but that of the enactment itself with any compromises that may have been built into it. But this is one of these semantic reconciliations that gives no satisfaction to the practically minded. Purposive interpretation is useless if the purposes cannot be discerned, and the presence of compromise makes the discernment of purpose difficult and often impossible. Notice, finally, the attraction of the deals approach to the legal positivist: brisk and confident judicial enforcement of the nakedly, amorally redistributive statute exemplifies the separation of law and morals.

Indeterminate Statutory Cases

When imaginative reconstruction fails, when purposive interpretation fails, or when these techniques reveal simply that the matter in question has been left to the courts to decide according to their own lights, statutory interpretation is transformed into judicial policy making, and the usual problems of judicial objectivity arise. This helps explain the enduring appeal of the plain-meaning approach; it avoids the uncertainties of interpretation. But it does so at a high price: that of refusing to take seriously the communicative intent, and broader purposes alike, of the legislators in the many cases in which that intent can be discerned, and of refusing to play a constructive role in the development of sound public policies in the remaining cases.

In the first two eventualities with which I began this section (cases of interpretive failure, one might call them), we have no clue to what the legislature wanted, and in the third one we know or think we know that it wanted the judges to make up their own minds. So the last is a matter of delegation and might be thought to vest the courts with common law rule-making powers, while the first two raise questions of legitimacy—who has authorized the courts to decide statutory cases when the meaning of the statute is unknown? But practically the three cases are the same. The fact that a legislature is unable to resolve a policy issue, such as whether a particular statute should be enforceable by suits for damages, does not warrant an inference that it *wanted* the courts to resolve it or that the courts should accept the role of supplementary legislature. The legislature may have had neither desire nor opinion as to whether the courts should try to close the gaps and dispel the ambiguities in its handiwork. Whether a gap in legislation arises because the legislators lacked foresight or because they were unable to agree on how to close the gap or because they lacked the time to deal with the question or because they just did not care does not dictate what attitude the courts should take toward the gap. Cases where legislatures explicitly delegate policy-making tasks to courts are rare, so the difference between the accidental and the deliberate gap has little practical significance. In either case the court must decide whether to fill it. If it does fill it, the court will be exercising the kind of discretion that a common law court uses to decide a question not ruled by precedent.
. . .

Is Communication Ever Possible?

By stressing the negative I risk leaving the impression that I think *all* statutory and constitutional interpretations are policy decisions by judges. That would amount to a denial of the possibility of written communication. Some people do deny this possibility—though in the same spirit, which is to say purely speculative, in which some people deny the existence of an external world. The communication skeptics think, or rather say, that the possibility of communication depends on the outmoded epistemology in which I have a mental picture (say, of the tree in front of my house) that I want to convey to you, I therefore encode it in a sign that you will recognize (the spoken words "tree in front of my house"—assuming we are both normal English speakers), you use the sign to create the identical picture in your head, and in that way an idea is conveyed intact from one mind to another. If this theory were correct, it would indeed make communication "objective" in a strong sense; communication would be a method of conveying an object from sender to recipient. Although properly emphasizing the importance of symbols in communication, the theory is not correct, or at least is radically incomplete.[13] It fails to recognize that most communication is conducted without any mental images; that simple, easily visualizable physical objects are an infrequent subject of communication—yet successful communication is not infrequent; that successful communication depends on a host of unspoken understandings; that (illustrating the last point) to insist on the sharing of mental images leads to the absurdity of the assistant in MacCallum's example[14] who failed to bring back any ashtrays because he was not sure which of the ones he had seen were the ones his boss had "in mind"; and that, as the same example also shows, communication is possible even when the communicants have different mental images of the objects being discussed.

We know that spoken communication works not because we can peer into the minds of the speaker and the listener and observe "intersubjectivity" but because we observe that the listener does what the speaker wanted him to do (the assistant fetched the ashtrays, and without tearing any off the walls, either). Written communication works too,[15] even though the recipient of a written communication will not have the cues provided by inflection and facial expression and may have no opportunity to ask the writer to repeat or explain the message.[16] We can show this by the same type of evidence by which we show that oral communication works. Consider the assembly of a piece of equipment from a set of written directions. With patience, common sense, and some understanding of the purpose of the equipment, the reader of the directions can construct the equipment without conferring with the author, and the successful construction verifies the hypothesis that written as well as oral communication is possible—sometimes, anyway. Although it cannot be proved that written communication can also work when the writer is dead, or is a committee (all of whose members may be dead), or wrote in a language different from that of the reader,[17] none of these conditions, or even all taken together, is inconsistent with the possibility of effective communication. Once we get away from the idea that communication requires being able to peek into the sender's mind, we need no longer fear that the fact that there are no group minds, and hence no "legislative intent" in a literal sense, makes the communication of statutory commands impossible. . . .

Beyond Interpretation

Despite my brave words in the previous section in defense of interpretation against attacks by extreme text skeptics, I readily acknowledge that the concept may be too various and loose to guide the application of statutes and the Constitution, and that we might be better off without it. Interpretation can be decoding of communications (and there it is least problematic), understanding, translation, extension, completion, transformation, even inversion. All that the term means concretely is that there is a text in the picture, the text is authoritative, and the decision must be related in some way to the text. Although this formulation may be slightly more directive than a definition of interpretation as the mediation of reality by language, it is not a formula for distinguishing sound interpretations from unsound ones. Maybe there is no formula, no methodology. Correctness in interpretation depends on the goal of the particular kind of interpretation, which may be why, for example, musical interpretation is not a useful analogy to statutory interpretation. But there is no agreement on what the goal of statutory or constitutional interpretation is. Maybe there are plural goals—fidelity to framers' intent, certainty, coherence, pragmatically good results. These are related, but different interpreters will give them different weights.

We could translate interpretive questions into questions about consequences. I come to a street crossing and the traffic light says "Walk." What does this mean? It certainly is not a command. It is not permission, either, for that would imply that "Wait" is a prohibition, which it is not in a realistic sense. If I cross the street when the light says "Wait," I am not going to be punished unless I am in one of the very few cities in the world in which jaywalking laws are enforced. "Wait" is a warning against the danger of crossing when vehicles have the right of way. What "Walk" means, as a practical matter, is that vehicles are unlikely to enter the crossing (other than by turning into it), because if they do they will be running a red light, a type of conduct that, unlike jaywalking, is punished. Thus the meaning of a green or a red light is discerned by imagining the consequences of alternative interpretations (for example, interpreting "Wait" to mean "Walk"). "I'll eat my hat"

. . . is a sentence that is interpreted ironically because of the consequences of interpreting it literally. Gerald MacCallum's ashtray examples are of the same character. Maybe the best thing to do when a statute is invoked is to examine the consequences of giving the invoker what he wants and then estimate whether those consequences will on the whole be good ones.[18]

This approach, which is pragmatic, does not justify, much less entail, ignoring the text. Not only is the text a source of information about the consequences of alternative "interpretations," but among the consequences to be considered is the impact that unpredictable statutory applications will have on communication between legislature and court. Normally, indeed, if communicative intent or legislative purpose can be discerned—in other words, if imaginative reconstruction works—that will be the end of the case.

Everything that now gets discussed in terms of interpretation would still get discussed but a term that seems no longer to have a useful meaning would be avoided, a fig leaf removed. The activist judge could not deny personal responsibility for his decisions by saying that all he was doing was interpretation, albeit loose rather than strict; neither could the restrained judge deny personal responsibility for his decisions by saying that all *he* was doing was interpretation, albeit strict rather than loose.

The approach is no cure-all. All too often, pragmatism without science is mush. The consequences foreseeable to a judge equipped only with legal training and experience, life experiences, and some common sense will be heavily influenced by the judge's personal values. The more diverse the judiciary is, the more difficult it will be to predict the outcome of statutory and constitutional cases if outcome depends on a projection and comparison of consequences. But since the American judiciary is and will remain diverse, would renewed dedication to "interpretation" be a better solution—or an evasion?. . .

A Case Study of Politics and Pragmatism

One of the most famous "interpretive" decisions in our history is the decision outlawing public school segregation. Fixed star in our judicial firmament that it is, *Brown v. Board of Education*[19] cannot be shown to be correct as a matter of interpretation.[20] As is so often true of legal decisions, its correctness is political rather than epistemic, pragmatic rather than apodictic.

The proposition that racial segregation in public schools denies black schoolchildren the "equal protection of the laws" guaranteed by section 1 of the Fourteenth Amendment does not have the inevitability of interpreting the age thirty-five provision to "mean what it says." The words "equal protection" are not obviously incompatible with a system of segregated schools, provided that the black schools are as good as the white ones. If they are not as good, the natural remedy, one might think, would be to order them improved. Since the motive for segregated schools was to keep blacks from mixing with whites, segregation stamped blacks with a mark of inferiority that common sense suggests could be very damaging to their self-esteem. But there is little evidence on this point, perhaps because the real damage was (and continues to be) done by the discriminatory attitudes that underlie racial discrimination rather than by the fact of segregation, which is an expression of those attitudes. Notice, by the way, that if this is right, it is further evidence against the view that law changes the attitudes of Americans as well as their behavior.

There is of course much more to be said about the issue of public school segregation. Apart from the psychological damage segregation may have caused blacks, it denied them the opportunity for valuable associations with whites—associations actually more valuable for blacks than for whites[21]—and probably produced more racial segregation than a free market in education would have done. Segregation had costly spillover effects in the northern states to which many blacks migrated in order to get away from it. And no doubt a white majority that insisted on segregation would have been unwilling to support truly equal public schools for blacks, yet the disparity would have been difficult to remedy by judicial decree. A goal of "separate but equal" might as a practical matter have been unattainable.

Against this powerful case for interpreting the equal protection clause to forbid public school segregation, however, it can be and was argued that the framers of the Fourteenth Amendment did not intend to bring about true equality between whites and blacks, but merely wanted to give the blacks certain fundamental political rights, not including the right to attend public schools on a footing of equality with whites.[22] Many white Northerners, as well as almost all white Southerners, would have thought it right and natural in 1868 that black people should attend segregated and inferior schools. Moreover, in 1896 the Supreme Court held that racial segregation in public facilities was constitutional,[23] and the public institutions of the South were built on that ruling. Any change, one could argue, should come from Congress, with its broad powers under the commerce clause and under section 5 of the Fourteenth Amendment (which empowers Congress to enforce the substantive provisions of the amendment).[24] It is true that congressional action was out of the question; southern Democrats controlled the key committees by virtue of their seniority. They owed their seniority to their safe seats, the consequence of the South's one-party system—

which in turn was the consequence in part of discrimination against blacks and in part of the South's continued resentment of Reconstruction. But a formalist would argue that a court should not consider such things; the opinion in *Brown* does not allude to them.

The "on the one hand, on the other hand" character of this analysis suggests that the ultimate justification for the *Brown* decision must be sought not in technical legal materials but in such political and ethical desiderata as improving the position of blacks; adopting a principle of racial (and implicitly also religious and ethnic) equality to vindicate the ideals for which World War II had recently been fought; raising public consciousness about racial injustice; promoting social peace through racial harmony; eradicating an institution that was an embarrassment to America's foreign policy;[25] reducing the social and political autonomy of the South ("completing the work of the Civil War"); finding a new institutional role for the Supreme Court to replace the discredited one of protecting economic liberty; breathing new life into the equal protection clause. If such considerations are not admissible, as on certain formalist accounts they are not, the decision in *Brown* is questionable.

I am not a formalist and do not regard the considerations I have mentioned as being out of bounds; nor do I think it was improper for the Court to consider the infeasibility of congressional action in the matter. . . . My central point is that *Brown* is not correct by virtue of being a demonstrably correct *interpretation* of the Constitution. . . .

Nor am I saying that the only possible dispositions toward *Brown* are interpretive certainty and utter agnosticism. In addition to (but related to) the natural law justification offered earlier (*Brown* as vindication of a moral norm that was influential then and that now commands a consensus), consider what we would think of a decision by the Supreme Court overruling *Brown* tomorrow on the ground that the decision was an incorrect interpretation of the Fourteenth Amendment. We would pronounce such a decision wrong even if we agreed that it rested on a defensible theory of constitutional interpretation. The decision would be an enormous provocation, stirring racial fears and hostilities in a nation more rather than less racially heterogeneous than when *Brown* was decided; it would be promptly overruled by Congress in the exercise of its powers under section 5 or the commerce clause; it would unsettle all of constitutional law, most of which rests on interpretive grounds no more powerful (and often much less so) than those of *Brown;* and whatever its actual motivations it would be thought to bespeak the politicization of the Court. It would in short be socially, politically, and legally destabilizing.

The example suggests that our legal certitudes are pragmatically rather than analytically grounded. The strongest defense of *Brown is* that the consequences of overruling it would be untoward. To borrow William James's formula, we believe that *Brown is* correct because that is a good, a useful, thing to believe. This may be true of most judicial decisions whose authority we are not disposed to question, whether they are ostensibly interpretive decisions or are leading cases in common law fields. . . .

Notes

1. "The Theory of Legal Interpretation," 12 *Harvard Law Review* 417-418 (1899). He is talking about contract interpretation but later makes clear that he thinks statutes should be interpreted the same way. See id. at 419-420.

2. For an illustration, see Zechariah Chafee, Jr., "The Disorderly Conduct of Words," 41 *Columbia Law Review* 381, 400 (1941).

3. The issue in *Nix v. Hedden,* 149 U.S. 304 (1893). The court answered "yes."

4. [22. N. E. 188 (1889).]

5. See my book *Law and Literature: A Misunderstood Relation,* ch. 5 (1988). I do think there are some fruitful analogies. . . . I also think that the interpretive disarray in the two fields may have common causes. See id. at 265-266. But no specific techniques of literary interpretation seem usable in the statutory arena.

6. "The Theory of Legal Interpretation," note 1 above, at 419.

7. See T. Alexander Aleinikoff, "Updating Statutory Interpretation," 87 *Michigan Law Review* 20, 21-22 (1988).

8. In California, legislators can be called as witnesses to testify regarding the intended meaning of a statute. See Comment, "Statutory Interpretation in California: Individual Testimony as an Extrinsic Aid," 15 *University of San Francisco Law Review* 241 (1980). The danger is that a legislator may try to alter the statute by offering an interpretation that was or would have been rejected by a majority of the legislators when the statute was passed; the interpretation may not correspond to the legislature's current preferences either.

9. Cf. Gilbert Ryle, *The Concept of Mind* 92 (1949).

10. Compare *Commonwealth v. Maxwell,* 271 Pa. 378, 114 Atl. 825 (1921), holding that they do, with People ex rel. *Fyfe v. Barnett,* 319 Ill. 403, 150 N.E. 290 (1926), and *Commonwealth v. Welosky,* 276 Mass. 398, 177 N.E. 656 (1931), holding that they do not.

11. The interest-group theory of legislation, and its bearing on statutory interpretation, are the subject of a vast scholarly literature in law, economics, and political science. See, for example, Arthur F. Bentley, *The Process of Government: A Study of Social Pressures* (1908); David B. Truman, *The Governmental Process: Political and Public Opinion* (1951); James M. Buchanan and Gordon Tullock, *The Calculus of Consent: Logical Foundations of Constitutional Democracy* (1962); George J. Stigler, *The Citizen and the State: Essays on Regulation* (1975); Gary S. Becker, "Pressure Groups and Political Behavior," in *Capitalism and Democracy: Schumpeter Revisited* 120 (Richard D. Coe and Charles K. Wilbur eds. 1985); "Symposium on the Theory of Public Choice," 74 *Virginia Law Review* 167 (1988).

12. The general point has been well stated by the Supreme Court: "No legislation pursues its purposes at all costs. Deciding what competing values will or will not be sacrificed to the achievement of a particular objective is the very essence of legislative choice—and it frustrates rather than effectuates legislative intent simplistically to assume that *whatever* furthers the statute's primary objective must be the law." *Rodriguez v. United States*, 480 U.S. 522 (1987) (per curiam). Unfortunately, the Court rather spoils things by relying heavily in the same opinion on canons of construction whose artificiality is in stark contrast to the realism of the passage just quoted.

13. As emphasized by the modern hermeneutic school of Gadamer and others. For useful discussions, see Joseph Rouse, *Knowledge and Power: Toward a Political Philosophy of Science*, ch. 3 (1987) (esp. pp. 42-47); Peter Goodrich, *Reading the Law: A Critical Introduction to Legal Method and Techniques*, ch. 4 (1986). Cf. Hilary Putnam, *Representation and Reality* 6-7, 24-25 (1988).

14. [MacCallum, "Legislative Intent," in *Essays in Legal Philosophy* 237, 256-257 (Robert S. Summers ed. 1968).]

15. "The possibility of filling mail orders correctly depends on a critically innocent use of language." Peter Caws, "Critical Innocence and Straight Reading," 17 *New Literary History* 165, 167 (1985).

16. Yet life might be simpler if legislation were spoken! For then we might know whether there is indeed such a thing as the "negative" or "dormant" commerce clause—that is, whether the commerce clause not only empowers Congress to regulate interstate and foreign commerce but also forbids the states to interfere with such commerce without Congress's authorization. Article I, §8, cl. 3 of the Constitution provides so far as pertinent here that "The Congress shall have Power . . . to regulate Commerce with foreign Nations, and among the several States." If the emphasis is placed on "Commerce," this is just a grant of power. If it is placed on "Congress," maybe the clause can be understood to be also allocating power between the states and Congress (an alternative, however, is that it is allocating power between Congress and the executive branch). Another way to look at this particular interpretive puzzle is with the aid of Collingwood's dictum that "every statement that anybody ever makes is made in answer to a question." R. G. Collingwood, *An Essay on Metaphysics* 23 (1940). The meaning of the commerce clause may depend on whether it is an answer to the question Who can regulate interstate commerce? or to the question Can Congress regulate interstate commerce? or to both questions.

17. But anyone who thinks deconstruction has *dis*proved these things does not understand deconstruction, on which see my discussion in *Law and Literature: A Misunderstood Relation*, ch. 5 (1988), and references there; also Reed Way Dasenbrock, "Accounting for the Changing Certainties of Interpretive Communities," 101 *Modern Language Notes* 1022 (1985); Alexander Nehamas, "Truth and Consequences: How to Understand Jacques Derrida," *New Republic*, Oct. 5, 1987, at 31.

18. See Max Radin, "Statutory Interpretation," 43 *Harvard Law Review* 863, 884 (1930), for a similar formulation.

19. 347 U.S. 483 (1954).

20. Do not forget the contemporary criticisms of the result by distinguished jurists. See Learned Hand, *The Bill of Rights: The Oliver Wendell Holmes Lectures, 1958* 54-55 (1958); Herbert Wechsler, "Toward Neutral Principles of Constitutional Law," 73 *Harvard Law Review* 1, 31-34 (1959).

21. See my book *The Economics of Justice* 355 (1981), criticizing the argument by Wechsler, note 20 above, that the costs which segregation imposed on blacks by preventing them from associating with whites were symmetrical with the costs that integration imposed on whites of unwanted association with blacks.

22. On the framers' intent, see Alexander M. Bickel, "The Original Understanding and the Segregation Decision," 69 *Harvard Law Review* 1, 56-59 (1955); Raoul Berger, *Government by Judiciary: The Transformation of the Fourteenth Amendment*, ch. 7 (1977); Aviam Soifer, "Protecting Civil Rights: A Critique of Raoul Berger's History," 54 *New York University Law Review* 651, 705-706 (1979).

23. See *Plessy v. Ferguson*, 163 U.S. 537 (1896).

24. It is questionable whether Congress could lawfully use section 5 to overrule a Supreme Court decision; that would not be *enforcing* the amendment, at least if the Court is considered the authoritative interpreter of the Constitution's meaning. See *Oregon v. Mitchell*, 400 U.S. 112, 128-129 (1970) (opinion of Justice Black). But this problem would disappear if Congress based legislation outlawing segregation on the commerce clause as well as on section 5 of the Fourteenth Amendment, as it did in the Civil Rights Act of 1964.

25. This point is emphasized in Mary L. Dudziak, "Desegregation as a Cold War Imperative," 41 *Stanford Law Review* 61 (1988).

5

LAW AS INTEGRITY

Ronald Dworkin is considered by many to be the most influential contemporary legal philosopher in both the United States and Great
Britain. Known to the general public primarily as a champion of liberal causes, he is best known to law professors as the proponent of the
view that law is essentially an interpretive enterprise. He is also a political philosopher whose critique of utilitarianism and defense of a
rights-based theory of justice have had significant impact.

Dworkin's approach to constitutional interpretation, law as integrity, holds that interpretations of the law should both fit and justify legal practice. As Dworkin explains in the selection below, legal
history imposes constraints on judges' and others' interpretations since
the legal enterprise requires consistency and coherence, like the game of
writing a chain novel. But Dworkin adds that "[a] successful interpretation must not only fit but also justify the practice it interprets," by understanding legal history in light of principles that make it "the best
it can be."

In Dworkin's view, judges must use moral theory in interpreting the
Constitution. Whereas legislators can appropriately base their decisions on judgments of what policy best serves some social goal, judges
must rely on moral principles in determining whether policy-based legislation violates constitutionally protected rights. The most fundamental principle in Dworkin's view is the "abstract egalitarian principle,"
which holds that citizens have a right to equal respect and concern on
the part of the government.

In order to illustrate how his theory works, Dworkin constructs a
mythical judge, Hercules, possessed of "superhuman intellectual power
and patience who accepts law as integrity." Hercules knows not only all

of legal history but also all relevant facts. In the following selection from **Law's Empire**, *Dworkin shows how Hercules would apply the abstract egalitarian principle to the debate about what theory of racial equality is implicit in the Fourteenth Amendment's requirement of "equal protection of the laws." Dworkin defends the view that the equal protection clause prohibits legal distinctions based on racial prejudice, although it does not prohibit racial classifications, such as those employed in affirmative action programs, that are not derived from what he calls "banned sources."*

Law as integrity is supposed to provide an explanation of the legitimacy of the coercive power of the law. Critics have argued that it fails to do this since judges who apply this method must rely on their own subjective moral views, especially in adjudicating hard cases where there may be no present consensus about which moral theory yields the right answer. It has also been argued that Hercules, or any judge employing Dworkin's method, is a usurper of democratic power. Some of Dworkin's responses to these objections can be found in the selection below.

S.J.B.

Integrity and Interpretation

Ronald   Dworkin

A Large View

. . . Law as integrity denies that statements of law are either the backward-looking factual reports of conventionalism[1] or the forward-looking instrumental programs of legal pragmatism.[2] It insists that legal claims are interpretive judgments and therefore combine backward- and forward-looking elements; they interpret contemporary legal practice seen as an unfolding political narrative. So law as integrity rejects as unhelpful the ancient question whether judges find or invent law; we understand legal reasoning, it suggests, only by seeing the sense in which they do both and neither.

Integrity and Interpretation

The adjudicative principle of integrity instructs judges to identify legal rights and duties, so far as possible, on the assumption that they were all created by a single author—community personified expressing a coherent conception of justice and fairness. We form our third conception of law, our third view of what rights and duties flow from past political decisions, by restating this instruction as a thesis about the grounds of law. According to law as integrity, propositions of law are true if they figure in or follow from the principles of justice, fairness, and procedural due process that provide the best constructive interpretation of the community's legal practice. Deciding whether the law grants Mrs. McLoughlin compensation for her injury,[3] for example, means deciding whether legal practice is seen in a better light if we assume the community has accepted the principle that people in her position are entitled to compensation.

Law as integrity is therefore more relentlessly interpretive than either conventionalism or pragmatism. These latter theories offer themselves *as* interpretations. They are conceptions of law that claim to show our legal practices in the best light these can bear, and they recommend, in their postinterpretive conclusions, distinct styles or programs for adjudication. But the programs they recommend are not themselves programs *of* interpretation: They do not ask judges deciding hard cases to carry out any further, essentially interpretive study of legal doctrine. Conventionalism requires judges to study law reports and parliamentary records to discover what decisions have been made by institutions conventionally recognized to have legislative power. No doubt interpretive issues will arise in that process: For example, it may be necessary to interpret a text to decide what statutes our legal conventions construct from it. But once a judge has accepted conventionalism as his guide, he has no further occasion for interpreting the legal record as a whole in deciding particular cases. Pragmatism requires judges to think instrumentally about the best rules for the future. That exercise may require interpretation of something beyond legal material: A utilitarian pragmatist may need to worry about the best way to understand the idea of community welfare, for example. But once again, a judge who accepts pragmatism is then done with interpreting legal practice as a whole.

Law as integrity is different: It is both the product of and the inspiration for comprehensive interpretation of legal practice. The program it holds out to judges deciding hard cases is essentially, not just contingently, interpretive; law as integrity asks them to continue interpreting the same material that it claims to have successfully interpreted itself. It offers itself as continuous with—the initial part of—the more detailed interpretations it recommends. . . .

Integrity and History

History matters in law as integrity: Very much but only in a certain way. Integrity does not require consistency in principle over all historical stages of a community's law; it does not require that judges try to understand the law they enforce as continuous in principle with the abandoned law of a previous century or even a previous generation. It commands a horizontal rather than vertical consistency of principle across the range of the legal standards the community now enforces. It insists that the law—the rights and duties that flow from past collective decisions and for that reason license or require coercion—contains not only the narrow explicit content of these decisions but also, more broadly, the scheme of principles necessary to justify them. History matters because that scheme of principle must justify the standing as well as the content of these past decisions. Our justification for treating the Endangered Species Act as law, unless and until it is repealed, crucially includes the fact that Congress enacted it, and any justification we supply for treating that fact as crucial must itself accommodate the way we treat other events in our political past.

Law as integrity, then, begins in the present and pursues the past only so far as and in the way its contemporary focus dictates. It does not aim to recapture, even for present law, the ideals or practical purposes of the politicians who first created it. It aims rather to justify what they did (sometimes including, as we shall see, what they said) in an overall story worth telling now, a story with a complex claim: That present practice can be organized by and justified in principles sufficiently attractive to provide an honorable future. Law as integrity deplores the mechanism of the older "law is law" view as well as the cynicism of the newer "realism." It sees both views as rooted in the same false dichotomy of finding and inventing law. When a judge declares that a particular principle is instinct in law, he reports not a simple-minded claim about the motives of past statesmen, a claim a wise cynic can easily refute, but an interpretive proposal: That the principle both fits and justifies some complex part of legal practice, that it provides an attractive way to see, in the structure of that practice, the consistency of principle integrity requires. Law's optimism is in that way conceptual; claims of law are endemically constructive, just in virtue of the kind of claims they are. This optimism may be misplaced: Legal practice may in the end yield to nothing but a deeply skeptical interpretation. But that is not inevitable just because a community's history is one of great change and conflict. An imaginative interpretation can be constructed on morally complicated, even ambiguous terrain.

The Chain of Law

The Chain Novel

[C]reative interpretation takes its formal structure from the idea of intention, not (at least not necessarily) because it aims to discover the purposes of any particular historical person or group but because it aims to impose purpose over the text or data or tradition being interpreted. Since all creative interpretation shares this feature, and therefore has a normative aspect or component, we profit from comparing law with other forms or occasions of interpretation. We can usefully compare the judge deciding what the law is on some issue not only with the citizens of courtesy deciding what that tradition requires, but with the literary critic teasing out the various dimensions of value in a complex play or poem.

Judges, however, are authors as well as critics. A judge deciding *McLoughlin* or *Brown*[4] adds to the tradition he interprets; future judges confront a new tradition that includes what he has done. Of course literary criticism contributes to the traditions of art in which authors work; the character and importance of that contribution are themselves issues in critical theory. But the contribution of judges is more direct, and the distinction between author and interpreter more a matter of different aspects of the same process. We can find an even more fruitful comparison between literature and law, therefore, by constructing an artificial genre of literature that we might call the chain novel.

In this enterprise a group of novelists writes a novel *seriatim;* each novelist in the chain interprets the chapters he has been given in order to write a new chapter, which is then added to what the next novelist receives, and so on. Each has the job of writing his chapter so as to make the novel being constructed the best it can be, and the complexity of this task models the complexity of deciding a hard case under law as integrity. The imaginary literary enterprise is fantastic but not unrecognizable. Some novels have actually been written in this way, though mainly for a debunking purpose, and certain parlor games for rainy weekends in English country houses have something of the same structure. Television soap operas span decades with the same characters and some minimal continuity of personality and plot, though they are written by different teams of authors even in different weeks. In our example, however, the novelists are expected to take their responsibilities of continuity more seriously; they aim jointly to create, so far as they can, a single unified novel that is the best it can be.[5]

Each novelist aims to make a single novel of the material he has been given, what he adds to it, and (so far as he can control this) what his successors will want or be able to add. He must try to make this the best novel it can be construed as the work of a single author rather than, as is the fact, the product of many different hands. That calls for an overall judgment on his part, or a series of overall judgments as he writes and rewrites. He must take up some view about the novel in progress, some working theory about its characters, plot, genre, theme, and point, in order to decide what counts as continuing it and not as beginning anew. If he is a good critic, his view of these matters will be complicated and multifaceted, because the value of a decent novel cannot be captured from a single perspective. He will aim to find layers and currents of meaning rather than a single, exhaustive theme. We can, however, . . . give some structure to any interpretation he adopts, by distinguishing two dimensions on which it must be tested. The first is . . . the dimension of fit. He cannot adopt any interpretation, however complex, if he believes that no single author who set out to write a novel with the various readings of character, plot, theme, and point that interpretation describes could have written substantially the text he has been given. That does not mean his interpretation must fit every bit of the text. It is not disqualified simply because he claims that some lines or tropes are accidental, or even that some events of plot are mistakes because they work against the literary ambitions the interpretation states. But the interpretation he takes up must nevertheless flow throughout the text; it must have general explanatory power, and it is flawed if it leaves unexplained some major structural aspect of the text, a subplot treated as having great dramatic importance or a dominant and repeated metaphor. If no interpretation can be found that is not flawed in that way, then the chain novelist will not be able fully to meet his assignment; he will have to settle for an interpretation that captures most of the text, conceding that it is not wholly successful. Perhaps even that partial success is unavailable; perhaps every interpretation he considers is inconsistent with the bulk of the material supplied to him. In that case he must abandon the enterprise, for the consequence of taking the interpretive attitude toward the text in question is then a piece of internal skepticism: That nothing can count as continuing the novel rather than beginning anew.

He may find, not that no single interpretation fits the bulk of the text, but that more than one does. The second dimension of interpretation then requires him to judge which of these eligible readings makes the work in progress best, all things considered. At this point his more substantive aesthetic judgments, about the importance or insight or realism or beauty of different ideas the novel might be taken to express, come into play. But the formal and structural considerations that dominate on the first dimension figure on the second as well, for even when neither of two interpretations is disqualified out of hand as explaining too little, one may show the text in a better light because it fits more of the text or provides a more interesting integration of style and content. So the distinction between the two dimensions is less crucial or profound than it might seem. It is a useful analytical device that helps us give structure to any interpreter's working theory or style. He will form a sense of when an interpretation fits so poorly that it is unnecessary to consider its substantive appeal, because he knows that this cannot outweigh its embarrassments of fit in deciding whether it makes the novel better, everything taken into account, than its rivals. This sense will define the first dimension for him. But he need not reduce his intuitive sense to any precise formula; he would rarely need to decide whether some interpretation barely survives or barely fails, because a bare survivor, no matter how ambitious or interesting it claimed the text to be, would almost certainly fail in the overall comparison with other interpretations whose fit was evident.

We can now appreciate the range of different kinds of judgments that are blended in this overall comparison. Judgments about textual coherence and integrity, reflecting different formal literary values, are interwoven with more substantive aesthetic judgments that themselves assume different literary aims. Yet these various kinds of judgments, of each general kind, remain distinct enough to check one another in an overall assessment, and it is that possibility of contest, particularly between textual and substantive judgments, that distinguishes a chain novelist's assignment from more independent creative writing. Nor can we draw any flat distinction between the stage at which a chain novelist interprets the text he has been given and the stage at which he adds his own chapter, guided by the interpretation he has settled on. When he begins to write he might discover in what he has written a different, perhaps radically different, interpretation. Or he might find it impossible to write in the tone or theme he first took up, and that will lead him to reconsider other interpretations he first rejected. In either case he returns to the text to reconsider the lines it makes eligible. . . .

[*Hercules*]

Law as integrity asks a judge deciding a common-law case like *McLoughlin* to think of himself as an author in the chain of common law. He knows that other judges have decided cases that, although not exactly like his case, deal with related problems; he must think of their decisions as part of a long story he must interpret and then continue, according to his own judgment of how to make the developing story as good as it can be. (Of course the best story for him means best from the standpoint of political morality, not aesthetics.) We can make a rough distinction once again between two main dimensions of this interpretive judgment. The judge's decision—his postinterpretive conclusions—must be drawn from an interpretation that both fits and justifies what has gone before, so far as that is possible. But in law as in literature the interplay between fit and justification is complex. Just as interpretation within a chain novel is for each interpreter a delicate balance among different types of literary and artistic attitudes, so in law it is a delicate balance among political convictions of different sorts; in law as in literature these must be sufficiently related yet disjoint to allow an overall judgment that trades off an interpretation's success on one type of standard against its failure on another. I must try to exhibit that complex structure of legal interpretation, and I shall use for that purpose an imaginary judge of superhuman intellectual power and patience who accepts law as integrity.

Call him Hercules.[6] [We will] follow his career by noticing the types of judgments he must make and tensions he must resolve in deciding a variety of cases. But I offer this caution in advance. We must not suppose that his answers to the various questions he encounters *define* law as integrity as a general conception of law. They are the answers I now think best. But law as integrity consists in an approach, in questions rather than answers, and other lawyers and judges who accept it would give different answers from his to the questions it asks. You might think other answers would be better. (So might I, after further thought.) You might, for example, reject Hercules' views about how far people's legal rights depend on the reasons past judges offered for their decisions enforcing these rights, or you might not share his respect for what I shall call "local priority" in common-law decisions. If you reject these discrete views because you think them poor constructive interpretations of legal practice, however, you have not rejected law as integrity but rather have joined its enterprise. . . .

Hercules on Olympus

Hercules is promoted, in spite of the extraordinary and sometimes tedious length of his opinions in courts below. He joins the Supreme Court of the United States as Justice Hercules. Suppose *Brown* . . . has not yet been decided. It now comes before Hercules' Court in the posture of 1953. The plaintiff school children say that the scheme of racially segregated public schools of Kansas is unconstitutional because it denies them equal protection of the law, in spite of the long history of that scheme throughout the southern states and in spite of the Court's own apparently contrary decision in a case raising the same issues of principle, *Plessy v. Ferguson*, which has been standing since 1896.[7] How does the champion of law as integrity reply to these claims?

The Constitution is, after all, a kind of statute, and Hercules has a way with statutes. He interprets each one so as to make its history, all things considered, the best it can be. This requires political judgments, but these are special and complex and by no means the same as those he would make if he were himself voting on a statute touching the same issues. His own convictions about justice or wise policy are constrained in his overall interpretive judgment, not only by the text of the statute but also by a variety of considerations of fairness and integrity. He will continue to use this strategy in his new position, but since the Constitution is a very unusual statute he will work out a special application of the strategy for constitutional cases. He will develop his strategy for statutes into a working theory of constitutional adjudication.

The Constitution is different from ordinary statutes in one striking way. The Constitution is foundational of other law, so Hercules' interpretation of the document as a whole, and of its abstract clauses, must be foundational as well. It must fit and justify the most basic arrangements of political power in the community, which means it must be a justification drawn from the most philosophical reaches of political theory. Lawyers are always philosophers, because jurisprudence is part of any lawyer's account of what the law is, even when the jurisprudence is undistinguished and mechanical. In constitutional theory philosophy is closer to the surface of the argument and, if the theory is good, explicit in it.

It is high time to repeat one of the cautions I offered earlier, however. Hercules serves our purpose because he is free to concentrate on the issues of principle that, according to law as integrity, constitute the constitutional law he administers. He need not worry about the press of time and docket, and he has no trouble, as any mortal judge inevitably does, in finding language and argument sufficiently discriminating to bring whatever qualifications he senses are necessary into even his initial characterizations of the law. Nor, we may now add, is he worried about a further practical problem that is particularly serious in constitutional cases. An actual justice must sometimes adjust what he believes to be right as a matter of principle, and therefore as a matter of law, in order to gain the votes of other justices and to make their joint decision sufficiently acceptable to the community so that it can continue to act in the spirit of a community of principle at the constitutional level. We use Hercules to abstract from these practical issues as any sound analysis must, so that we can see the compromises actual justices think necessary as compromises with the law.

Theories of Racial Equality

We are interested now in Hercules' working theory of those parts of the Constitution that declare individual constitutional rights against the state, and in particular in his theory of the equal protection clause. He will begin with the abstract egalitarian idea . . . [which] holds that government must treat all its citizens as equals in the following sense: Political decisions and arrangements must display equal concern for the fate of all. . . .

We [must distinguish] between the overall collective strategies a government uses to secure the general interest as a matter of policy and the individual rights it recognizes, as a matter of principle, as trumps over these collective strategies. Hercules now asks a neglected question of fundamental importance for constitutional theory. How far does the Constitution limit the freedom of Congress and the several states to make their own decisions about issues of policy and principle? Does the Constitution, properly interpreted, set out a particular conception of equality that every state must follow in its collective judgments of policy, in its general scheme of distributing and regulating property, for example? If not, does it stipulate, in the name of equality, certain individual rights every state must respect, as trumps over its collective decisions of policy, whichever conception of equality the state has chosen?

These are separate questions, and the distinction is important. Hercules will answer the first in the negative. The Constitution cannot sensibly be read as demanding that the nation and every state follow a utilitarian or libertarian or resource-egalitarian or any other particular conception of equality in fixing on strategies for pursuing the general welfare. The Constitution does insist that each jurisdiction accept the abstract egalitarian principle that people must be treated as equals, and therefore that each respect some plausible conception of equality in each of its decisions about property and other matters of policy. (That relatively permissive constitutional standard is at least part of what constitutional lawyers call, somewhat misleadingly, the "rationality" requirement.) The second question, about individual constitutional rights over any collective justification, is a different matter. For Hercules will certainly draw this conclusion from constitutional history and practice: Though the Constitution leaves each state free in matters of policy, subject only to the constraint just described, it insists that each state recognize certain rights qualifying any collective justification it uses, any view it takes of the general interest. The crucial interpretive question is then what rights these are.

Hercules is now concerned with one set of putative constitutional rights. It seems plain that the Constitution mandates some individual right not to be the victim of official, state-imposed racial discrimination. But what is the character and what are the dimensions of that right? He constructs three accounts of a right against racial discrimination. He will test each as a competent interpretation of constitutional practice under the Fourteenth Amendment.

1. *Suspect classifications.* The first account supposes that the right against discrimination is only a consequence of the more general right people have to be treated as equals according to whichever conception of equality their state pursues. It supposes, in other words, that people have no distinct right not to be the victim of racial or other discrimination beyond what the rationality restraint already requires. If a state generally adopts some view of the general welfare, like that proposed by utilitarianism or equality of resources on the market model, in which gains to some are balanced against losses to others, then it meets the Constitutional standard against discrimination simply by counting everyone's welfare or choices in the same way. Race and similar grounds of distinction are special, on this account, only because history suggests that some groups are more likely than others to be denied the consideration due them, so political decisions that work to their disadvantage should be viewed with special suspicion. Even though the courts will not ordinarily review political decisions that benefit some groups more than others, unless these are shown to be "irrational" in the sense just described, it will inspect these decisions more carefully when historically mistreated minorities are disadvantaged.

Nevertheless, the standard requires only that these groups receive the right consideration in the overall balance, and a state may meet that standard even though it treats them differently from others. It might justify segregated schools, for example, by showing that integration would provide an inferior educational environment because it would outrage long-standing traditions of racial separation and that the damage to white children would then more than offset any gains to black children, even counting these gains as equally important in themselves, child by child. It might add that the facilities it has assigned to blacks, though separate, are nevertheless equal in quality. Or, even if they are not equal, that they cannot be improved except through special expense that would count the interests of each black child as more important, in the overall calculation, than the interests of each of the larger number of white children.

2. *Banned categories.* The second theory on Hercules' list insists that the Constitution does recognize a distinct right against discrimination as a trump over any state's conception of the general interest. This is the right that certain properties or categories, including race, ethnic background, and perhaps gender, not be used to distinguish groups of citizens for different treatment, even when the distinction would advance

the general interest on an otherwise permissible conception. A racially segregated school system is, on this account, unconstitutional under all circumstances.

3. *Banned sources.* The third theory recognizes a different special right against discrimination. Most conceptions of equality, including utilitarianism and resource-egalitarianism, make the public interest, and therefore proper policy, sensitive to people's tastes, preferences, and choices. A community committed to such a conception will think that certain decisions of policy are sound simply because preferences and choices are distributed in a certain way: The fact that more people want a sports stadium than an opera house, or that those who want the stadium want it much more, will justify choosing it, without any assumption that those who prefer it are worthier or their preferences more admirable. The third theory insists that people have a right, against this kind of collective justification, that certain sources or types of preferences or choices not be allowed to count in that way. It insists that preferences that are rooted in some form of prejudice against one group can never count in favor of a policy that includes the disadvantage of that group. This right, like the right proposed by the second theory, condemns the program of racially segregated education presented in *Brown*, though not quite so automatically. Segregation treats blacks differently, and history shows that the seat of the different treatment lies in prejudice. So segregation cannot be saved, according to the third account, by the kind of argument we supposed might save it under the first. It would not matter that a calculation counting all the preferences of each person as equally important, including those rooted in prejudice, might show that segregation was in the general interest, so understood.

When Hercules considers each of these theories about the force of the Fourteenth Amendment's requirement of equal protection he will . . . distinguish between the academic and the practical elaboration of each theory; he will ask not only how attractive each theory is in the abstract, as it would be elaborated and applied by a sophisticated political philosopher, but how well each one could be put into practice in a community like his, as a constitutional standard courts could use effectively in deciding what legislation it disqualifies. I took the requirements of practical elaboration into account in describing the first theory. It sets out certain "suspect" classifications which, when used in legislation, raise a presumption that the interests of some group have not been taken into account in the proper way. But that presumption can be rebutted, and it is rebutted by showing that the classification does in fact give equal effect to all the preferences displayed in the community, with no distinction as to the character or source of these preferences.

The second theory, of banned categories, needs no distinct practical elaboration, because its academic elaboration is already practical enough. It sets out particular categories and insists that the constitutional right has been violated whenever the law makes distinctions among groups of citizens using any of those categories. The second theory insists (in the odd maxim often used to express it) that the Constitution is color-blind and blind also to certain other listed properties that distinguish different groups. The third theory, of banned sources, does need a distinct practical elaboration, because its fundamental principle would be extremely difficult for judges and other officials to apply directly case by case. That principle prohibits legislation that could be justified only by counting, within the overall calculation determining where the general interest lies, preferences directly or indirectly arising from prejudice. Even in theory it will often be difficult to decide which preferences these are, because people's desires usually have complex and sometimes even indeterminate sources. It will also be difficult to decide, case by case, which legislation would have been justified even if tainted preferences had not been counted in the calculation. It might be impossible to decide, for example, how far some particular parent's wish that his children be educated with other children from a similar background expresses a racially neutral view that education is always more effective in these circumstances and how far it reflects racial prejudice.

So judges who accepted the banned sources theory would have to construct a practical elaboration based on judgments about the kinds of preferences that often or typically have been generated through prejudice, and about the kinds of political decisions that in normal circumstances could not be justified were such preferences not counted as part of the justification. This practical elaboration would designate a set of "suspect" classifications much like those of the first theory, classifications that usually cause disadvantage to groups, like blacks or Jews or women or homosexuals, that have historically been the targets of prejudice; it would raise a presumption that any political decision that causes special disadvantage to these groups violates the constitutional right against discrimination. But the case necessary to rebut that presumption, according to the practical elaboration of the third theory, would be very different from the case necessary to rebut the suspicion of violation under the first theory. According to the first, the suspicion can be put to rest by showing that a calculation neutral among all preferences would justify the distinction of race. Under the third, this would not suffice: It would be necessary either to show that the classification was justified by popular preferences unstained by prejudice, or to provide some different form of justification that did not rely on preferences at all. The third theory, even when practically elaborated in this way, is also different from the second theory, of banned categories. The two come apart in confronting legislation whose purpose and effect is to benefit people who have historically been the victims of prejudice, not to harm them. The banned sources theory would distinguish between affirmative action programs designed to help blacks and Jim Crow laws designed to keep them in a state of economic and social subjugation. The banned categories theory would treat both in the same way.

Deciding *Brown*

Which Theory Is the Constitution's Theory?

Hercules is now ready to test these three accounts of the constitutional right against discrimination by asking how far each fits and justifies, and so provides an eligible interpretation of, American constitutional structure and practice. He will reject the first theory, which denies any special right against discrimination and insists only that the welfare or preferences of each citizen be counted in the same scale without restriction as to source or character. Perhaps this theory would have been adequate under tests of fairness and fit at some time in our history; perhaps it would have been adequate when *Plessy* was decided. It is not adequate now, nor was it in 1954 when Hercules had to decide *Brown*. It gains little support from ideals of political fairness. The American people would almost unanimously have rejected it, even in 1954, as not faithful to their convictions about racial justice. People who supported racial segregation did not try to justify it by appealing just to the fact of their preferences, as people might support a decision for a sports stadium rather than an opera house. They thought segregation was God's will, or that everyone had a right to live with his own people, or something of that sort. And those who opposed segregation did not rest their case on unrestricted preference calculations either: They would not have thought the case for segregation any stronger if there were more racists or if racists took more pleasure in it. Hercules will think the first account inadequate in justice as well, and so he will discard it if either of the other two fit constitutional practice well enough to be eligible.

He needs to develop his working theory of constitutional adjudication only in enough detail to decide *Brown*, so he would not have to choose between banned categories and banned sources, the second and third theories on his list. Both condemn officially sponsored racial segregation in schools. Both fit the past pattern of Court decisions and the general structure of the Constitution well enough to be eligible. Both were consistent, in 1954, with ethical attitudes that were widespread in the community; neither theory fit these attitudes noticeably better than the other, because the difference between them appears only at a level of analysis popular opinion had not yet been forced to reach. America's growing sense that racial segregation was wrong in principle, because it was incompatible with decency to treat one race as inherently inferior to another, can be supported either on grounds of banned sources, that some preferences must be disregarded in any acceptable calculation of what makes the community better off on the whole, or on grounds of banned categories, that some properties, including race, must never be made the basis of legal distinction.

Hercules is therefore ready to decide, for the plaintiffs, that state-imposed racial segregation in education is unconstitutional. He knows that the congressmen who proposed the Fourteenth Amendment had a different view, which they declared in official legislative history. But . . . he does not believe that this much matters now. It cannot be evidence of any deep and dominant contemporary opinion to which he must refer, as one aspect or dimension of interpretation, for reasons of fairness. The old legislative history is no longer an act of the nation personified declaring some contemporary public purpose. Nor is this the kind of issue in which it is more important that institutional practice be settled than that it be settled in the right way. The Court had already, in earlier cases, given people reason to doubt that established patterns of racial distinction would be protected much longer.[8] The plaintiff schoolchildren are being cheated of what their Constitution, properly interpreted, defines as independent and equal standing in the republic; this is an insult that must be recognized and removed. So if *Plessy* is really precedent against integration, it must be overruled now. Everything conspires toward the same decision. Racially segregated public schools do not treat black children as equals under any competent interpretation of the rights the Fourteenth Amendment deploys in the name of racial equality, and official segregation is therefore unconstitutional. . . .

Deciding *Bakke*

I will not pursue the history of *Brown*'s progeny. . . . We turn instead to a different problem, a child of the success rather than the failures of the revolution *Brown* began. The conscience of American business and education, and its prudence as well was stirred by the racial wars of the 1960s, and programs collectively called affirmative action or reverse discrimination were part of their response. We can settle for a very rough description of these programs: They aimed to improve the place and number of black and other minorities in labor, commerce, and the professions by giving them some form of preference in hiring, promotion, and admission to college and professional schools. The preference was sometimes indistinct, a matter of counting a person's race or ethnic background as an advantage that could secure him a place, "all else being equal," which it never was. But sometimes the preference was both explicit and mechanical.

The medical school of the University of California at Davis, for example, used a bifurcated system for judging applicants: A quota was set apart for minority applicants who competed only among themselves for a designated number of places, with the consequence that some blacks were accepted whose test scores and other conventional qualifications were far below those of whites who were rejected. Alan Bakke was one of the latter, and it was conceded, in the litigation he provoked, that he would have been accepted had he been black. He said that this quota system was unlawful because it did not treat him as an equal in the contest for places, and the Supreme Court, justifying its decision in a divided and somewhat confused set of opinions, agreed.[9]

How would Justice Hercules have voted? The case forces him to confront the issue he found unnecessary to decide for *Brown*. Is the banned categories theory a more successful interpretation of the pertinent constitutional practice, all things considered, than the banned sources theory? A practical constitutional standard enforcing the banned sources theory would designate certain racial classifications as suspect. But it would not be necessary to include in the list of suspect classifications a distinction obviously designed to aid historical victims of prejudice. Perhaps institutions that used racial quotas should have the burden, under that theory, of showing that these did not reflect covert prejudice against some other group. But Davis could have met that burden, so under the banned sources theory it would not have violated Bakke's constitutional right. It would have violated his rights according to the banned categories theory, however. The academic as well as practical elaboration of that theory is just a list of properties that must not be used to distinguish groups one of which thereby gains an advantage over the other. Race must be prominent in any such list, and Davis used racial classifications that disadvantaged whites like Bakke.

So Hercules must choose between the two theories, and he will prefer the banned sources to the banned categories theory. Though banned categories fits the decisions about racial discrimination up to *Bakke* as well as banned sources does—it fits the language used in these decisions better—it does not fit constitutional or political practice more generally. Banned categories, as it stands, is too arbitrary to count as a genuine interpretation under law as integrity. It must be supported by some principled account of why the particular properties it bans are special, and the only principle available is that people must never be treated differently in virtue of properties beyond their control. This proposition has been decisively rejected throughout American law and politics. Statutes almost invariably draw lines along natural differences of geography and health and ability: They subsidize workers who have by chance come to work in one industry or even firm rather than another, for example, and restrict licenses to drive or practice medicine to people with certain physical or mental abilities. Educational opportunities in universities and professional schools, in particular, have always and without constitutional challenge been awarded in flat violation of the supposed principle. Candidates are chosen on the basis of tests that are thought to reveal difference in natural ability, and in many schools they are also chosen to promote geographical balance in classes or even the school's athletic success. Candidates are no more responsible for their ability to score well on conventional intelligence tests or for their place of birth or skill at football than for their race; if race were a banned category because people cannot choose their race, then intelligence, geographic background, and physical ability would have to be banned categories as well. Racial discrimination that disadvantages blacks is unjust, not because people cannot choose their race but because that discrimination expresses prejudice. Its injustice is explained, that is, by the banned sources theory, not the banned categories theory.

Suppose Bakke's lawyers argue that the banned categories strategy must be accepted for race (and perhaps for certain other special cases like ethnic background and sex as well) even though it cannot be supported by any general principle that people must never be divided according to properties they cannot control. They must not say that this special standing for race and a few other properties is just a matter of constitutional fact, that the Constitution picks out and disqualifies race and these other properties alone. For that begs the question: The correct interpretation of our constitutional practice is exactly what is now in issue, and they need an argument that justifies their claim about what the Constitution means, not an argument that begins in that claim. Suppose they say: The framers of the equal protection clause had race particularly in mind because the Fourteenth Amendment followed and was provoked by slavery and the Civil War. This is . . . a particularly feeble form of historicism in this context. For we know that the framers of the Fourteenth Amendment did not believe they were making *any* racial discrimination in education unconstitutional, even segregation aimed at blacks, and we can hardly take their opinions as an argument that *all* racial distinction, even that designed to help blacks, is outlawed.

Suppose Bakke's lawyers now say that whatever the framers might or might not have intended, wise constitutional statecraft argues for the banned category theory for race and a few other categories alone because admissions or hiring programs that use racial classifications in any way will exacerbate racial tension and so prolong discrimination, hatred, and violence. This is exactly the kind of complex, forward-looking calculation of policy that even a weakened, sensible form of passivism would leave to the judgment of elected officials or of executives appointed by and responsible to these officials. If Congress decides that a national policy prohibiting any affirmative action is desirable, it has the power to enact a statute that will partly achieve this.[10] The Supreme Court should not take that judgment of policy upon itself.

So Hercules will reject the banned categories theory of equality, both in its general form, which cannot be made to fit, and in its special form, which is too arbitrary to count as principled. He will accept the banned sources theory as the best interpretation available,[11] then construct a suitable practical elaboration of that theory for constitutional purposes by selecting a list, open to revision as social patterns change, of "suspect" classifications whose use to disadvantage a group historically the target of prejudice is prima facie unconstitutional. The list he constructs would not outlaw affirmative action programs in principle, because these do not work to the disadvantage of any such group.

But Bakke has one more possible argument that the equal protection clause, interpreted as Hercules now understands it, does outlaw the particular quota-based form of affirmative action Davis used. The banned sources theory explicates a special right as a supplement to the general requirement of the Fourteenth Amendment, the requirement that any state's calculation of the general interest must take into account the interests of all citizens even though it disadvantages some; it must be in that sense a "rational" calculation understood as serving some acceptable conception of how people are treated as equals. Government violates this more general requirement whenever it ignores the welfare of some group in its calculation of what makes the community as a whole better off. Even though Bakke finds no help in the special right against racial discrimination Hercules recognizes, he might fall back on the general requirement. Davis argues that its quota system plausibly contributes to the general welfare by helping to increase the number of qualified black doctors. Bakke might argue to the contrary that Davis's quota system prevented it from even attending to the impact of its admissions decisions on people in his position. Hercules would decide (I believe) that this claim is confused: A quota system gives the same consideration to the full class of applicants as any other system that relies, as all must, on general classifications.[12] But reasonable judges might disagree with that part of his overall conclusion in the case.[13]

Is Hercules a Tyrant?

We have followed Hercules through only one chain of decisions, because here as everywhere in jurisprudence detail is more illuminating than range. But the argument . . . gives some idea of his attitudes to other Constitutional issues,[14] and enough has emerged about his Constitutional methods to justify a minor summary. Hercules is not a historicist, but neither is his the buccaneer style sometimes lampooned under the epithet "natural law." He does not think that the Constitution is only what the best theory of abstract justice and fairness would produce by way of ideal theory. He is guided instead by a sense of constitutional integrity; he believes that the American Constitution consists in the best available interpretation of American constitutional text and practice as a whole, and his judgment about which interpretation is best is sensitive to the great complexity of political virtues bearing on that issue.

His arguments embrace popular conviction and national tradition whenever these are pertinent to the sovereign question, which reading of constitutional history shows that history overall in its best light. For the same reason and toward the same end, they draw on his own convictions about justice and fairness and the right relation between them. He is not a passivist because he rejects the rigid idea that judges must defer to elected officials, no matter what part of the constitutional scheme is in question. He will decide that the point of some provisions is or includes the protection of democracy, and he will elaborate these provisions in that spirit instead of deferring to the convictions of those whose legitimacy they might challenge. He will decide that the point of other provisions is or includes the protection of individuals and minorities against the will of the majority, and he will not yield, in deciding what those provisions require, to what the majority's representatives think is right.

He is not an "activist" either. He will refuse to substitute his judgment for that of the legislature when he believes the issue in play is primarily one of policy rather than principle, when the argument is about the best strategies for achieving the overall collective interest through goals like prosperity or the eradication of poverty or the right balance between economy and conservation.[15] He would not have joined the *Lochner* majority, for example, because he would have rejected the principle of liberty the Supreme Court cited in that case as plainly inconsistent with American practice and anyway wrong and would have refused to reexamine the New York legislature's judgment on the issues of policy that then remained.[16]

Hercules, then, escapes the standard academic classifications of justices. If he fell neatly into any of the popular categories he would not be Hercules after all. Is he too conservative? Or too liberal or progressive? You cannot yet say, because your judgment would depend on how closely your convictions matched his across the wide spectrum of different kinds of convictions an interpretation of constitutional practice engages. I have not exposed enough of what his convictions are, or how these would be deployed in due process cases about criminal procedure, or free speech cases, or cases about fair electoral districting and procedures, for you to tell. Nor have I discussed, as a distinct problem in the constitutional context, his convictions about the role of precedent, about past decisions of the Supreme Court. You will have some sense of this attitude . . . from the fact that he was untroubled about overruling *Plessy* in deciding *Brown*; but this is not the whole story, because his attitude toward precedents would be more respectful when he was asked to restrict the constitutional rights they had enforced than when he was asked to reaffirm their denials of such rights. So you must reserve your overall political judgments for the careers of justices you know more about.

But we have seen enough to know that one charge some lawyers would urge against Hercules is unfair and, what is even worse, obscurantist. Hercules is no usurping tyrant trying to cheat the public of its democratic power. When he intervenes in the process of government to declare some statute or other act of government unconstitutional, he does this in service of his most conscientious judgment about what democracy really is and what the Constitution, parent and guardian of democracy, really means. You may disagree with the few judgments I have reported in his name; if I told you more of his career on Olympus you would probably disagree with more. But if Hercules had renounced the responsibility I have described, which includes the responsibility to decide when he must rely on his own convictions about his nation's character, he would have been a traitor, not a hero of judicial restraint.

Notes

1. [On p. 116 of *Law's Empire*, Dworkin defined "conventionalism" by two claims: "The first is positive: That judges must respect the established legal conventions of their community except in rare circumstances. . . . The second claim, which is at least equally important, is negative. It declares that there is no law—no right flowing from past political decisions—apart from the law drawn from those decisions by techniques that are themselves matters of convention, and therefore that on some issues there is no law either way."]

2. [On p. 151 of *Law's Empire,* Dworkin defined "pragmatism" as follows: "The pragmatist . . . denies that past political decisions in themselves provide any justification for either using or witholding the state's coercive power. He finds the necessary justification for coercion in the justice or efficiency or some other contemporary virtue of the decision itself. . . ."]

3. [*McLoughlin v. O'Brian* (1983) 1 A.C. 410, reversing (1981) Q.B. 599. Mrs. McLoughlin's husband and four children were in an automobile accident. She suffered emotional injury two hours later at the hospital when she saw the survivors and learned that her daughter had died. She sued the negligent driver for compensation for her emotional injury.]

4. [*Brown v. Board of Educ.,* 347 U.S. 486 (1954). In *Brown,* the Court ruled racially segregated schools unconstitutional.]

5. Perhaps this is an impossible assignment; perhaps the project is doomed to produce not just an impossibly bad novel but no novel at all, because the best theory of art requires a single creator or, if more than one, that each must have some control over the whole. (But what about legends and jokes? What about the Old Testament, or, on some theories, the *Iliad?)* I need not push that question further, because I am interested only in the fact that the assignment makes sense, that each of the novelists in the chain can have some grasp of what he is asked to do, whatever misgivings he might have about the value or character of what will then be produced.

6. Hercules played an important part in [Ronald Dworkin,] *Taking Rights Seriously* [(Cambridge, Mass.: Harvard University Press, 1977)] chap. 4.

7. 163 U.S. 537 (1896).

8. See *McLaurin v. Oklahoma State Regents,* 339 U.S. 637 (1950); *Sweatt v. Painter,* 339 U.S. 629 (1950); *Sipnel v. Board of Regents,* 332 U.S. 631 (per curiam); *Missouri ex rel. Gaines v. Canada,* 305 U.S. 337 (1938).

9. *Regents of the University of California v. Bakke,* 438 U.S. 265 (1978).

10. It did not do so in the Civil Rights Act of 1964. See [Ronald Dworkin,] *A Matter of Principle* [(Cambridge, Mass.: Harvard University Press, 1977)] chap. 16.

11. Id. at chap. 14.

12. Id. at chap. 15.

13. See Justice Powell's opinion in *Bakke,* 438 U.S. 215.

14. See my "Reagan's Justice," *New York Review of Books,* Nov. 8, 1984, and "Law's Ambitions for Itself," 71 *University of Virginia Law Review* 73 (1985).

15. He will not substitute his judgment, that is, on constitutional grounds when his techniques of statutory construction have yielded a conclusion about what the statute properly interpreted says. His convictions about policy will, however, have a role in this latter decision. . . .

16. *Lochner v. New York,* [198 U.S. 45 (1905)]. The opinion in that case treats the issue as one of principle, about whether bakers and their employers have a right to contract for longer hours if they wish. Hercules would have replied that the particular interpretation of the principle of freedom of contract this assumes cannot be justified in any sound interpretation of the Constitution.

6

CRITICAL RACE THEORY

This selection by Patricia Williams represents an approach to constitutional interpretation known as critical race theory. This approach is distinguished from others by both method and subject matter. Its method is characterized by the use of first person narratives (sometimes autobiographical and sometimes fictional) that are designed to put constitutional issues into the context of people's lives and to increase the reader's ability to imagine how the law looks from the perspective of a member of a racial minority. Its subject has been our nation's history of racism and injustice toward racial minorities, a history that, as their stories and examples show, continues into the present.

In contrast to both liberal and conservative theorists who argue for their interpretations of the Constitution by invoking abstract, universally applicable principles of justice, critical race theorists maintain that this talk of universality can be just a mask for a particular perspective, namely, that of those in power. The assumption that it is possible to write constitutional theory in a genuinely universal voice has been present in our legal history since the writing of the "We the People" preamble of the Constitution, when the "we" clearly excluded slaves. Critical race theorists have argued that the use of the apparently all-embracing "we" in legal theory continues to silence minority voices that have different stories to tell.

Patricia Williams has used autobiography, allegory, legal and literary theory, case studies, and cultural criticism to expose everyday racism and analyze how it affects legal practice and interpretation. Her essay in this anthology begins with a critique of the Court's decision in a recent affirmative action case, City of Richmond v. J. A. Croson Co., that analyzes the ways in which an interpretation of the Constitution advocating purely formal equality of opportunity perpetuates, in reality, unequal opportunities for women and people of color.

Her essay probes, among other things, the Court's rhetoric of "equality" in Croson, *reactions to an incident of racist hate speech at Stanford University, and examples of "ordinary," insidious racial prejudice and discrimination.*

Some critics of critical race theory have taken issue with what they believe to be one of its assumptions, namely that there is a distinct, shared "voice of color." Critical race theorists, however, need not be committed to the view that those who have for so long been silenced, if finally allowed to be heard, will speak in unison.

S.J.B.

The Obliging Shell:
An Informal Essay on
Formal Equal Opportunity

Patricia Williams

I. Introduction

We live in an era in which women and people of color compose and literally define both this society's underclass and its most underserved population. Remedying this therefore ought to be, must be, this society's most pressing area of representational responsibility; not only in terms of fairly privatized issues like "more pro bono" or more lawyers taking on more cases of particular sorts, but in really examining the ways in which the law operates to omit women and people of color at all levels, including the most subtle—to omit them from the literature of the law, from the ranks of lawyers, and to omit them from the numbers of those served by its interests.

In this regard, I have been thinking a lot about the recent Supreme Court decision in *City of Richmond v. J.A. Croson Co.*,[1] which presented a challenge, as well as its own model of resistance, to the pursuit of "[p]roper findings . . . necessary to define both the scope of the injury [in race and gender cases] and the extent of the remedy."[2]

That case, if you will recall, involved a minority set-aside program in the awarding of municipal contracts. The city of Richmond, Virginia,

with a black population of just over 50%, set a 30% goal in the awarding of city construction contracts, based on its findings that local, state
and national patterns of discrimination had resulted in all but complete
lack of access for minority-owned businesses. In fact, theretofore, only
0.67% of municipal contracts had been awarded to minority-owned
businesses. The Supreme Court held:

> We, therefore, hold that the city has failed to demonstrate a compelling
> interest in apportioning public contracting opportunities on the basis of
> race. To accept Richmond's claim that past societal discrimination alone
> can serve as the basis for rigid racial preferences would be to open the door
> to competing claims for "remedial relief" for every disadvantaged group.
> The dream of a Nation of equal citizens in a society where race is
> irrelevant to personal opportunity and achievement would be lost in a
> mosaic of shifting preferences based on inherently unmeasurable claims of
> past wrongs. "Courts would be asked to evaluate the extent of the prejudice
> and consequent harm suffered by various minority groups. Those whose
> societal injury is thought to exceed some arbitrary level of tolerability then
> would be entitled to preferential classifications. . . ." We think such a result
> would be contrary to both the letter and spirit of a constitutional provision
> whose central command is equality.[3]

What strikes me most about this holding are the rhetorical devices
the court employs to justify its outcome:

(1) It sets up a "slippery slope" at the bottom of which lie hordes-in-
waiting of warring barbarians: An "open door" through which would
flood the "competing claims" of "every disadvantaged group." It prob-
lematizes by conjuring mythic dangers.

(2) It describes situations for which there are clear, hard statistical
data as "inherently unmeasurable." It puts in the diminutive that
which is not; it makes infinite what in fact is limited.

(3) It puts itself in passive relation to the purported "arbitrariness"
of others' perceptions of the intolerability of their circumstances (ie.,
"those whose societal injury is thought to exceed some arbitrary level
of tolerability."[4])

These themes are reiterated throughout the opinion: Societal discrimination is "too amorphous";[5] racial goals are labelled
"unyielding";[6] goals are labelled "quotas";[7] testimony becomes mere
"recitation";[8] legislative purpose and action become "simple legislative assurances of good intention";[9] lower court opinion is disregarded as
just "blind judicial deference";[10] and statistics are rendered
"generalizations."[11] This adjectival dismissiveness alone is sufficient
to hypnotize the reader into believing that the "assumption that
white prime contractors simply will not hire minority firms" is completely "unsupported."[12]

And as I think about the *Croson* opinion, I cannot help but marvel at how, against a backdrop of richly textured facts and proof on both local and national scales, in a city where more than 50% of the population is black and in which fewer than 1% of contracts are awarded to minorities or minority-owned businesses, interpretive artifice alone allowed this narrow vision that not only was 30% too great a set-aside but that there was no proof of discrimination.

I think, moreover, that the rhetorical devices that accomplished this astonishing holding are comprehensible less from the perspective of traditionally conceived constitutional interpretive standards— whether rational relationship or strict scrutiny—than by turning to interpretive standards found in private law. The process by which the Court consistently diminished the importance of real facts, real figures, is paralleled only by the process of rendering "extrinsic" otherwise probative evidence under the Parol Evidence Rule.[13]

In particular, I am struck by the Court's use of the word "equality" in the last line of its holding.[14] It seems an extraordinarily narrow use of "equality," when it excludes from consideration so much clear inequality. It, again, resembles the process by which the Parol Evidence Rule limits the meaning of documents or words by placing beyond the bounds of reference anything that is inconsistent, or depending on the circumstances, even that which is supplementary: It is this lawyerly language game of exclusion and omission that is the subject of the rest of this essay.

II. A Quick Review of the Parol Evidence Rule

Before I went into teaching, I practiced consumer protection. I remember one trial in particular, a suit against a sausage manufacturer for selling impure and contaminated products. The manufacturer insisted that the word "sausage" meant "pig meat and lots of impurities." Here are my notes from my final argument to the jury:

> You have this thing called a sausage-making machine. You put pork and spices in at the top and crank it up, and because it is a sausage-making machine, what comes out the other end is a sausage. Over time everyone knows that anything that comes out of the sausage-making machine is known as a sausage. In fact, there is law passed that says that it's indisputably sausage.
>
> One day, we throw in a few small rodents of questionable pedigree and a teddy bear and a chicken. We crank the machine up and wait to see what comes out the other end. (1) Do we prove the validity of the machine if we call the product a sausage? (2) Or do we enlarge and enhance the meaning of "sausage" if we call the product a sausage? (3) Or do we have any

success in breaking out of the bind if we call it something different from "sausage"?

In fact, I'm not sure it makes any difference whether we call it sausage or if we scramble the letters of the alphabet over this . . . this thing that comes out, full of sawdust and tiny claws. What will make a difference, however, is a recognition of our shifting relation to the word "sausage," by either:

(1) enlarging the authority of sausage-makers and enhancing the awesome, cruel inevitability of the workings of sausage machines—i.e., everything they touch turns to sausage or else it doesn't exist; or by

(2) expanding the definition of sausage itself to encompass a wealth of variation: chicken, rodent, or teddy bear sausage; or, finally, by

(3) challenging our own comprehension of what it is we really mean by sausage—i.e., by making clear the consensual limits of sausage, and reacquainting ourselves with the sources of its authority and legitimation.

Realizing that there are at least three different ways to relate to the facts of this case, to this product, this thing, is to define and acknowledge your role as jury and as trier of fact; is to acknowledge your own participation in the creation of reality.

(At this point there was an objection, overruled, from the sausage-maker's lawyer based upon too much critical theory in the courtroom.)

[Sausage-maker's] suit is an attempt to devour the meaning of justice in much the same way that this machine has devoured the last shred of common-sense meaning from sausage itself. But the ultimate interpretive choice is yours: Will you allow the machine such great transformative power that everything which goes in it is robbed of its inherency, so that nonconformity ceases to exist? Or will you choose the second alternative, to allow the product to be so powerful, that "sausage" becomes all-encompassing, so engorged with alternative meaning as to fill a purposeful machine with ambiguity and undecidability. Or will you wave that so-called sausage, sawdust and tiny claws spilling from both ends, in the face of that machine and shout: This is not Justice! For now is the time to revolt against the tyranny of definition-machines and insist on your right to name what your senses well know, to describe what you perceive to be the limits of sausage-justice, and the beyond of which is this *thing*, this clear injustice.

(There was a spattering of applause from the gallery as I thanked the ladies and gentlemen of the jury and returned to my seat at counsel table.)

Since that time, I have used sausages to illustrate and illuminate a whole range of problems: I just substitute "Constitution" or "equality" or "black" or "freedom of speech" instead of the word "sausage." It helps me think about a whole range of word-entanglements, on theoretical as well as prosaic levels. For one thing, the three levels of meaning correspond to:

(1) a positivist mode of interpretation in which the literal meaning of words is given great authority;

(2) a legal realist, as well as mainstream feminist and civil rights mode of interpretation (squeezing room into meaning for "me too"); and

(3) what is often (inaccurately) attributed to a "nihilistic" critical interpretive stance ("I don't know what it is, but I do know what it isn't"). I think a better way of describing this last category is that it is that part of interpretive discourse that explores the limits of meaning, that gives meaning by knowing its bounds. (I think, by the way, that an accurate understanding of critical theory requires recognition of the way in which the concept of "indeterminacy" questions the authority of definitional cages; it is not "nihilism," but a challenge to contextualize, by empowering community standards and the democratization of interpretation.)

It also corresponds to the three levels of "integration" of contracts under the Parol Evidence Rule: (1) Written contracts that are found by a judge to be "totally integrated" are limited to their "plain meaning,"[15] just as the dominant social contract as understood by the Reagan Court is limited in its meaning and will not suffer any additions or variation of interpretation from evidence of prior or contemporaneous circumstance, events, or sources of meaning. (2) Contracts that are found to be only "partially integrated" allow for multiplicities of meaning and may have their terms supplemented by additional extrinsic evidence.[16] (3) And contracts that are found "not integrated" at all may be altogether undone by a range of possible meaning that includes the wholly inconsistent.[17]

Law and life are all about the constant assessment of where on the scale one's words are meant; and by which level of the scale to evaluate and interpret the words of others. I think however that the game is more complicated than choosing a single level in which to settle for all time. That truth exists on all three levels is the theme that I want to pursue from here.

III. The Truth About Equality

I think of situational sausage-machine analysis as a way of reexamining what is lost by too narrow interpretive ideologies, and of rediscovering those injuries made invisible by description of them beyond the bounds of legal discourse. For example, affirmative action programs, of which minority set-asides are but one example, were designed to remedy a segregationist view of equality in which positivistic categories of race reigned supreme. "White" had an ironclad definition that was

the equivalent of "good," or "deserving." "Black" had an ironclad definition that was the equivalent of "bad," or "unworthy of inclusion."

While the most virulent examples of such narrow human and linguistic interpretations have been removed from code books, much of this unconsciously filtered vision remains with us in subtler form. An example
of this subtler manifestation may be found in the so-called "Ujamaa
House incidents" that took place on Stanford University's campus last
October [1988].

A brief bit of background is in order first:

Ujamaa House is one of several "theme" houses at Stanford, set up
with the idea of exposing students to a variety of live-in cultural and
racial exchanges. There is an Hispanic theme house, a Japanese theme
house; Ujamaa is the African-American theme house.

On the night of September 29, 1988, a white student, identified only
as "Fred," and a black student, called "QC," had an argument about
whether or not the composer Beethoven "had black blood." QC insisted
that he did; Fred thought the very idea was "preposterous."

> The following night, the white students said that they got drunk and
> decided to color a poster of Beethoven to represent a black stereotype. They
> posted it outside the room of [QC], the black student who had originally
> made the claim about Beethoven's race.
>
> Later, on Oct[ober] 14, after the defacing but before the culprits had been
> identified, a black fraternity's poster hanging in the dorm was emblazoned
> with the word "niggers." No one has admitted to that act, which prompted
> an emergency house staff meeting that eventually led to the identification [of
> Fred as one] of the students who had defaced the Beethoven poster.[18]

In subsequent months, there was an exhaustive study conducted by
the university, which issued a report of its fact findings on January 17,
1989.[19] There were three things about Fred's explanation that I found
particularly interesting in that report:

(1) Fred said that he was upset by all the emphasis on race, on difference. "He wanted others to 'relax and focus on the humanistic aspect
of everyone' and could not see why race or diversity was such a 'big
deal.'"[20] I was struck by the word boxes by which "race," "difference,"
and "humanity" were structured to be inconsistent concepts.

(2) Fred was a descendant of German Jews, and was schooled in
England. Fred described incidents of what he referred to as "teasing"—
and what I would call humiliation, even torture—by his schoolmates
about his being Jewish. They called him miserly, and his being a Jew
was referred to as a weakness. Fred said that he had learned not to
mind it and indicated that the poster defacement at Ujamaa House had
been in the spirit of that teasing. He wondered that the black students
couldn't respond to it in the "spirit" in which it was meant—nothing se-

rious, just "humor as a release." It was just a little message he said, to stop all this divisive black stuff and be human.[21] In these facts, Fred appeared to me to be someone who was humiliated into conformity, and who in the spirit of the callousness and displaced pain which humiliation ultimately engenders, passed it on.

(3) Fred found the assertion that Beethoven was black not just annoying but preposterous. In the wake of the defacement, he was assigned to do some reading on the subject and found that indeed Beethoven was mulatto. This discovery upset him deeply, so deeply, in fact, that his entire relation to the music changed:[22] "Fred said that 'before [he] knew Beethoven was black he had had a certain image of Beethoven and hearing he was black changed his perception of Beethoven and made him see Beethoven as the person he drew in the picture.'"

Ultimately, Stanford's Disciplinary Board found no injury to QC and recommended no discipline of Fred because it was felt that would victimize him, depriving him of his first amendment rights. As to this remedy, I was struck by the following issues:

(1) The privatization of remedy to QC alone,

(2) The invisibility of any injury to anyone, whether to QC or to the Stanford community, whether to whites or to blacks, and

(3) The pitting of the first amendment against other forms of injury— i.e., If it's speech then there *can't* be any harm emanating from it.[23]

As in *Croson's* definition of "equality," I think that the resolution of the Ujamaa House incident rested on a definition of "harm" that was so circumscribed in scope as to conceal from any consideration—legal or otherwise—a range of serious but "extrinsic" harms felt by the decisionmakers to be either inconsistent with the first amendment, or beside the point ("additional to," according to the Parol Evidence Rule). To illustrate this point, I will try to recount my own sense of the injury in this case.

I relate to the Beethoven injury in the following way: Personally, I am the first black female [lots of things] [in lots of circumstances]. I am a first black pioneer just for speaking my mind. The only problem is that every generation of my family has been a first black something or other, an experimental black, a "different" black—a hope, a candle and a credit to our race. Most of my black friends' families are full of generations of pioneers and exceptions to the rule. (How else would we have grown up to such rarified heights of professionalism? Nothing is ever really done in one generation, or alone.) It is not that we are that rare in time, it is that over time our accomplishments have been co-opted and have disappeared; the issue is when can we stop being perceived as "firsts"? I wonder when I and the millions of other people of color who have done great and noble things and small and courageous things and creative and scientific things—when our achievements will become generalizations about our race and seen as contributions to the larger culture, rather than exceptions to the rule, as privatized and isolated abnormalities. (If only there were more of you! I hear a lot. The truth is, there are lots more of me, and better of me, and always have been.)

The most deeply offending part of the injury of the Beethoven defacement is its message that if I ever manage to create something as significant, as monumental, and as important as Beethoven's music, or the literature of the mulatto Alexandre Dumas or the mulatto Aleksander Pushkin—if I am that great in genius, and perfect in ability—then the best reward to which I can aspire, and the most cherishing gesture with which my recognition will be preserved, is that I will be remembered as white. Maybe even a white man. And perhaps my tribe will hold a candle in honor of my black heart over the generations—for blacks have been teaching white people that Beethoven was a mulatto for over a hundred years now—and they will be mocked when they try to make some piece of a claim to me. If they do press their point, the best that they can hope for is that their tormenters will be absolved based on the fact that it was a reasonable mistake to assume that I was white: They just didn't know. But it is precisely the appropriation of knowledge, the authority of creating canon, revising memory, of declaring boundary beyond which lies the "extrinsic" and beyond which ignorance is reasonably suffered, that is the issue. It is not only the individual and isolating fact of that ignorance: It is the violence of claiming in a way that denies, of creating property that fragments and dehumanizes.

This should not be understood as a claim that Beethoven's music is exclusively black music, or that white people have no claim to its history or enjoyment; it is about the ability of black and brown and red and yellow people to name their rightful contributions to the universe of music or any other field. It is the right to claim that we are, after all, part of Western Civilization. It is the right to claim our existence.

The determination that Beethoven was not-black is an unspoken determination that he was German and therefore he could not be black. To acknowledge his mulatto ancestry is to undo the supposed purity of the Germanic empire. It is the sanctification of cultural symbols that are rooted in notions of racial purity. I think that one of the most difficult parts of the idea that Beethoven was not pure white has to do with the implication that this has for notions for the words of the purity of all Western civilization: If Beethoven, that most Aryan of musicians, is not really Aryan, if the word "German" also means "mulatto," then some of the most powerfully uplifting, inspiring, limbically unifying of what we call "Western" moments come crashing down to the aesthetic of vaudevillian blackface. The student who defaced the poster said

that "before [he] knew Beethoven was black he had a certain image of
Beethoven and hearing he was black changed his perception of
Beethoven and made him see Beethoven as the person he drew in the
picture."[24]

All of this is precisely the reasoning that leads so many to assume
that the introduction of African-American, or South American, or feminist literature into Stanford's curriculum is a threat to the very concepts
of what is meant by "Western" or "Civilization." It is indeed a threat.
The most frightening discovery of all will be the eventual realization
of the degree to which people of color have always been part of
Western Civilization.

When Fred's whole relationship to the music changed once he discovered that Beethoven was black, it made me think of how much my
students' relationship to me is engineered by my being black, how much
I am marginalized based on a hierarchy of perception, by my relation to
definitional canons which exercise superhuman power in my life. When
Beethoven is no longer Übermensch, but real and really black, he falls
to debasement beneath contempt; for there is no racial midpoint between the polarities of adoration and aversion. When some first-year
law students walk in and see that I am their contracts teacher, I have
been told that their whole perception of law school changes. The failure of Stanford to acknowledge this level of the harm in the Ujamaa
House incident allows students to deface me. In the margins of their
notebooks, or unconsciously perhaps, they deface me; to them, I "look
like a stereotype of a black [person]"[25] (as Fred described it), not a
black academic. They see my brown face and they draw lines
"'emphasizing [enlarging]' the lips, and coloring in 'black, frizzy
hair.'"[26] They add "red eyes, 'to give . . . a demonic look.'"[27] In the
margins of their notebooks, I am obliterated.

IV. The Truth About Neutrality

The Beethoven controversy is an example of an analytic paradigm in
which "white=good and black=bad." While that paradigm operated
for many years as a construct in United States law, it cannot be said to
exist as a formal legal matter today.

Rather, an interpretive shift has occurred, as though our collective
social reference has been enlarged somewhat, by slipping from what I
described above as the first level of sausage analysis to the second: By
going from a totally segregated system to a "partially integrated" one.
In this brave new world, "white" still retains its ironclad (or paradigmatic) definition of "good," but a bit of word-stretching is allowed to
include some few consistent additional others: Blacks, whom we all

now know can be good too, must therefore be "white." Blacks who refuse the protective shell of white goodness and insist that they are black are inconsistent with the paradigm of goodness, and therefore they are bad. As silly as this sounds as a bare-bones schematic, I think that it is powerfully hypostatized in our present laws and in Supreme Court holdings: This absurd type of twisted thinking, this racism-in-drag is propounded not just as a theory of "equality" but as a standard of "neutrality." (I also think that this schematic is why equality and neutrality have become such constant and necessary companions; they are two sides of the same coin. "Equal . . ." has as its unspoken referent ". . . to whites"; "neutral . . ." has as its hidden subtext ". . . to concerns of color.")

Consider, for example, the case of the Rockettes. In October 1987, the Radio City Music Hall Rockettes hired their first black dancer in the history of that troupe. Her position was "to be on call for vacancies." (Who could have thought of a more quintessentially postmodern paradox of omission within the discourse of omission?) As of December 26, 1987, she had not yet performed, but, it was hoped, "she may soon do so."[28] Failure to include blacks before this was attributed not to racism, but to the desire to maintain the aesthetic of "mirror image" uniformity and precision.[29] I read this and saw allegory—all of society mirrored in that one statement.

Mere symmetry, of course, could be achieved by hiring all black dancers. It could be achieved by hiring light-skinned black dancers, in the tradition of the Cotton Club's grand heyday of condescension. It could be achieved by hiring an even number of black dancers and then placing them like little black anchors at either end; or like hubcaps at the center; or by speckling them throughout the lineup at even intervals, for a nice checkerboard, melting pot effect. . . . It could be achieved by letting all the white dancers brown themselves in the sun a bit, to match the black dancers—something they were forbidden to do for many years, because the owner of the Rockettes didn't want them to look "like . . . colored girl[s]."[30]

There are infinite ways to get a racially mixed lineup to look like a mirror image of itself. Hiring one black, however, is not the way to do it. Hiring one and sticking her third to the left is a sure way to make her stick out. She will stand out like a large freckle and the imprecision of the whole line will devolve upon her. Hiring one black dancer and pretending that her color is invisible is the physical embodiment of the sort of emptiness and failure of imagination that more abstract forms of so-called neutral or "color-blind" remedies represent. As a spokeswoman for the company said: "[Race is not] an issue for the Rockettes—we're an equal opportunity employer."[31]

An issue that is far more difficult to deal with than the simple omission of those words which signify racism in the law and in society is the underlying yet dominant emotion of racism—i.e., the feeling, the perception that introducing blacks into a lineup will make it ugly ("unaesthetic"), imbalanced ("nonuniform") and sloppy ("imprecise"). The ghostly power of this perception will limit everything the sole black dancer does—it will not matter how precise she is in feet and fact, her presence alone will be construed as imprecise; for it is her inherency which is unpleasant, conspicuous, unbalancing.

The example of the Rockettes is a lesson in why the limitation of original intent as a standard of constitutional review is problematic particularly where the social text is an "aesthetic of uniformity"—as it appears to be in a formalized, strictly-scrutinized but color-blind, liberal society. Uniformity nullifies or at best penalizes the individual. Noninterpretive devices, extrinsic sources and intuitive means of reading may be the only ways to include the reality of the unwritten, unnamed, nontext of race.

In *Croson*, the Supreme Court responded to a version of this latter point by proclaiming that the social text, no matter how uniform and exclusive, could not be called exclusionary in the absence of proof that people of color even want to be recipients of municipal contracts,[32] or want to be Rockettes, or whatever.

But the nature of desire and aspiration as well as the intent to discriminate are quite a bit more complicated than that, regulated as they are by the hidden and perpetuated injuries of racist words. The black power movement notwithstanding, I think many, many people of color still find it extremely difficult to admit, much less prove, our desire to be included in alien and hostile organizations and institutions, even where those institutions also represent economic opportunity. I think, moreover, that even where that desire to be included is acknowledged, the schematic leads to a simultaneous act of race-abdication and self-denial.

Last January, for example, on the day after Dr. Martin Luther King's birthday, the *New York Times* featured a story that illustrates as well as anything the paradoxical, self-perpetuating logic of this form of subordination and so-called neutrality. In Hackensack, New Jersey, African-American residents resisted efforts to rename their street after Dr. King because it would signal to "anyone opening up the Yellow Pages" that it was a black neighborhood. It was feared that no white person would ever want to live there, and that property values would drop. "It stigmatizes an area."[33]

The Hackensack story struck a familiar chord with me. I grew up among the clutter of such opinions, just such uprisings of voices, riotous, enraged, middle-class, picky, testy, living and brash. Our house was in

Boston on the edge of the predominantly black section of Roxbury; for years the people on my street fought and argued about whether they were really in Roxbury or whether they were close enough to be considered part of the (then) predominantly white neighborhood of Jamaica Plain.

It seems to me that the "stigmatum" of "Dr. Martin Luther King Boulevard" or "Roxbury" is reflective of a deep personal discomfort among blacks, a wordless and tabooed sense of self that is identical to the discomfort shared by both blacks and whites in even mentioning words like "black" and "race" in mixed company. Neutrality is from this perspective a suppression, an institutionalization of psychic taboos as much as segregation was the institutionalization of physical boundaries. What the middle-class, propertied, upwardly mobile black striver must do, to accommodate a race-neutral world view, is to become an invisible black, a phantom-black, by avoiding the label "black" (it's OK to be black in this reconfigured world as long as you keep quiet about it) because the words of race and the knowledge and controversy they bear are like windows into the most private vulnerable parts of the self; the world looks in, and the world will know by the awesome, horrific revelation of a name.

I remember with great clarity the moment I discovered that I was "colored." I was three. I already knew that I was a "negro"; my parents had told me to be proud of that. But "colored" was something else; it was the totemic evil I had heard my little white friends talking about for several weeks before I finally realized that I was one of them. I still remember the crash of that devastating moment of union, the union of my joyful body and the terrible power-life of that devouring symbol of negritude. I have spent the rest of my life recovering from the degradation of being divided against myself, within myself; I am still trying to overcome the polarity of my own vulnerability. The tense poised trembling whirling joy of my mortality. The immortal unrelenting finality of my dangerous bottomless black fate.

Into this breach of the division-within-ourselves falls the helplessness of our fragile humanity. Unfortunately, the degree to which it is somewhat easier in the short run to climb out of the pit by denying the mountain labelled "colored" than it is to tackle the sheer and risky cliff that is our scorned mortality, is the degree to which blacks internalize the mountain labelled colored. It is the degree to which blacks remain divided along all sorts of categories of blackness, including class, turning the speech of helplessness upon ourselves like a fire hose. We should do something with ourselves, say the mothers to the daughters and the sons to the fathers, we should do something. So we rub ointments on our skin and pull at our hair and wrap our bodies in silk and gold. We remake and redo and we sing and we pray that the ugliness will be hidden and that our beauty will shine through like light and be accepted. And we work and we work and we work at ourselves. Against ourselves. In spite of ourselves, and in subordination of ourselves.

And we resent those of us who do not do the same. We resent those who are not well-groomed and well-masked, and have not reined in the grubbiness of their anger, who have not sought the shelter of the best assimilation we know how, the most decorative denial-art forms. So confusing are the "colored" labels, so easily do they masquerade as real people, that we frequently mistake the words for one another.

When segregation was eradicated from the American lexicon, its omission led many to actually believe that racism therefore no longer existed. Race-neutrality in law was the presumed antidote for race bias in real life. With the entrenchment of the notion of race-neutrality came attacks on the concept of affirmative action and the rise of reverse discrimination suits. Blacks, for so many generations deprived of jobs based on the color of our skin, are now told that we ought to find it demeaning to be hired based on the color of our skin. Such is the silliness of simplistic either-or inversions as remedies to complex problems.

What *is* truly demeaning in this era of double-speak-no-evil is going on interviews and not getting hired because someone doesn't think we'll be comfortable. It is demeaning not to be promoted because we're judged "too weak," then putting in a lot of energy the next time and getting fired because we're "too strong." It is demeaning to be told what we find demeaning. It is very demeaning to stand on street corners unemployed and begging. It is downright demeaning to have to explain why we haven't been employed for months and then watch the job go to someone who is "more experienced." It is outrageously demeaning that none of this can be called racism, even if it happens to disproportionately large numbers of black people; as long as it's done with a smile, a handshake and a shrug; as long as the phantom-word "race" is never used.

The image of race as a phantom-word came to me after I moved into my late godmother's home. In a respectful attempt to make it my own, I cleared the bedroom for painting. The following morning the room asserted itself, came rushing and raging at me through the emptiness, exactly as it had been for twenty-five years. One day filled with profusion and overwhelming complexity, the next day filled with persistently recurring memories. The shape of the past came to haunt me the shape of the emptiness confronted me each time I was about to enter the room. The force of its spirit still drifts like an odor throughout the house.

The power of that room, I have thought since, is very like the power of racism as status quo: It is deep, angry, eradicated from view but strong enough to make everyone who enters the room walk around the bed that isn't there, avoiding the phantom as they did the substance, for fear of bodily harm. They do not even know they are avoiding; they defer to the unseen shapes of things with subtle responsiveness, guided by an impulsive awareness of nothingness, and the deep knowledge and denial of witchcraft at work.

The phantom room is to me symbolic of the emptiness of what formal equal opportunity as promised has actually turned out to be. It is the creation of a space that is filled in by a meandering stream of unguided hopes, dreams, fantasies, fears, recollections. It is the presence of the past in imaginary, imagistic form. What is required in the law of opportunity is some acknowledgement of the room as an empty room before we can stop filling the void with the perpetuated racism of the past. The law must see the room for its actuality as an empty room before we can stop filling it with unfulfilled promises of the future. The real room must be filled with the actuality of our vision, and our wisdom—not the phantom-roomed exile of our longing.

My dispute is perhaps not with formal equal opportunity at all. So-called formal equal opportunity has done a lot but misses the heart of the problem. It put the vampire back in its coffin, but it was no silver stake. The rules may be color-blind but people are not. The question remains, therefore, whether the law can truly shed, or exist apart from the color-conscious society in which it exists, as a skeleton is devoid of flesh; or whether law is the embodiment of society, either the creation or the reflection of a particular citizenry's arranged complexity of relations.

All this is to say I strongly believe in the efficacy not just of programs like affirmative action but affirmative action as a socially and professionally pervasive concept. Not because blacks or women—or anyone—can prove we are holy in our suffering, but because black individuality is subsumed in a social circumstances—an idea, a stereotype—that pins us to the underside of this society and keeps us there, out of sight and out of mind—out of the knowledge of mind which is law. Blacks and women are the objects of a constitutional omission which has been incorporated into a theory of neutrality. It is thus that omission is really a form of expression, as oxymoronic as that sounds: Racial omission is a literal part of original intent; it is the fixed, reiterated prophecy of the Founding Fathers. It is thus that affirmative action is an affirmation; the affirmative act of hiring—or hearing—blacks is a recognition of individuality that re-places blacks as a social statistic, that is profoundly interconnective to the fate of blacks and whites and women and men either as subgroups of each other or as one group. Affirmative action in this sense is as mystical and beyond-the-self as an initiation ceremony. It is an act of verification and of vision; an act of social as well as professional responsibility.

V. The Truth About Truth

In the last ten or fifteen years, there has been increasing movement to expand racial paradigms beyond what has been discussed in the first parts of this essay. A standard allowing increased differentiation, and celebrating "difference," is more frequently touted as a desirable social norm. This is, I think, very much like yet another shift in the sausage-machine analogy, from the second level of "partial integration" to the third level, where whole new worlds of meaning are allowed to coexist, and to contradict one another. In this happily cacophonous universe, white is white and white is good, and black is good and black is really black.

I think that it is this paradigm that has given us so many of the instructional and cultural diversity experiments, in academia as elsewhere—such as Stanford's theme houses. Soul food nights. Salsa dances. Or, at one institution with which I was associated, even Real White Men's Day, celebrated on the occasion of the first blizzard of the season. (Real White Men would go out to the parking lot, set up grills, and barbecue Real Red Meat in their shirtsleeves. We, the rest of the community, would be there rooting them on from the warmth of the cafeteria, always ready to acknowledge anyone's difference, but most particularly theirs.)

All of this is good, with the possible problem that in the exclusive celebration of difference, difference becomes a property launching us back into a complicated version of the first level of parol-evidence-sausage, so that: If white is good and black is good and white and black are different, then goodness must be different for each—or goodness becomes a limited property which is the subject of intense competition, as though it were some physical thing, a commodity or object whose possession can know only one location.

I think, by the way, that this latter is pure silliness—goodness, like humanity, is a concept full of generosity and delights in its multiplicity of voice, and grows strong with each different manifestation. But silly though it may be, it is, again, an attitude that is quite powerful and very pervasive in law, and in society.

Let me give you an example, shifting from race to gender, of how this third-level "difference" can get complicated and overlap with first-level exclusion of the "extrinsic." Once upon a time, when I was living in California, I had a student, S., who was very unhappy being a man. S. came to me and informed me of his intention to become a woman. He said he wanted to talk to me before anyone else at the school because I was black, and that as a black person, I might be more understanding. I had never thought about transsexuality at all;[34] I remember finding myself at a complete loss for words.

After the sex-change operation, S. began to use the ladies room. There was enormous outcry from women students of all political persuasions, who "felt raped"—in addition to the more academic assertions of some, who "feared rape." In a complicated blizzard of homophobia, the men of the student body let it be known that they too "feared rape," and vowed to chase her out of any and all men's rooms. Ultimately, the oppositional forces of men and women reached a compromise. S. should use the dean's bathroom. Alas, in the dean's bathroom, no resolution was to be found, for indeed the suggestion had not been an honest one, but merely an integration of the fears of each side. Thus, in his turn, the dean, circumspection having gotten him this far in life, expressed polite, well-modulated fears about "the appearance of impropriety" in having "students" visit his inner sanctum, and a bunch of other things that I think were related to fear of a real compromise of hierarchy.

I remember thinking about how peculiar and revealing were the scripts that people shook in the face of poor S. Gender as property. Gender as privilege. Hierarchy as sexualized oppression. "I am not a homosexual," I remember S. crying out at one point in the middle of all that mess.

Those words echo in me still. She was "not homosexual" first and foremost as to her best friend, a man with whom she was in love and for whom she had had the operation. She was not homosexual as to the women, whose outcry she took for fear of lesbianism. She was not homosexual as to the men, for this would have been an ultimate betrayal of her bitter, hard-won love. She was not homosexual as to the dean, as though this bit of clarity would save him from some embarrassment, or reassure him that his power or status would not be lowered by the ambivalence of her identity.

At the vortex of this torment, S. as human being who needed to go to the bathroom was lost. Devoured by others, she carved and shaped herself to be definitionally acceptable. She aspired to a notion of women set like jewels in grammatical mountings, fragile and display-encased. She had not learned what society's tricksters and dark fringes have had to, in order to survive: To invert, to hollow and to stretch meaning, rather than oneself. She to whom words meant so much, was not given the room to appropriate them into warm skins and protective shields. S. as "transsexual," S. as "not homosexual," thus became mere floating signifiers, a deconstructive polymorph par excellence.

In retrospect, I see clearly the connection between S.'s fate and my being black, her coming to me because I was black. S.'s experience was a sort of Jim Crow mentality applied to gender.[35] Lots of men, women, blacks and certainly anyone who self-identifies with the term "white" are caught up in the perpetuation and invisible privilege of this game; for "black," "female," "male," and "white" are every bit as much "properties" as the buses, private clubs, neighborhoods and schools which provide the extra-corporeal battlegrounds of their expression. S.'s experience, indeed, was a reminder of the extent to which property is nothing more than the mind's enhancement of the body's limitation. (This is true to some extent in all cultures, I think, but particularly in ours, where our possessions become the description of who we are and the reflection of our worth; and where land usually is referred to not for or by its use, but by the name of its owner [i.e.: Queens, Victoria, Washington, Pennsylvania]—as though the greater the expanse of an estate, the greater in personhood will its master become.)

Another dimension of my resistance was that, for me, the property of my blackness was all about my struggle to define myself as "somebody." Into the middle of that struggle, S. was coming to me because others had defined her as "nobody." Initially, it felt as though she were seeking in me the comfort of another nobody, I was a bit put off inside by the implication that my distinctive somebody-ness was being ignored; I felt in some way that I was being used, an apparency of me being rendered invisible through her refusal to see all of me. (In fact in the suits and situations that give rise to the question of whether all-black and all-women's organizations should admit whites and men, I often feel as though there is a good deal of just such "I'm lonely therefore I'm oppressed too" presumptiveness, that treats such organizations not just as access to power or collegiality, but as empty wilderness to be filled in by the mere comfort of belonging just for belonging's sake; it is thus that the desire to become "one" often disguises appropriation for the mere sake of convenience and the denial of real difference; it is thus that this sometimes noble sentiment comes very close to perpetuating a quite demeaning form of paternalism.)

Very quickly, however, I realized that a literal designation of "black" in my self-definition was probably not appropriate in this situation. While all of the above may be true, I realized that a simultaneous truth existed also: That a discursive property of black somebody-ness was being part of a community of souls who had experienced being permanently invisible nobodies; that "black" was a designation for those who had no place else to go; that we were both nobody and somebody at the same time, if for different purposes.

This is not an easy concept, I think. I am not saying that my blackness is unimportant, or not different. Under other circumstances it might be presumptuous for S. to "become black" in effect, or for me to feel obligated to stretch the definition to include her.

What I *am* saying is that my difference was in some ways the same as her difference; and that simultaneously her difference was in some ways very different from my difference, and that simultaneously we were in all ways the same.

VI. Conclusion: In Which All Things Are One,
Things Fall Apart, and Nothing Is Ever the Same

Not long ago, a white acquaintance of mine described a boyfriend of hers as "having a bit of the Jewish in him." She meant that he was stingy with money. I said, "Oh, don't talk like that! I know you didn't mean it *that way,* but I think that there are harmful implications from thinking *like that.*" She responded with profuse apologies, phone calls, tears, then anger. She said repeatedly that she had no wish to offend me or anyone: that it was just a cultural reality, that there was no offense in it, and that she had heard Jewish people say the same thing, that it was just the way things were, just a group characteristic, nothing personal. There was an odd moment in all this at which I thought we were in agreement, when she said she was sorry, that it was "just cultural reality": I thought that she was referring to racism being so deeply imbedded in culture that it was unconscious, but what she meant was that stinginess was a Jewish "thing."

As we argued, words like "overly sensitive," "academic privilege," and "touchy" began to creep into her description of me. She accused me of building walls, of being unrealistic, of not being able to loosen up and just be with people. She did not use the word "righteous" but I know that that is what she meant. I listened and we talked; I tried to reassure her that I did not mean to put her on the defensive, that I had not meant to attack or upset her, and that I deeply valued her friendship. But I did not back down.

Eventually I felt our friendship being broken apart. She would be consoled with nothing less than a retraction of my opinion, an admission that I was wrong. She did not want me to understand merely that she meant no harm, she wanted me to confess ultimately that there was no harm. Moreover, I realized that she perceived the very raising of the subject matter as an act of hostility, while I perceived my mention of it as an attempt to take our friendship to newer and franker levels of conversation, risking showing what was truly important to me.

About this time, my sister sent me an article about the difficulties of blacks and whites discussing racial issues in social settings. It included warnings of Shelby Steele, a black professor of English at San Jose State University ("If you are honest and frank, then you may come to be seen as belligerent, arrogant, a troublemaker"),[36] and the advice of Harvard professor Dr. Alvin Poussaint ("Defuse the situation—devise a way of getting out of it very quickly. Develop some humorous responses . . . and take charge by steering the conversation in another direction.")[37]

Not long after that, I went shopping for a sweatshirt in the emptiness of nearly-closing-time at Au Coton, a clothing store near my home. The three young salespeople told me that the waffle weave sweater would make me look "really fly." I told them that I'm too old to be fly. The young woman closest to me persisted: "Well, all the really fly people are wearing waffle weave."

As I continued to shop, I could hear them laughing among themselves. It wasn't until I came closer to the counter that I realized that they were joking about Jews. They laughed about "princesses" and imitated "Jewish" accents—New Yorkers imitating other New Yorkers. To an outsider like me, they sounded like they were imitating themselves. "Speak of the devil," said one of them as four other young people came into the store. I don't know why the three young salespeople had decided that the four newcomers were Jews—again, it was as though they were pointing fingers at themselves. They all wore waffle weave tops. They wore denim jackets with the collars turned up. They wore their hair in little moussed spikes and lacquered ringlets. Each and every one of them wore a colorful little kerchief knotted at their throats.

"Tell that girl to get a job," murmured one of the salesgirls of one of the new girls. There was both playfulness and scorn in her voice. Her friends tittered.

The designated Jews wandered around the store, held clothes on hangers up to their chins, and generally looked as youthfully fly as could be.

One of the salesgirls said, "Can I help you guys?" Her voice was high-pitched and eager. Then she turned her head and, behind their backs, winked at her friends.

I didn't say anything. I wanted to say something, and since I am usually very outspoken about these things, I was surprised when no words came out. It is embarrassing but worthwhile nonetheless, I think, to run through all the mundane, even quite petty components of the self-consciousness that resulted in my silence. I think such silence is too common, too institutionalized, and too destructive not to examine it in the most nuanced way possible.

My self-consciousness, I think, was a powerful paralyzer. I was self-conscious about being so much older than they. I was afraid of sounding so maternally querulous that they would dismiss my words, not hear their substance.

I was self-conscious, too, about shopping in a store that had posters that said "As advertised in *Seventeen* magazine. . . ." As old as I was, I felt very young again—young in a sticky, tongue-tied awful adolescent way. In some odd way that is extremely hard to admit in print, I wanted their approval. I was on the edge of their group, the odd person out (as I always was as a teen—that time in one's life when one's attitudes about everything social, including race, are most powerfully reinforced). I did not want to be part of them, but I did not want to be the object of their derision, either. The whole room was filled with adolescent vanity, social pressure and a yearning to belong. The room was ablaze with the cross fire of self-assertive groupings. The four who wandered in, preening and posing and posturing, pretending self-confidence. The three who worked there, lounging and diffident, pretending they owned the place. It was like meeting up with a smoking gun; for those brief, childish, powerful moments, I wasn't sure I could survive being on the wrong side.

I was also caught short because they were so open about their anti-Semitism. They smiled at me and commented on the clothing I was looking at; they smiled and commented on the clothing being looked at by the others. Their anti-Semitism was smiling, open, casually jocular, and only slightly conspiratorial or secretive. They were such nice young people; how could they possibly mean any harm? This little piece of cognitive dissonance was aided and abetted by my blackness, by the fact that I am black: I grew up in a neighborhood where blacks were the designated Jews. I can think of few instances, therefore, in which I have ever directly heard the heart, the source, the uncensored, undramatic day-to-day core of it—heard it as people think it, and heard it from the position of an "insider." And it was irresistible, forbidden, almost sexually thrilling to be on the inside.

I have, of course, heard the message too often to recount as an outsider, by words or acts ranging from hostile to insincere to unconscious. But this time, the salespeople drew their circle with me on the inside. I was "privileged" to hear what they really thought. I was earmarked as someone who would not reveal them; I was designated "safe." I was also designated as someone who didn't matter.

What they had constructed around me was the architecture of trust. As strange as it sounds, I realized that breaking the bond of my silence was like breaking the bond of our silence, was like breaking the heart of a friend. At the same time, I realized that the very fact of their faith in me was oppressively insulting. I became an anti-Semite by the stunning audacity of their assumption that I would remain silent. If I was "safe" I was also "easy" in my desire for the illusion of inclusion, in my capitulation to the vanity of mattering enough even to be included. It did not occur to me that I was simply ignored. I could have been Jewish as much as the four random souls who wandered into the store; but by their designation of me as "not Jewish" they made property of me, as they made wilderness of the others. I became colonized as their others were made enemies.

I left a small piece of myself on the outside, beyond the rim of their circle. I was those others on the other side of the store—as they made fun of the others, they also made light of me; I was watching myself be made fun of. I became "them." In this way, I transformed myself into the third person; I undermined the security of my most precious property, "I." It would be a long time before I would be able to trust in the same way again; I would give much power to the wilderness of strangers, some few of whom I would feel as reflections of my lost property by being able to snare them in the strong bear traps of my own familiarizing labels.[38]

I have thought a lot about this incident since. Part of my reaction was premised on the peculiarities of my own history. Although I was quite young, I remember the Woolworth's sit-ins; I remember my father walking trepidatiously into stores in Savannah, Georgia, shortly after desegregation, cautiously disbelieving of his right to be there, disproportionately grateful for the allowance to just be. Very much my father's daughter, I am always grateful when storekeepers are polite to me; I do not expect courtesy. I value it in a way that resembles love that resembles trust. I value it in a way that is like finding shelter. I value it in a way that is frequently misleading, for it is neither love nor trust nor shelter.

I know that this valuing is a form of fear. I am afraid of being alien, of being suspect, of being thrown out at any moment; I am relieved when I am not. At the same time, I am enraged by the possibility of this subsurface drama-waiting-to-happen. My rage feels dangerous, trapped by necessity, full of physical violence, like something that will get me arrested. And at the same time I am embarrassed by all these feelings, ashamed to reveal in them, through their frequent disproportion, the truth of my insignificance.

All this impermissible danger floating around in me, so boiling so exhausting. I can't kill. I can't teach everyone. I can't pretend it doesn't bother me; it eats me alive. There is no place to dump this toxic rage. So I protect myself. I don't venture into the market very often. I don't deal with other people if I can help it. I don't risk exposing myself to the rage that will get me arrested.

The dilemma, and the distance between the "I" on this side of the store and the me that is "them" on the other side of the store, is marked by an emptiness in myself. Frequently such emptiness is reiterated by a hole in language, by a gap in the law, or a chasm of fear.

I think that the hard work of a non-racist sensibility is the boundary-crossing, from safe circle into that wilderness: The testing of boundary, the consecration of sacrilege. The willingness to spoil a good party and break an encompassing circle, to travel from the safe to the unsafe. It is the courage to realize something beyond bounds. The transgression is dizzyingly intense, a reminder of what it is to be alive. It is a sinful pleasure, this willing transgression of a line, that takes one into new and heightened awareness, a secret, lonely and tabooed world—to survive that transgression is terrifying and addictive. To know that everything has changed and yet that nothing has changed, and in leaping the chasm of this impossible division of the self, a discovery of the self surviving, still well, still strong, and, as a curious consequence, renewed.

But as I said earlier, I think that the perspective we must learn to acquire is one beyond these three boxes that have been set up. It is a perspective that exists on all three levels and eighty-five more levels besides—simultaneously.

It is this perspective, the ambivalent, multivalent way of seeing that is, I think, at the heart of what is called critical theory, feminist theory, and the so-called minority critique. It has to do with a fluid positioning that sees back and forth across boundary, that acknowledges that in certain circumstances I can be black and good and black and bad, and that I can also be black and white, male and female, yin and yang, love and hate.

Nothing is simple. Each day is a new labor.

Ursula Le Guin, in her novel, *The Lathe of Heaven*, writes that making love is like baking bread: Each time it must be done with care and from the beginning.[39]

Each day is a new labor.

Notes

1. 109 S. Ct. 706 (1989).

2. 109 S. Ct. at 730.

3. 109 S. Ct. at 727 (emphasis added; citation omitted) (quoting *Regents of the University of California v. Bakke*, 438 U.S. 265, 296-97 [1478] [Powell, J.]).

4. 109 S. Ct. at 723 (quoting *Bakke*, 438 U.S. at 296-97 [Powell, J.]).

5. 109 S. Ct. at 724.

6. 109 S. Ct. at 716 passim.

7. 109 S. Ct. at 719, 722, 724, 729.

8. 109 S. Ct. at 724.

9. 109 S. Ct. at 725.

10. 109 S. Ct. at 724.

11. 109 S. Ct. at 725.

12. 109 S. Ct. at 725.

13. Restatement (Second) of Contracts § 43 (1979); U.C.C. § 2-202 (1987).

14. 109 S. Ct. at 727.

15. Restatement (Second) of Contracts § 215 (1979).

16. Restatement (Second) of Contracts § 216 (1979); see also U.C.C. § 2-202 (1987).

17. *See* Restatement (Second) of Contracts § 215 (1979).

18. O'Toole, *Ujamaa Incident a "Gripping Study" in Race Relations*, Stan. Univ. Campus Rep., Jan. 18, 1989, at 1, col. 1, 19, cols. 1 & 2.

19. Board Of Trustees, Stanford Univ., Final Report on Recent Incidents at Ujamaa House (1989).

20. *Id.* at 2.

21. *Id*. at 2.

22. *Id*. at 5.

23. This is always a hard point to make without being misunderstood: I am not arguing against the first amendment; what I am insisting upon, however, is some appreciation for the power of words and for the other forms of power abuses that may be lurking behind the "defense" of free speech.

24. Board of Trustees, Stanford Univ., *supra* note 19, at 5 (bracketed material in original).

25. *Id*. at 2.

26. *Id*.

27. *Id*.

28. Lambert, *Rockettes and Race, Barrier Slips*, N.Y. Times, Dec. 26, 1987, at 25, col. 6.

29. As recently as five years ago, the director of the Rockettes, Violet Holmes, defended the all-white line on artistic grounds. She said that the dancers were supposed to be "mirror images" of each other, and added: "One or two black girls in the line would definitely distract. You would lose the whole look of precision, which is the hallmark of the Rockettes." *Id*. at 27, col. 1.

30. Russell Markert, the late founder of the Rockettes, "acknowledged before his death that he . . . forbade suntans for a white dancer because 'it would make her look like a colored girl.'" *Id*.

31. *Id*. at cols. 1 & 2.

32. *See City Of Richmond v. J.A. Croson Co.*, 109 S. Ct. 706, 729-30 (1989).

33. Winerip, *A City Struggles Over an Honor for Dr. King*, N.Y. Times Jan. 19, 1988, at B1, col. 1.

34. I have tried to do a fair amount of reading on the subject since. I by no means want to imply, in my recounting of S., any implication that this was all there was to her story, or that her story explains transsexuality. I want most explicitly to acknowledge a range of transsexuality beyond S. herself, as well as an S. who exists beyond my limited characterization or experience of her.

35. When they changed trains in Birmingham for the last leg of the trip, they discovered what luxury they had been in through Kentucky and Tennessee, where the rest stops had all had colored toilets. After Birmingham there were none. Helene's face was drawn with the need to relieve herself, and so intense was her distress she finally brought herself to speak to a black woman with four children who had got on in Tuscaloosa.

"Is there somewhere we can go to use the restroom?"

The woman looked up at her and seemed not to understand. "Ma'am?" Her eyes fastened on the thick velvet collar, the fair skin, the high-tone voice.

"The restroom." Helene repeated. Then, in a whisper, "The toilet."

The woman pointed out the window and said, "Yes, ma'am. Yonder."

Helene looked out of the window halfway expecting to see a comfort station in the distance; instead she saw gray-green trees leaning over tangled grass. "Where?"

"Yonder," the woman said. "Meridian . . ."

. . . .

At Meridian the women got out with their children. While Helene looked about the stationhouse for a door that said COLORED WOMEN, the other woman stalked off to a field or high grass on the far side of the track. Some white men were leaning on the railing in front of the stationhouse. It was not only their tongues curling around toothpicks that kept Helene from asking information of them. She looked around for the other women and, seeing just the top of her head rag in the grass, slowly realized where "yonder" was.

Toni Morrison, *Sula* 23-24 (1974).

36. Williams, *Uneasy Mingling: When Small Talk at Parties Tackles Larger Issues*, N.Y. Times, Oct. 21, 1988, at A15, col. 1.

37. *Id.*

38. The corollary of historiographic metafiction's challenge to the realist assumption of the transitivity of language and of narrative as an unmediated way to represent history (or some reality that exists outside the discourse) is its challenge to the traditional transparency of the first-person pronoun as a reflection of subjectivity and of the third-person pronoun as the guarantee of objectivity.

L. Hutcheon, *A Poetics Of Postmodernism: History, Theory, Fiction,* 177 (1988).

39. U. Le Guin, *The Lathe Of Heaven* 158 (1971).

7

FEMINIST LEGAL THEORY

One of the most innovative and influential recent developments in constitutional law is known as feminist legal theory. This approach first gained prominence in the 1980s, fueled by the gains (and the setbacks) of the women's movement and by the increased representation of women in law. Informed by multidisciplinary feminist scholarship and inspired by new methods such as consciousness raising and speaking out, feminist legal theory has addressed a wide variety of issues concerning women and the law, including abortion, new reproductive technologies, sex discrimination, affirmative action, pregnancy leaves, gay and lesbian rights, pornography, sexual harassment, battering, and rape.

In applying their approach to constitutional interpretation, feminist legal theorists have focused on the ways in which women have been—and still are—denied equal treatment under the law. They have also developed strategies for ensuring that women's rights are granted constitutional protection.

Like critical race theory, feminist legal theory employs what Mari Matsuda has termed "outsider jurisprudence." It pays attention to women's formerly silenced voices and to the ways in which constitutional issues have been framed with men's interests and perspectives in mind. Exploding the myth of the genderless legal subject, feminist legal theorists have shown how this apparently neutral construct has led to the neglect, in law and in legal theory, of women's needs and perspectives.

In the following selection, Martha Minow discusses the challenge of coming up with a fair, truly impartial interpretation of the Constitution that takes into account differences among groups of people—not only gender differences but also differences in race, ethnicity, religion, and physical ability. She argues—and illustrates this argument by means of many revealing examples—that treating people as equals sometimes means not treating them equally.

This insight leads to a problem that Minow labels the "dilemma of difference." On the one hand, if the law takes difference into account, it may perpetuate the history of oppression based on difference. (Requiring employers to grant pregnancy leaves could, for example, reinforce stereotypes about women as primarily child-bearers rather than employees, which in turn could be used to justify discriminatory hiring practices.) But on the other hand, not taking difference into account in, as Minow puts it, "a world that has made difference matter," could also lead to unjust laws and practices. (Not granting pregnancy leaves forces women but not men to choose between continuing in a job and having a child.) An ongoing challenge for feminist legal theorists is to elaborate how the law can take into account gender and other differences without further entrenching them and thereby contributing to gender stereotyping and discrimination.

S.J.B.

Justice Engendered

Martha Minow

The problem of freedom is the problem of how to divest our categories of their halo of eternal truth.
—Mary Douglas[1]

The truth is that we are all responsible, even if we are not to blame.
—Sarah Burns[2]

The nineteenth-century American legal system recognized only three races: "white," "Negro," and "Indian." Californian authorities faced an influx of Chinese and Mexicans and were forced to confront the now complicated question of racial categorization. They solved the problem of categorizing Mexicans by defining them as "whites" and by according them the rights of free white persons. Chinese, however, were labeled "Indian" and denied the political and legal rights of white persons.[3] Similarly, in 1922, a unanimous Supreme Court concluded that Japanese persons were not covered by a federal naturalization statute applicable to "free white persons," "aliens of African nativity," and "persons of African descent."[4]

In retrospect, these results seem arbitrary. The legal authorities betrayed a striking inability to reshape their own categories for people who did not fit. Of course, it is impossible to know what might have happened if some piece of history had been otherwise. Still, it is tempting to wonder: What if the California legal authorities had changed their racial scheme, rather than forcing the Chinese and Mexican applicants into it? The officials then might have noticed that nationality, not race, distinguished these groups. What if these officials and the Justices in 1922 had tried to take the point of view of the people they were labeling? Perhaps, from this vantage point, the Justices would have realized the need for reasons—beyond racial classification—for granting or withholding legal rights and privileges.

. . . [T]rying to take seriously the point of view of people labeled "different" is a way to move beyond current difficulties in the treatment of differences in our society. This last statement, like much of the article, is addressed to people in positions of sufficient power to label others "different" and to make choices about how to treat difference.[5] If you have such power,[6] you may realize the dilemma of difference: By taking another person's difference into account in awarding goods or distributing burdens, you risk reiterating the significance of that difference and, potentially, its stigma and stereotyping consequences. But if you do not take another person's difference into account—in a world that has made that difference matter—you may also recreate and reestablish both the difference and its negative implications. If you draft or enforce laws, you may worry that the effects of the laws will not be neutral whether you take difference into account or you ignore it. If you employ people, judge guilt or innocence, or make other decisions affecting lives, you may want and need the discretion to make an individualized assessment, free from any focus on categorical differences. But if that discretion is exercised without constraint, difference may be taken into account in a way that does not treat that person as an individual—and in a way that disguises this fact from view.

These dilemmas . . . become less paralyzing if you try to break out of unstated assumptions and take the perspective of the person you have called "different." Once you do that, you may glimpse that your patterns for organizing the world are both arbitrary and foreclose their own reconsideration. You may find that the categories you take for granted do not well serve features you had not focused upon in the past. You may see an injury that you had not noticed, or take more seriously a harm that you had otherwise discounted. If you try to take the view of the other person, you will find that the "difference" you notice is part of the relationship or comparison you draw between that person and someone else, with reference to a norm, and you will then get the chance to examine the reference point you usually take for granted. Maybe you will conclude that the reference point itself should change. Employers do not have to treat pregnancy and parenthood as a disability, but instead as a part of the lives of valued workers. You may find that you had so much ignored the point of view of others that you did not realize that you were mistaking your point of view for reality. Perhaps you will find that the way things are is not the only way things could be— that changing the way you classify, evaluate, reward, and punish may make the differences you had noticed less significant, or even irrelevant, to the way you run your life.

. . . [H]owever, . . . we often forget how to take the perspective of another. We forget even that our point of view is not reality and that our conceptual schemes are simplifications, serving some interests and uses rather than others. We forget because our minds—and probably our hearts—cannot contain the whole world, and so we reduce the world to short-hand that we can handle. Our short-hand—because it is our short-hand—reflects what we thought we needed, where we stood, and who we are. We treat our divisions of the world as though they were real and universal. We do not see that they embody our early experiences of discovering how we are both the same as and different from our parents. We forget how we learned from them to encode the world into the same classifications they used to serve their own needs. We forget that things may appear frightful only because they are unfamiliar. We look at people we do not know, and think they are different from us in important ways. We forget that even if they are different, in a way that matters to them, too, they also have a view of reality, and ours is as different from theirs as theirs is from ours.

We think we know what is real, what differences are real, and what really matters, even though sometimes we realize that our perceptions and desires are influenced by others.[7] Sometimes we realize that television, radio, classes we had in school, or the attitudes of people who matter to us affect our inclinations. Every time we wear an item of clothing that we now think is fashionable, but used to think was ugly, we brush up against the outside influences on what we think inside. Yet we think that we think independently. We forget that widely held beliefs may be the ones most influenced from the outside.[8]

The more powerful we are, the less we may be able to see that the world coincides with our view precisely because we shaped it in accordance with those views.[9] That is just one of our privileges. Another is that we are able to put and hear questions in ways that do not question ourselves. In contrast, the more marginal we feel from the world, from the groups we know, the more likely we are to glimpse a contrast between some people's perceptions of reality and our own. Yet we still may slip into the world view of the more powerful, because it is more likely to be validated. We prefer to have our perceptions validated; we need to feel acknowledged and confirmed. But when we fail to take the perspective of another, we deny that very acknowledgment and confirmation in return.

If we want to preserve justice, we need to develop a practice for more knowing judgments about problems of difference. We must stop seeking to get close to the "truth" and instead seek to get close to other people's truths. The question is, how do we do this? In this Section, I argue that we must persuade others as much as they must persuade us about the reality we should construct. Justice can be impartial only if judges acknowledge their own partiality. Justice depends on the possibility of conflicts among the values and perspectives that justice pursues. Courts, and especially the Supreme Court, provide a place for the contest over realities that govern us—if we open ourselves to the chance that a reality other than our own may matter. Justice can be engendered when we overcome our pretended indifference to difference and instead people our world with individuals who surprise one another about difference.

A. Impartiality and Partial Truths

[T]he ultimate sources of moral value are not one, but many.
—*Charles Larmore*[10]

By closing your eyes you become . . . impartial. . . .
—*Hannah Arendt*[11]

It is a paradox. Only by admitting our partiality can we strive for impartiality.[12] Impartiality is the guise partiality takes to seal bias against exposure. It looks neutral to apply a rule denying unemployment benefits to anyone who cannot fulfill the work schedule, but it is not neutral if the work schedule was devised with one religious Sabbath, and not another, in mind. The idea of impartiality implies human access to a view beyond human experience, a "God's eye" point of view. Not only do humans lack this inhuman perspective, but humans who claim it are untruthful, trying to exercise power to cut off conversation and debate. Doris Lessing argues that a single absolute truth would mean the end of human discourse, but that we are happily saved from that end because any truth, once uttered, becomes immediately one truth among many, subject to more discourse and dispute. If we treat other points of view as irritants in the way of our own vision, we are still hanging on to faulty certainty. Even if we admit the limits of our view, while treating those limits as gaps and leaving the rest in place, we preserve the pretense that our view is sufficiently rooted in reality to resist any real change prompted by another.

Acknowledging partiality may cure the pretense of impartiality. But unless we have less capacity to step outside our own skins than I think we do, we then have a choice of which partial view to advance or accept. Whose partial view should resolve conflicts over how to treat assertions of difference, whether assigned or claimed? Preferring the standpoint of an historically denigrated group can reveal truths obscured by the dominant view, but it can also reconfirm the underlying conceptual scheme of the dominant view by focusing on it. Similarly, the perspective of those who are labeled "different" may offer an important challenge to the view of those who imposed the label, but it is a corrective lens, another partial view, not absolute truth. We then fight over whether to prefer it. "Standpoint theories" may also deny the multiple experiences of members of the denigrated group and create a new claim of essentialism.

Instead of an impartial view, we should strive for the standpoint of someone who is committed to the moral relevance of contingent particulars.[13] Put in personal terms, if I pretend to be impartial, I hide my partiality; however, if I embrace partiality, I risk ignoring you, your needs, and your alternate reality—or, conversely, embracing and appropriating your view into yet another rigid, partial view. I conclude that I must acknowledge and struggle against my partiality by making an effort to understand your reality and what it means for my own. I need to stop seeking certainty and acknowledge the complexity of our shared and colliding realities, as well as the tragic impossibility of all prevailing at once. It is this complexity that constitutes our reciprocal realities, and it is the conflict between our realities that constitutes us, whether we engage in it overtly or submerge it under a dominant view.

Moral action, then, takes place in a field of complexity, and we act ethically when we recognize what we give up as well as what we embrace. The solution is not to adopt and cling to some new standpoint, but instead to strive to become and remain open to perspectives and claims that challenge our own. Justice, like philosophy, ought

> to trust rather to the multitude and variety of its arguments than to the conclusiveness of any one. Its reasoning should not form a chain which is no stronger than its weakest link, but a cable whose fibers may be ever so slender, provided they are sufficiently numerous and intimately connected.[14]

We who judge should remove the removal of ourselves when we either ignore or notice a difference. We can and should confront our involvement in and responsibility for what happens when we act in a reality we did not invent but still have latitude to discredit or affirm. We should have the humility and the courage to act in each situation anew, rather than applying what we presume to know already, as though each case were merely a repetition of an episode from the past.

The plea for judges to engage with perspectives that challenge their own is not a call for sympathy or empathy, nor a hope that judges will be "good" people. Sympathy, the human emotion, must be distinguished from equal respect, the legal command. As one philosopher puts it: "Whereas sympathy involves an imaginative extension of our own person, our beliefs and perspective, respect heeds the distinctness of persons. . . . [W]e can respect [another's] views without sympathizing with them. We can find them justified from his perspective, without believing that they would be ours in that situation."[15]

The obligation to pursue multiple perspectives as developed here is not identical to the Golden Rule. Despite its historic place in ethics, and across cultural and religious groups, the Golden Rule is subject to two risks: First, we may assume that we know the perspective of the other, when we do not; second, we may assume that the other person is too different for us to know his or her perspective. The first risk creates a false unity or universalism, treating another as though he or she were just like us, a replica with no different qualities. The second risk creates a false dichotomy, treating the other as though he or she were sharply and essentially different from us. The difference dilemma recurs.

Nothing in the Rule challenges the notion that difference resides in those who are different; if anything, the Rule reinforces the use of the individual actor's own experience as the reference point for treating a different person. Do not do unto others as you would not have them do unto you. The unstated reference point for treating the other is the self, and it is from the self's point of view, not the other's, that treatment is to be evaluated. Competing perspectives are invisible and difference may continue to seem intrinsic to the other. The status quo can remain unchallenged, too, in the face of the Golden Rule. Treating me as you would want to be treated could be transformed, in your mind, into the phrase, "treating me as you would want to be treated if you were someone in my position." Assume a world of sharply hierarchical social class. You are an elite, I am your servant. What does the Golden Rule command? Treat me as you would wish to be treated if you were in my position. By this formulation, you may rest unperturbed in the view that someone in my position, lower than yours, expects no better or would even be embarrassed if you accorded an unfamiliar kind of equal respect. Thus, even sincere commitments to taking the perspective of the other cannot undo the grip of the unstated assumptions about difference, points of reference, and the privileged position given to the status quo. George Bernard Shaw aptly reformulated the Rule in this vein: "Do not do unto others as you would that they should do unto you. Their tastes may not be the same."[16]

The problem is as much whether anyone *can* know the perspective of another as whether anyone can know the meaning of difference in a given context. The very assumption that one can know the other may so stamp in place the unstated assumptions about what reference point and what point of view matters as to shield any action from confirming or disconfirming tests. Thus, even though the commitment to take the perspective of another, especially a "different" person, can expose and challenge the unstated assumptions that exacerbate legal dilemmas in treating difference, this commitment may also reinforce those assumptions.

It takes practice to make a habit of glimpsing the perspectives of others. A pessimistic view suggests that we can never glimpse another's world, because our self-absorption limits our own self-knowledge. A more hopeful view maintains that through emotional maturity we can learn to identify with others, even those we have treated as different from ourselves. This goal demands a continual process of taking stock of the barriers we erect out of self-interest.

Two exercises can help those who judge to glimpse the perspectives of others and to avoid a false impartiality. The first is to explore our own stereotypes, our own attitudes toward people we treat as different —and, indeed, our own categories for organizing the world. Audre Lorde put it powerfully: "I urge each one of us here to reach down into that deep place of knowledge inside herself and touch that terror and loathing of any difference that lives there. See whose face it wears. Then the personal as the political can begin to illuminate all our choices."[17] This is a call for applying "strict scrutiny" not just to a defendant's reasons for burdening a protected minority group, but also to ourselves when we judge those reasons.[18] It is a process that even we who see ourselves as victims of oppression need to undertake, for devices of oppression are buried within us. We must also examine and retool our methods of classification and consider how they save us from questioning our instincts, ourselves, and our existing social arrangements. Putting ourselves in the place of those who look different can push us to challenge our ignorance and fears and to investigate our usual categories for making sense of the world. This is an opportunity to enlarge judges' understanding and abilities to become better practitioners in the business of solving problems.

The second exercise is to search out differences and celebrate them, constructing new bases for connection. We can pursue the possibilities of difference behind seeming commonalities and seek out commonalities across difference, thereby confronting the ready association of sameness with equality and difference with inferiority. One route is to emphasize our common humanity, despite our different traits. Another tack is to disentangle difference from the allocation of benefits and burdens in society—a tack that may well require looking at difference to alter how people use it. The Court's effort to assure equality for women and men in the conjunction of work and family life in *CalFed* represents such an effort to disentangle institutional arrangements from the difference they create.[19] A third approach is to cherish difference and welcome anomaly. Still another is to understand that which initially seems strange and to learn about sense and reason from this exercise—just as philosophers, anthropologists, and psychologists have urged us to take seriously the self-conceptions and perceptions of others. In the process of trying to understand how another person understands, we may even remake our categories of understanding. Other persons may not even define "self" the same way we do, and glimpsing their "self-concepts" thus challenges us to step beyond our operating assumptions. A further skill to practice is to recognize commonality in difference itself: In the relationships within which we construct difference and connect and distinguish ourselves from one another.

These exercises in taking the perspective of the other will deepen and broaden anyone's perspective. For judges, who debate the use of the coercive forces of the law in relation to issues of difference, these exercises are critical. Judges can and should act as representatives, standing in for others and symbolizing society itself. Judicial acts of representation must also be responsive to the demands of the people they govern, in order to secure apparent legitimacy and, ultimately, to remain effective. One judge explained that law's coercive power must be applied to assure "the viability of a pluralistic democracy," which "depends upon the willingness to accept all of the 'thems' as 'us.' Whether the motives of the framers be considered moralistic or pragmatic, the structure of the Constitution rests on the foundational principle that successful self-governance can be achieved only through public institutions following egalitarian policies."[20]

This exhortation—that we must take the perspective of another, while remembering that we cannot really know what another sees, and must put our own categories up for challenge, without ceding the definition of reality over to others—sounds quite complicated. What do we do with the sense of complexity?

B. Complexity, Passivity, and the Status Quo: The Problem of Deference

Will all those who feel powerless to influence events please signify by maintaining their usual silence.
—Ashleigh Brilliant[21]

We are mistaken when we hold onto simple certainties. Yet complexity seems both overwhelming and incapacitating. By bearing into complexity rather than turning away from it, by listening to the variety of voices implicated in our problems, we may lose a sense of ready solutions and steady certainties. But clear answers have been false gods, paid homage to in the coinage of other people's opportunities, and also at cost to our own character. We harden ourselves when we treat our categories as though they were real, closing off responses to new facts and to challenges to how we live and think. Our certainties also leave unresolved conflicts among incompatible but deeply held values. In the face of complexity, "[t]he politics of difference can all too easily degenerate into the politics of 'mutual indifference. . . .'"[22] If we care about justice, the biggest mistake would be to respond to complexity with passivity. That response is not impartial; it favors the status quo, those benefited by it, and the conception of reality it fosters.

1. Forms of Passivity

Four forms of judicial passivity may be tempting in the face of complexity: deference, intent requirements, reliance on apparent choices or concessions of the parties, and reliance on doctrine. I will consider each in turn.

Respect for other institutions and persons is a critical part of judging, but there are particular risks when the Court, while acknowledging the complexity of a problem of difference, defers to other branches or levels of government, to private actors, or even to the parties before the Court. One risk is that the Court will pretend that it has no power over or responsibility for what results. When the Court defers to Congress, the executive, a state government, or a private actor, the Justices are saying, let's not make a decision, let's leave it to others, or let's endorse the freedom or respect the power of others. It is surely important for the Justices to understand their relationship with other people or institutions with interests in a matter, but such understanding is quite different from ceding responsibility for what ensues. This principle is important for everybody, but especially for a judicial body, which has parties with genuine conflicts before it. As Frank Michelman put it, "attention [to other branches of government] cannot mean deference, or talismanic invocation of authority. The norm of justice to parties itself commands that no other norm should ever take a form that preempts questions or exempts from reason-giving."[23]

Problems also arise when the Court takes on the second form of passivity: Focusing on the intentions of the parties before it. When the Court demands evidence of intentional discrimination before upholding a plaintiff's charges, the Justices are deferring to and thereby entrenching the perspective of the defendant, thus rejecting the perspective of the plaintiff-victim. Asking only about the sincerity of the motive behind a statute whose effect is challenged is also an act that takes sides, defines which reality will govern, and avoids the real challenge of responding to the perspective of the plaintiff.

It is equally problematic for the Court, in a third form of passivity, to point to apparent choices made by plaintiffs, victims, or members of minority groups, as Justice Scalia did in *Johnson*,[24] as a justification for holding against them. The Court may presume incorrectly that the choices are free and uncoerced, or the Court may wrongly attribute certain meanings to a choice.[25] Similarly, judicial references to litigants' concessions during litigation, including during oral argument,[26] are not without risk. Although the Court may be trying to take the perspective of others seriously, its reliance on litigants' concessions as the peg for a judicial decision may also be the Court's way of reducing the task of deciding on its own. Reliance on concessions of the lawyer may be especially troubling in cases involving the rights of minorities, because it is unclear for whom the lawyer speaks at that moment: the client, the cause, or others unrepresented there who will be affected in the future by the Court's ruling.

The fourth form of passivity is perhaps one of the most effective circumventions of responsibility: The Court's reliance on its own doctrinal boundaries and categories to resolve the cases before it. This [article] has demonstrated that the difference dilemma poses similar problems in a wide variety of contexts, including cases involving religion, gender, race, and sexual preference.[27] Yet when the Court takes the boundaries between doctrines as given, filling the doctrines with operative tests and lines of precedent, it obscures these potential similarities across contexts. By the time a case reaches an appellate court, the adversary process has so focused on specific issues of doctrinal disagreement that the competing arguments have come under one framework, not under competing theories. Legal analogy is typically inseparable from precedential reasoning, telescoping the creative potential of a search for surprising similarities into a narrow focus on prior rulings that could "control" the instant case. The Court's practice vividly demonstrates how fabricated categories can assume the status of immutable reality. Of course, law would be overwhelming without doctrinal categories and separate lines of precedent. Yet by holding to rigid categories, the Court denies the existence of tensions and portrays a false simplicity amid a rabbit warren of complexity. The Court's strict segregation of doctrines also cloisters lines of thought and insights, thereby restricting the Court's ability to use larger frames of judgment.[28]

2. Avoiding Passivity

Besides resisting tempting forms of passivity—which do not lessen judicial responsibility—the Court can and should challenge rigid patterns of thought. What if litigants argued more emphatically across contexts, and reminded members of the Court, "you have seen something like this before"? Litigants can help the Court to avoid the dangers of complacency and complexity by searching out analogies and developing unfamiliar perspectives. At the same time, litigants may gain a tactical advantage, because they may persuade a member of the Court of their point of view by analogizing to something the Justice has glimpsed elsewhere. This practice also has some support in epistemology. The difficulties each of us has in seeing around the bend of our own thought can be eased with the help of insights from others who are positioned differently. Given the relationship between knowledge and power, those with less privilege may well see better than those with more.

Surprisingly, traditional legal techniques actually provide fruitful starting points for avoiding passivity. One noted feature of the legal system that can be used to mount this challenge is analogical reasoning. The existence of encrusted practices and categories, however, frustrates the full use of these tools. Litigants and judges should search out unexpected analogies to scrape off barnacles of thought and to challenge views so settled that they are not thought to be views. This process may persuade particular judges, in particular cases, to see a different angle on a problem. It also holds promise as a method for finding surprising commonalities that can nudge us all to reassess well-established categories of thought.

The promise of reasoning by analogy is lost if it becomes an arid conceptualist enterprise. Yet when immersed in the particulars of a problem, we sometimes are able to think up analogies that break out of ill-fitting conceptual schemes. As one observer of creative processes in art, science, and philosophy has commented, "'in the history of human thinking the most fruitful developments frequently take place at those points where two different lines of thought meet.'"[29] By seeing something in a new light, seeing its similarity to something else once thought quite different, we are able to attribute different meanings and consequences to what we see. A glimpse of difference in one context may enable litigants and judges better to appreciate it in another context.

The adversarial process is another feature of the legal system that, with some modification, can be used to challenge judicial complacency. In fact, the values of thinking through analogies bear a striking similarity to the virtues of reasoning in dialogue. The dialogue form puts the student in a position to follow the connections and divergences in argument and invent for herself ways to think anew, rather than simply internalizing the monologue of inherited knowledge. Barbara Johnson notes that "[l]earning seems to take place most rapidly when the student must respond to the contradiction between two teachers. And what the student learns in the process is both the power of ambiguity and the non-innocence of ignorance."[30] Similarly, dialogue in legal briefs and courtroom arguments can stretch the minds of listeners, especially if they are actively forming their own position and not simply picking between the ones before them.[31]

The introduction of additional voices may enable adversary dialogue to expand beyond a stylized, either/or mode, prompting new and creative insights. Consequently, the Court can, and should, seek out alternative views in amicus briefs. Inventive approaches can bring the voices of those who are not present before the Court, as in the recent brief filed with the Court that collected the autobiographical accounts of men and women who believed their lives had been changed by the availability of legalized abortion.[32] Similarly, the famous "Brandeis brief" in *Muller v. Oregon*[33] marked a creative shift for the Court, introducing the use of vivid, factual detail as a way to break out of the formalist categories dominating the analysis. Seeking unusual perspectives enables justices to avail themselves of the "partial superiority"[34] of other people's views and to reach for what is unfamiliar and perhaps suppressed under the dominant ways of seeing. Bringing in a wider variety of views can also make the so-called "counter-majoritarian" Court more "democratic."

Besides seeking out unfamiliar perspectives and analogies new to the law, all judges should also consider the human consequences of their decisions in difference cases, rather than insulating themselves in abstractions. Such engagement encourages the judge to fill in textual gaps based on his or her own experiences. It may seem paradoxical to urge those who judge to bring their own experiences to the problems before them, after identifying the dangerous ways in which we all confuse our own perceptions and interests for reality. In the process of personal reflection, however, the judge may stretch faculties for connection, while engaging in dialogue with the parties over their legal arguments and analogies. I petition all judges to open up to the chance that someone may move them[35]—the experience will not tell them what to do, but it may give them a way outside of routinized categories to forge new approaches to the problem at hand.

This call to be open, to canvass personal experience, applies to all legal controversies, but it is especially important in the context of cases that present the dilemma of difference. Here the judicial mainstays of neutrality and distance prove most risky, for they blind judges to their own involvement in recreating the negative meanings of difference. Yet the dangers of making differences matter also argue against categorical solutions. By struggling to respond humanly to the dilemma in each particular context, the judge can supply the possibility of connection otherwise missing in the categorical treatments of difference.

C. Choosing Among Divergent Demands

If what we change does not change us we are playing with blocks.
—Marge Piercy[36]

Urging judges to allow themselves to be moved by the arguments may seem misguided. A judge who identifies with every perspective may simply feel indecisive and overburdened. Would feeling the tugs in all directions render us powerless to choose? It may be just this fear that explains our attachment to simplifying categories, stereotypes, and fixed ways of thought. Some of us may fear being overwhelmed by the world, others fear being too moved by it, others fear being powerless before it. Challenging familiar categories and styles of reasoning may threaten the search for order, decisiveness, and manageability that maintain the predictability in our lives. But there are other ways to hold things together than the methods we have used in the past.

Some may aspire to a jurisprudence of individualism, never treating any individual as a member of a group. Yet, resonant as it is with many American traditions, individualization is a myth: Because our language is shared and our categories communally invented, any word I use to describe your uniqueness draws you into the classes of people sharing your traits. Even if ultimately I produce enough words so that the intersection of all classes you belong in contains only one member—you—we understand this through a language of comparison with others. This language, however, seems to embroil us in the dilemma of difference.

What could we do instead? I believe we should welcome complexity and challenge complacency—and stop fearing that we will be unable to make judgments. We can and do make judgments all the time, in a way committed to making meaning, rather than recreating or ignoring difference. We make commitments when we make decisions; we reconfirm or remake current understandings by reflecting so deeply and particularly about a new situation that we challenge presumptive solutions. Instead of trying continually to fit people into categories, and to enforce or deny rights on that basis, we can and do make decisions by immersing in particulars to renew commitments to a fair world. Martha Nussbaum described such a process of decision this way:

> We reflect on an incident not by subsuming it under a general rule, not by assimilating its features to the terms of an elegant scientific procedure, but by burrowing down into the depths of the particular, finding images and connections that will permit us to see it more truly, describe it more richly; by combining this burrowing with a horizontal drawing of connections, so that every horizontal link contributes to the depth of our view of the particular, and every new depth creates new horizontal links.[37]

I believe we can still decide, even when we are moved by competing views. We should be moved by [the story of Paul Johnson, who alleged he was unfairly passed over for a promotion, in *Johnson v. Transportation Agency*], as well as [the story of Diane Joyce, who received the promotion in question]; both worked hard for the chance of a promotion, both took risks, both, in some sense, deserved to be promoted. We can turn our sympathy for Johnson into respect for his personal efforts, and sorrow for the world of incommensurable values in which we live. His story deepens our understanding of his individual perspective. But we can be moved by Johnson's story and still decide to deny his claim. Johnson is both an individual as well as a member of a group, a group whose members in the past had a 100% better chance of getting the job at issue than did members of Joyce's group. We can also reach an answer: Their employer should be empowered to do something about this past in order to usher in a more fair future. Substantive commitments—such as a commitment to expand employment participation by members of previously excluded groups— do not tell us what to do, but may help us select from plausible, competing choices in a given circumstance. Moving between specific contexts and general commitments, we can challenge unstated assumptions that might otherwise rule.

Thus, one reason we can still decide, amid powerfully competing claims, is that immersion in particulars does not require the relinquishment of general commitments. The struggle is not over the validity of principles and generalizations[38]—it is over which ones should prevail in a given context. The choice from among principles, in turn, implicates choices about which differences, and which similarities, should matter. These are moral choices, choices about which voices should persuade those who judge.

Even when we understand them, some voices will lose.[39] The fundamentalist Christians who supported the Balanced Treatment Act in Louisiana deserve respect and understanding: Their view of the world may well be threatened by the curriculum taught to their children in the public schools. However, this is what the fight is about. Whose view of reality should prevail in public institutions? This deep conundrum involves the conflicts between the world view animating any rule for the entire society, and the world views of subgroups who will never share the dominant views. I am tempted to propose a seemingly "neutral" rule, such as a rule that judges interpreting the commitment to respect difference should make the choice that allows difference to flourish without imposing it on others. If exclusion of their world view from the biology curriculum creates an intolerable choice for the fundamentalists, they do and they must have the choice to establish their own educational institutions, and their own separate community. Yet this seemingly "neutral" position is a comfortable view for a nonfundamentalist like myself, who cannot appreciate the full impact of the evolution science curriculum as experienced by at least some fundamentalists. Rather than pretending to secure a permanent solution through a "neutral" rule, I must acknowledge the tragedy of non-neutrality— and admit that our very commitment to tolerance yields intolerance toward some views. If the fundamentalists lose in this case, they can continue to struggle to challenge the meaning of the commitment to separate church and state, and they may convince the rest of us in the next round. Although it may be little solace for the minority group, its challenge achieves something even when it loses, by reminding the nation of our commitment to diversity, and our inability, thus far, to achieve it fully.

Thus, choices from among competing commitments do not end after the Court announces its judgment. Continuing skepticism about the reality endorsed by the Court—or any source of governmental power—is the only guard against tyranny.

The continuing process of debate over deeply held but conflicting commitments is both the mechanism and the promise of our governmental system. Within that system, the Supreme Court's power depends upon persuasion. As Hannah Arendt wrote: "The thinking process which is active in judging something is not, like the thought process of pure reasoning, a dialogue between me and myself, but finds itself always and primarily, even if I am quite alone in making up my mind, in an anticipated communication with others with whom I know I must finally come to some agreement."[40] The important question is, with whom must you come to agreement? In a society of diversity with legacies of discrimination, within a polity committed to self-governance, the judiciary becomes a critical arena for demands of inclusion.[41] I see the judicial arena as a forum for contests over competing realities. The question remains, however, whose definitions of realities will govern in a given case and over time.

Court judgments endow some perspectives, rather than others, with power. Judicial power is least accountable when judges leave unstated— and treat as a given—the perspective they select. Litigation before the Supreme Court sometimes highlights individuals who otherwise seldom imprint their perspective on the polity. In eliciting these perspectives, and accepting their challenge to the version of reality the justices otherwise would take for granted, the Court advances the fundamental constitutional commitment to require reasons before exercises of power, whether public or private. Growing from our history, wrought from many struggles, is the tradition we have invented, and it is a tradition that declares that the status quo cannot be immune from demands for justification. Litigation over the meanings of difference represents demands for such accountability. By asking how power influences knowledge, the Court can address whether a "difference" has been assigned through past domination or as a remedy for past domination. In this way, the Court can solicit information about contrasting views of reality without casting off the moorings of historical experience; and in this inquiry, the Court can assess the risk of creating new patterns of domination while remedying inequalities of the past. As we compete for power to give reality to our visions, we confront tragic limits in our abilities to make meaning together. Yet we must continue to seek a language to speak across conflicting affiliations.[42]

We need settings in which to engage in the clash of realities that breaks us out of settled and complacent meanings and creates opportunities for insight and growth. This is the special burden and opportunity for the Court: To enact and preside over the dialogue through which we remake the normative endowment that shapes current understandings.

When the Court performs these roles, it engenders justice. Justice is engendered when judges admit the limitations of their own viewpoints, when judges reach beyond those limits by trying to see from contrasting perspectives, and when people seek to exercise power to nurture differences, not to assign and control them. Rather than securing an illusory universality and objectivity, law is a medium through which particular people can engage in the continuous work of making justice. The law "is part of a distinctive manner of imagining the real."[43] Legal decisions engrave upon our culture the stories we tell to and about ourselves, the meanings that constitute the traditions we invent. Searching for words to describe realities too multiple and complex to be contained by their language, litigants and judges struggle over what will be revealed and what will be concealed in the inevitable partiality of human judgment. Through deliberate attention to our own partiality, we can begin to acknowledge the dangers of pretended impartiality. By taking difference into account, we can overcome our pretended indifference to difference, and people our worlds with those who can surprise and enrich one another. As we make audible, in official arenas, the struggles over which version of reality will secure power, we disrupt the silence of one perspective, imposed as if universal. Admitting the partiality of the perspective that temporarily gains official endorsement may embolden resistance to announced rules. But only by admitting that rules are resistible— and by justifying to the governed their calls for adherence—can justice be done in a democracy. "[I]t is only through the variety of relations constructed by the plurality of beings that truth can be known and community constructed."[44] Then we constitute ourselves as members of conflicting communities with enough reciprocal regard to talk across differences. We engender mutual regard for pain we know and pain we do not understand.

Notes

1. M. Douglas, IMPLICIT MEANINGS: ESSAYS IN ANTHROPOLOGY 224 (1975).

2. Burns, *Apologia for the Status Quo* (Book Review), 74 GEO. L.J. 1791, 1819 (1986).

3. *See* Omi & Winant, *By the Rivers of Babylon: Race in the United States, Part One,* SOCIALIST REV., Sept.-Oct. 1983 at 51–52.

4. *See Ozawa v. United States,* 260 U.S. 178 (1922).

5. If it is presumptuous for me to address judges and justices, and to expect them to hear me, that is the presumption of the substantive argument: That people in power should at least try to hear contrasting points of view, not necessarily so that my view will prevail, but so that we can pursue what happens in the back and forth. Moreover, I am responsible for what I do, and see, and given that, what else should I say here but what I see?

6. I do not mean solely official power, because many people engage in labeling and social stereotyping.

7. Indeed, we learned from others how to express our perceptions of others, and learned how to use language by watching the meanings given by others. *See* H. Pitkin, WITTGENSTEIN AND JUSTICE 222–25 (1973). Even Descartes, in the midst of doubting whether others exist or whether he himself existed, treated categories of thought for describing his experience as shared by readers who would understand his use of them. *See* R. Descartes, MEDITATIONS ON FIRST PHILOSOPHY (2d rev. ed. 1960).

8. This idea is the familiar and troubled concept of false consciousness. *See* G. Lukács, HISTORY AND CLASS CONSCIOUSNESS 256-59 (R. Livingstone trans. 1971).

9. One commentator has observed:

When Justice Stewart said of obscenity, "I know it when I see it," that is even more interesting than it is usually taken to be, if viewed as a statement connecting epistemology–what he knows through his way of knowing, in this case, seeing–with the fact that his seeing determines what obscenity is in terms of what he sees it to be, because of his position of power.

MacKinnon, *Pornography, Civil Rights, and Speech,* 20 Harv. C.R.-C.L. L. Rev. 1, 3 (1985) (footnote omitted) (quoting *Jacobellis v. Ohio,* 378 U.S. 184, 197 [1964] [Stewart, J., concurring]).

10. C. Larmore, PATTERNS OF MORAL COMPLEXITY 151 (1987).

11. H. Arendt, *Appendix: Judging: Excerpts from Lectures on Kant's Political Philosophy,* in THE LIFE OF THE MIND 266 (1978).

12. This does not mean abandoning the idea of a government of laws and not men—especially not men. *See* Michelman, *The Supreme Court, 1985 Term— Foreword: Traces of Self-Government,* 100 HARV. L. REV. 1, 17 (1986). Yet we cannot come close to this idea without recognizing that it is human beings, acting and thinking, who aspire to a government of laws and not men.

13. *See* M. Nussbaum, THE FRAGILITY OF GOODNESS: LUCK AND ETHICS IN GREEK TRAGEDY AND PHILOSOPHY 314 (1986). Nussbaum adds that the someone should be committed to "the value of the passions, and the incommensurability of the values that will tend to approve of this particular sort of judge as a guide." *Id* at 311. The point is that a judge must have a plurality of attachments and do justice in the tension among them. *Id.* at 314.

14. C.S. PEIRCE, *Some Consequences of Four Incapacities,* in COLLECTED PAPERS at 157 (C. Hartshorne & P. Weiss eds. 1931).

15. C. Larmore, *supra* note 10, at 63. Larmore also explores the meaning of respect for persons, not just their beliefs, and connects respect for persons to their capacity to work out a coherent view of the world for themselves. *See id.* at 64.

16. G.B. Shaw, *Maxims for Revolutionists,* in THE COLLECTED WORKS OF BERNARD SHAW 217 (1930).

17. Lorde, *The Master's Tools Will Never Dismantle the Master's House,* in THIS BRIDGE CALLED MY BACK: WRITINGS BY RADICAL WOMEN OF COLOR 98 (C. Moraga & G. Anzaldua eds. 1981). This is not sympathy, tolerance, or even compassion, each of which leaves the viewer's understanding fundamentally unchanged.

18. The burden should not always be on the minority to educate the judge or the majority, for such a task is a drain of energy and a distraction from the minority's projects. *See* A. Lorde, SISTER OUTSIDER 114–15 (1984); E. Spelman, INESSENTIAL WOMAN: PROBLEMS OF EXCLUSION IN FEMINIST THOUGHT, ch. 8 (1988).

19. [*California Federal Savings & Loan v. Guerra* 107 S. Ct. 683 (1987). In this case, "[p]etitioners, a collection of employers, argued that a California statute mandating a qualified right to reinstatement following an unpaid pregnancy disability leave amounted to special preferential treatment, in violation of title VII's prohibition of discrimination on the basis of pregnancy. Writing an opinion announcing the judgment for the Court, Justice Marshall transformed the question presented by the plaintiffs: instead of asking whether the federal ban against discrimination on the basis of pregnancy precluded a state's decision to require special treatment for pregnancy, the majority asked whether the state could adopt a minimum protection for pregnant workers, while still permitting employers to avoid treating pregnant workers differently by extending similar benefits to nonpregnant workers. Framing the problem this way, the majority ruled that "Congress intended the PDA (Pregnancy Discrimination Act of 1978) to be 'a floor beneath which pregnancy disability benefits may not drop—not a ceiling above which they may not rise.'" The majority acknowledged the risk that recognizing the difference of pregnancy could recreate its stigmatizing effects, but noted that "a State could not mandate special treatment of pregnant workers based on stereotypes or generalizations about their needs and abilities." Minow, *The Supreme Court—1986 Term—Foreword: Justice Engendered,* 101 HARV. L. REV. 10, 17-18 (citations omitted)].

... Studies of other cultures, whose work arrangements may be more hospitable to pregnancy and child-rearing, can sharpen such efforts to separate apparent differences from the institutional set-ups constructing them. *See* generally FAMILY POLICY: GOVERNMENT AND FAMILIES IN FOURTEEN COUNTRIES (S. Kamerman & A. Kahn eds. 1978).

20. *Keyes v. School Dist. No. 1,* 576 F. Supp. 1503, 1520 (D. Colo. 1983) (Matsch, J.).

21. A. Brilliant, *Post Card* (Brilliant Enterprises, Pot-Shots No. 2076, 1981).

22. Cornell, *The Poststructuralist Challenge to the Ideal of Community,* 8 CARDOZO L. REV. 989, 996 (1987). Talk of complexity smacks of futility, which absolves everyone from any obligation to try for anything better. Such talk may also assign the problem to the class of people "who benefit from problems being perceived as complex. That is the class of people who have the intellectual and organizational equipment to deal with complex problems" and therefore have a stake in seeing them remain unsolved. Rodes, *Greatness Thrust Upon Them—Class Biases in American Law,* 28 AM. J. JURIS. 1, 4 (1983).

23. Michelman, *The Supreme Court, 1985 Term—Foreword: Traces of Self-Government,* 100 HARV. L. REV. 1, 76 (1986).

24. *See Johnson v. Transportation Agency,* 107 S. Ct. 1442 (1987) [in which the Court upheld a voluntary affirmative action plan for women]. In *Hobbie v. Unemployment Appeals Commission,* 107 S. Ct. 1046, 1051 (1987), however, the Court's majority was sympathetic about constraints on choice, arguing that it is unlawful coercion to force an employee to choose between fidelity to religious belief and continued employment.

25. *See Plessy v. Ferguson,* 163 U.S. 537, 551 (1896) (suggesting that if Negroes attribute stigma to their segregation, it is because they choose to do so) . . . .

26. *See, e.g., Wimberly v. Labor & Indus. Relations Comm'n,* 107 S. Ct. 821, 824-25 (1987); *California Fed. Sav. & Loan Ass'n v. Guerra,* 107 S. Ct. 683, 695 (1987).

27. . . . [C]onservatives on the Court approve of accommodation for religious minorities despite neutrality problems . . . , while liberals sometimes object on neutrality grounds, . . . At the same time, liberals want accommodation for racial minorities and white women, while conservatives object on neutrality grounds. *See Johnson v. Transportation Agency,* 107 S. Ct. 1442 (1987). (The awkwardness of locution—whether to include women of color in the category of racial minorities or that of women—indicates some of the problems with categories that reflect someone else's experience.) There are, of course, doctrinal differences in religion and equality cases. However, there is more textual basis in the Constitution to support an objection on neutrality grounds to accommodation of religious minorities than to accommodation of racial and gender minorities, for neither the fourteenth amendment nor statutes like Title VII include an equivalent of the first amendment's ban against establishing religion.

28. The Court's rejection of the plaintiff's equal protection theory in *Roe v. Wade,* 410 U.S. 113 (1973), for example, constrained the emerging jurisprudence of privacy within a framework that produced inequalities. *See Harris v. McRae,* 448 U.S. 297 (1980) (upholding limits on governmental funding of abortions for poor women).

29. F. Capra, THE TAO OF PHYSICS xii (1984) (quoting Werner Weisenberg); *cf.* S. Harding, THE SCIENCE QUESTION IN FEMINISM 102, 235 (1986) ("'Analogies are

not aids to the establishment of theories; they are an utterly essential part of theories, without which theories would be completely valueless and unworthy of the name.'" (quoting N. Campbell, PHYSICS, THE ELEMENTS [1920]).

30. B. Johnson, A WORLD OF DIFFERENCE 83 (1987) (emphasis in original).

31. One way to formulate a new position is to salvage the power of seemingly antagonistic views, as in the old, and telling, joke of the rabbi who listened to the first disputant, thought a minute, and said, "You're right." Then he listened to the second disputant, and thought a while, and said, "You're right." The rabbi's wife, listening in the doorway, then said, "They can't both be right." The rabbi replied, "You're also right."

32. *See* Brief Amici Curiae, of National Abortion Rights Action League, et al., *Thornburgh v. American College of Obstetricians & Gynecologists*, 476 U.S. 747 (1986) (No. 84-495 and 84-1379).

33. 208 U.S. 412 (1908). The premise advanced by the brief–that women need kinds of protections from night labor that men do not–has been rejected legally, and current feminist efforts challenge any revival of this view. *See* Becker, *From Muller v. Oregon to Fetal Vulnerability Policies*, 53 U. CHI. L. REV. 1219, 1223-25 (1986). The brief itself, however, included evidence of not only special risks to women from long and hazardous employment, but also risks to the health of male workers. *See id.* at 1223 n.25. Many supporters of protective labor legislation for women conceived of this reform as only the first step toward general, sex-neutral reforms establishing an eight- or ten-hour day and safer working conditions. *See* Collins & Friesen, *Looking Back on* Muller v. Oregon, 69 A.B.A. J. 294, 298 (1983).

34. W. James, *On a Certain Blindness in Human Beings*, in ON SOME OF LIFE'S IDEALS 3, 46 (1912).

35. There are long-standing philosophic and jurisprudential debates about the legitimate roles of emotion and personal views in judging. I mean here to emphasize the view that "[b]y compartmentalizing our lives we implicitly accept individual responsibility for the failures that grow out of our collective oppression and absorb into ourselves the impact of these failures." Hartsock, *Political Change: Two Perspectives on Power*, in BUILDING FEMINIST THEORY: ESSAYS FROM QUEST 3, 16 (C. Bunch & J. Dolkart eds. 1981).

36. *Id.* at 6 (quoting Piercy).

37. M. Nussbaum, *supra* note 13, at 69. Nussbaum uses Heraclitus' image of a spider in a web, "able to feel and respond to any tug in any part of the complicated structure." *Id.* It is a vivid image of responsiveness to complexity in a world of practical choice. *Cf.* E.B. White, CHARLOTTE'S WEB 92-104 (1952) (discussing a spider who acts as a sensitive and involved creature, using her web to spell an important message).

38. *See* King, *I Sing Because I'm Happy: Some Random Thoughts on* "An Absolutely Positively True Story: Seven Reasons Why We Sing," 16 N.M. L. REV. 535, 539 (1986). I endorse the demand for reasons, after decisions are reached, that is represented by the rule of law, but ask here instead, what should be done before the decision-maker reaches judgment? What stance toward the arguments should the judge try to strike?

39. A real conundrum for me is whether ever to suppress some voices. Usual examples here are the views of Nazis and terrorists, and increasingly, pornography. Are these views unacceptably intolerant and debasing in their very

expression? Or does suppressing them without criticism leave them smoldering? I do not have an answer, but I believe that these, too, are matters that deserve and require struggle and debate.

40. H. Arendt, BETWEEN PAST AND FUTURE 220 (1961).

41. There is some risk of making a fetish about courts, as Frank Michelman has discussed. *See* Michelman, *supra* note 23, at 74. Building on the concept of idea of "paidea" developed by Michelman and by Robert Cover, *see* Cover, *The Supreme Court, 1982 Term—Foreword:* Nomos and Narrative, 97 HARV. L. REV. 4 (1983), we can view a model of self-government in not only the conduct of judges, but also in the conduct of litigants, the watching public, and the people debating the case at the corner drug store. All are part of the process, or should be in the minds of the justices as they consider whose approval they seek.

42. The rhetoric of rights is one such language. Its use in litigation has limitations, and yet it has proved malleable enough to be remade to express competing realities, even for those for whom rights were not initially intended. *See* Minow, *Interpreting Rights: An Essay for Robert Cover*, 96 YALE L.J. 1860 (1987); Schneider, *The Dialectic of Rights and Politics*, 61 N.Y.U. L. REV. 589 (1986); Williams, *Alchemical Notes: Reconstructing Ideals from Deconstructed Rights*, 22 HARV. C.R.–C.L. L. REV. 401 (1987).

43. C. Geertz, LOCAL KNOWLEDGE: FURTHER ESSAYS IN INTERPRETIVE ANTHROPOLOGY 184 (1983).

44. N. Hartsock, MONEY, SEX, AND POWER: TOWARD A FEMINIST HISTORICAL MATERIALISM 254 (1983) (describing the view of Hannah Arendt).

8

DECONSTRUCTION

Another current approach to constitutional interpretation has emerged from the recent movement in Continental philosophy and literary theory known as deconstruction. Although deconstruction has its roots in the philosophies of Hegel, Husserl, Heidegger, and Nietzsche, it was Jacques Derrida who first articulated the method of deconstruction and who has had the greatest influence on those applying it to the law. The term "deconstruction" has been taken up by popular culture and used in so many different ways that it has come to stand for just about anything—and for nothing at all. But as Derrida uses the term, "deconstruction" involves a distinctive method that, as Balkin and others argue, can be a helpful tool in interpreting the Constitution.

A deconstructive reading typically begins by pointing out a hierarchical opposition; for example, "A is the tradition and B is an aberration." In such an opposition, one of the terms is "privileged," that is, considered to be more fundamental or basic. A deconstructive interpretation reverses—or "deconstructs"—this hierarchy by showing that the supposedly foundational term, A, depends on the supposedly subordinate one, B. The "privileging" of A over B is then shown to be an ideological choice rather than a conceptual necessity.

In the following selection, J. M. Balkin applies the methods of deconstruction in analyzing the appeal to "tradition" in Justice Scalia's opinion in a case involving parental rights. This example of deconstruction at work illustrates its benefits, which Balkin summarized in an earlier article, "Deconstructive Practice and Legal Theory": "first, deconstruction provides a method for critiquing existing legal doctrines; in particular, a deconstructive reading can show how arguments offered to support a particular rule undermine themselves, and instead, support an opposite rule. Second, deconstructive techniques can show how doctrinal arguments are informed by and disguise ideological thinking. . . . Third, deconstructive techniques offer both a new kind of interpretive strategy and a critique of conventional interpretations of legal texts."

Whereas some have considered deconstruction to be a progressive political tool able to undermine entrenched but unjustifiable legal norms, others have argued that it is nihilistic and incapable of yielding a stable interpretation of the law or providing grounds for reform. For if any view can be deconstructed, what authorizes a theorist to settle on a particular interpretation? Balkin responds to this charge by suggesting that although the deconstruction of legal text could in principle be interminable, pragmatic considerations determine both when one starts to apply the technique and when one decides to stop.

S.J.B.

Tradition, Betrayal, and the Politics of Deconstruction

J. M. Balkin

Using deconstructive techniques to make political and legal arguments raises the obvious question whether there is any connection between deconstruction and politics or deconstruction and justice. In fact, I believe that there are important connections between deconstruction, justice, and politics. But deconstruction itself does not have a politics, or rather, it has only the politics of those who make use of it. And deconstruction itself is not just, although it may be used to pursue justice. These are controversial claims. In this essay I want to explore them by deconstructing a particular case that raises issues of Justice. It concerns the concept of tradition in constitutional law. I shall use deconstruction to explore this important and enigmatic concept, and, equally importantly, to consider what this deconstructive analysis tells us about the relationship of deconstruction to ethical and political choice.

I. Tradition and Betrayal

I begin with a recent decision of the United States Supreme Court, *Michael H. v. Gerald D.*[1] This case is especially interesting to constitutional scholars because its various opinions offer a number of contrasting theories about the meaning of the "liberty" protected by the due process clause of the Constitution. For those not familiar with the case, it involves an attempt by one Michael H. to establish parental rights to a little girl, Victoria, who Michael claimed was his biological daughter, and who had lived with him as his daughter on and off for three years. Michael sued to establish his paternity and obtain visitation rights. Victoria, however, was conceived and born while her mother Carole was married to another man, Gerald D. Michael H. offered genetic tests establishing to a 98.07 percent certainty that he, and not Gerald D., was the biological father. Nevertheless, the United States Supreme Court upheld a California statute which established a presumptive conclusion that a child is the offspring of the man who is married to the mother at the time of the child's birth, unless the mother or her husband wish to deny the husband's paternity.[2] Neither Gerald nor Carole wished to contest paternity in this case because they did not want Michael to visit Victoria.

Michael H. argued that California's statutory presumption denied him a liberty guaranteed by the due process clause of the fourteenth amendment. The Supreme Court held, in a plurality opinion written by Justice Scalia, that Michael had no liberty interest in a continuing relationship with Victoria. Justice Scalia argued that the concept of liberty is amorphous, and that to give it content one must refer to existing traditions of liberty in the United States.[3] He argued that one must look to "the most specific level at which a relevant tradition protecting, or denying protection to, the asserted right can be identified."[4] Thus, it was not enough for Justice Scalia that American society traditionally protected the interests of biological fathers in relationships with their children. Justice Scalia argued that there was no liberty interest in this case because society has not traditionally protected the parental rights of adulterous fathers of children born during marriage of the mother to another man.[5] Moreover, there was a traditional interest in the protection of what Justice Scalia called the "unitary family"—one husband, one wife, one or many children.[6] Therefore, despite the virtual certainty that Victoria was Michael's biological daughter, despite the fact that she lived with him over many months and he held her out as his own child, despite the fact that she even called him "Daddy," California was constitutionally justified in cutting off all of Michael's parental rights in the interest of preserving the unitary family.

I suspect that many people will think that this opinion is wrongheaded in the extreme. For some it will appear to be nothing more than the product of a rather intolerant jurist who apparently believes that familial relations have always been conducted according to the rules first laid down by June and Ward Cleaver. Indeed, one hardly needs all of the philosophical artillery of deconstruction to see why Justice Scalia's arguments are problematic. Nevertheless, I do think that one can learn something from deconstructing this opinion. But what one will learn is as much about deconstruction—and its possible political uses—as it is about constitutional law.

We could deconstruct this opinion in many ways. We might note that Justice Scalia's opinion relies upon a distinction between more and less specific traditions, a distinction which is, as Justice Brennan points out, manipulable and difficult to maintain.[7] I shall return to this criticism in a moment. Nevertheless, we should first take seriously the reasons why Justice Scalia wants to read the concept of tradition narrowly. He makes clear that the search for the most specific tradition is tied to his fears about the open-ended character of the concept of liberty and the great power given to judges who must interpret this concept. Justice Scalia is greatly concerned that courts will use such open-ended terms to make value-laden choices inappropriate to their institutional role.[8] The more specific the inquiry into tradition, the more likely it is that a court is protecting something that already is in place, rather than simply creating a tradition, or stretching an existing tradition further than is historically permissible.[9] For persons with the same general philosophy as Justice Scalia, an example of such an unwarranted extension of tradition might be extending the traditional respect for the privacy of marriage to protect extramarital sexual relations. Thus, specific traditions are more reliable guides to the contours of liberty than are general traditions because they are more easily identifiable, and because they involve less danger of countermajoritarian value choices by the judiciary.

Ultimately, however, these very justifications undermine Justice Scalia's test of the most specific tradition. His test assumes that constitutionally protected liberties match or do not match existing traditions in an unproblematic way. For each asserted right there either is or is not a specific tradition associated with its protection. Yet there are many different ways of describing a liberty, and many different ways of characterizing a tradition. For example, we might point out that under his test, there has been no established tradition in California for protecting Justice Scalia's own rights to visit his children, since there is no tradition of affording protection to fathers who are children of Italian immigrants and who graduated from Ivy League law schools before 1965, were appointed to the United States Supreme Court by former governors of the state of California and have more than two children but less than thirteen. Indeed, the question has hardly ever come up. Justice Scalia would no doubt respond that these are the wrong factors to consider in matching liberty to tradition. And we might reply: How do you, oh purveyor of neutral principles, know this?

To be sure, Justice Scalia has a plausible response. When Justice Scalia claims parental rights to his children, the liberty he claims is the parental right of fathers with respect to biological children born while the father was married to the child's mother. This has been traditionally protected.

The rights of adulterous fathers, however, have not been traditionally protected.[10]

But this answer reveals that Justice Scalia's theory is not simply a preference for narrower traditions over broader traditions. It rests upon an important metaphysical set of assumptions—that traditions or (more importantly) the absences of traditions, come in discrete units with discrete boundaries. To describe a tradition accurately is to respect the preexisting boundaries of the tradition. Similarly, to describe a liberty traditionally protected is to describe its actual contours. Thus, one cannot simply divide up traditions or liberties any way one wants. Like glass bottles, traditions and liberties come in premade sizes. One cannot cut them to fit, or else one will break the glass. Thus, there is a tradition of protecting marital privacy but not a tradition of protecting the marital privacy of a narrower class—for example, middle class persons, and certainly not a tradition of protecting the privacy of a broader class of persons that would include unmarried couples. Yet, under this logic, it is also historically clear that there is a tradition of protecting the marital right of privacy, but not a historical tradition of protecting married couples' right to purchase contraceptives. *Griswold v. Connecticut*[11] is thus a potential embarrassment for Justice Scalia.[12]

Moreover, Justice Scalia's vision of tradition assumes that traditions are not only discrete, but presumptively normatively correct. What is traditional is worthy of constitutional protection, and what is not traditional is not, whether it be marital privacy, the rights of married fathers to visit their children, sexual harassment in the workplace or racial segregation. This, too, is a potential source of embarrassment.

Justice Scalia's metaphysics of tradition produces sufficiently troublesome counter-examples that we must pause and consider whether we have stumbled upon a serious difficulty concerning the concept of tradition itself. What is tradition? How do we determine its boundaries or entailments, and what is its normative status? If there is a tradition of protecting marital privacy, but not a more specific tradition protecting marital purchase of contraceptives, how do we know whether the latter situation is nevertheless subsumed under the former for purposes of constitutionally protected liberty? Might one not conclude instead that the *real* historical tradition was protection of marital privacy in the home, so that the purchase of contraceptives in the open marketplace could be regulated or even proscribed consistent with the tradition? Would this not be more consistent with the experiences of Margaret Sanger and her followers, who publicly advocated birth control in the early twentieth century, and were met with incredible resistance?[13] Again, if sexual harassment directed toward women in the workplace and respect for marital privacy are both traditions, but only one is worth protecting, how do we tell the difference? If back alley abortions are a tradition in response to the "traditional" prohibition on abortion in America, does this make abortion (in or out of a back alley) a tradition worth protecting and sustaining? In short, what normative status should be assigned to a set of values given the fact that many people have held these values at one point or another in our nation's history?[14]

One of Justice Scalia's predecessors on the Supreme Court, the second Justice Harlan, was also enamored of tradition as an aid to understanding the content of the liberty protected by the due process clause. But he was more aware of its problems. In his dissent in *Poe v. Ullman*,[15] he spoke of the need for "regard to what history teaches are the traditions from which [this country] developed as well as the traditions from which it broke."[16] In alluding to the traditions from which America broke, Justice Harlan thus recognized, in a way that Justice Scalia appears not to, that the existence of a tradition may be a reason for rejecting it as controlling. Just as Learned Hand rejected the defense of custom in tort law on the ground that "a whole calling may have unduly lagged,"[17] so too the existing customs of the American people may not be appropriate for constitutional perpetuation. This is especially true, one might think, when they are impositions of values by a majority on a political, cultural, ethnic, religious, or ideological minority.

In fact, what is most troubling about Justice Scalia's call for respecting the most specific tradition available is that our most specific historical traditions may often be opposed to our more general commitments to liberty or equality. Curiously, then, different parts of the American tradition may conflict with each other. And indeed, this is one of the untidy facts of historical experience.

The fourteenth amendment's abstract commitment to racial equality was accompanied by simultaneous acceptance of segregated public schools in the District of Columbia[18] and acquiescence in antimiscegenation laws.[19] The establishment clause and the principle of separation of church and state have coexisted with presidential proclamations of national days of prayer,[20] official congressional chaplains,[21] and national Christmas trees.[22] Traditions do not exist as integrated wholes. They are a motley collection of principles and counterprinciples, standing for one thing when viewed narrowly and standing for another when viewed more generally. Tradition never speaks with one voice, although, to be sure, persons of particular predilections may hear only one.

Moreover, as the quote from Justice Harlan suggests, tradition is not an unmitigated good or an unalloyed source of constitutional wisdom. There are good and bad traditions, and one must choose between them. Nevertheless, a more realistic approach to tradition, along the lines of Justice Harlan, is cold comfort to Justice Scalia. It undermines the very reasons he has attempted to hew to tradition. It leads us back to the very value-laden inquiry that Justice Scalia sought to avoid by his theory of tradition. To follow tradition because it reflects the values of the many is insufficient—one must also believe that these values are justified, or not so unjustified that they must be contradicted. Inquiry into tradition leads us back, in other words, to the basic problem of constitutionalism all over again. It does not solve the problem of determining the boundaries of constitutionally protected liberty, but merely phrases the same question in a different way.

Tradition, it thus appears, rather than solving our problems, has proven to be a very troublesome concept. Traditions may be worthy or pernicious. Traditions may conflict. Traditions at a more abstract level may contradict traditions at a more concrete level. Here, perhaps, a deconstructive analysis might come to our aid. We might try to understand the logic of tradition, and its place in this opinion, and in constitutional law generally, by employing a familiar deconstructive technique—etymological analysis.

The word "tradition" is derived from the Latin *traditio,* which in turn is derived from the verb *tradere,* meaning to deliver or hand over.[23] Tradition is the delivery of something into the hands of another, as one might deliver a deed or an object, or even a set of teachings that are passed down from generation to generation. For the same reason, however, *tradere* also means to deliver someone into another's hands, from which we get the word "betrayal."[24] From *tradere* and *tratitio* we also get "treason,"[25] and "extradite"—that is to hand someone over to the authorities.[26]

This etymology leads us naturally to the word "traitor," and its alternative form, "traditor," both of which also come from *tradere.* Thus, "tradition" also means the crime of being a traitor or traditor. The term "traditor" was used by the early Christians especially during the Diocletian era, to describe persons who delivered holy vessels, or scripture, or more often, their fellow Christians, into the hands of the Romans.[27] Thus, Judas Iscariot is the first great traditor of Christian theology, which is also to say that he is the first great Christian traditionalist, the founder of the tradition of Christian tradition—that is, the handing over of Christians.

Indeed, Dante's ninth circle of hell—the lowest circle—is specifically reserved for betrayers (Dante uses the word *traditor*—the modern Italian equivalent is *traditore).*[28] He includes in the ninth circle those who have betrayed their friends, family, country, or (worst of all) their lords and benefactors. There one will find Judas Iscariot joined by Brutus and Cassius, who earned their place in Dante's Inferno by betraying Julius Caesar. Dante apparently thought that tradition—in the sense of betrayal—was the most grievous of sins, for in the ninth circle, Beelzebub himself gnaws at the heads of the *traditores,* the great traditionalists.[29]

It does not take us long to discover that tradition and betrayal are closely linked, and not only etymologically. To respect tradition is also to betray in at least three senses. First, it is to forsake other alternatives for the future, to hand them over to their enemies, to hinder and eliminate them in the name of social solidarity, propriety, order, or other goals. Tradition is always extradition. Second, to respect tradition is also to betray other existing and competing traditions, to submerge and extinguish them. It is to establish through this suppression the hegemony of a particular way of thinking, just as in *Michael H.* Justice Scalia tried to write 1950's white middle class theories of the family into the Constitution—thus establishing the hegemony of Ozzie and Harriet, if you will. There are, of course, other traditions of family life in this country. There are traditions of extended families, of spousal separations, of common law marriage and unmarried cohabitation—but apparently they don't count, since we didn't see them on "I Love Lucy."

Third, a tradition is often, in an uncanny way, a betrayal of itself. For Scalia's vision of the unitary family, as exemplified by television situation comedies of the 1950's, portrays a theory of the family that was hypocritical even in its own time—since even what white middle class families in the 1950's said one should do and not do sexually was not in fact what they always did, as we all found out later on. To establish and enshrine a tradition is thus at the same time to establish a countertradition—a seamy underside consisting of what society also does and perhaps cannot help but do, but will not admit to doing. The overt, respectable tradition depends upon the forgetting of its submerged, less respectable opposite, even as it thrives and depends on its existence in unexpected ways. For example, in the television and movies of the 1950's, one sees Rock Hudson and other homosexual or bisexual males playing the parts of monogamous heterosexual males, and implicitly endorsing a heterosexual lifestyle. These roles served to support and define the very tradition of sexual practices of which Justice Scalia speaks.[30] They furthered and reinforced a tradition of values that the persons playing these roles owed no fealty to, a tradition that indeed, made each of them a traditor, and required of each of them a particular form of self-betrayal.

Michael H. v. Gerald D., in this sense, is all about tradition and betrayal. It is about the sexual betrayal that led to the conception of Victoria. It is about the emotional betrayal of Michael H. by the mother, Carole, who, after living with him and allowing him to foster a relationship with his own daughter, denied him the right to continue that relationship. It is about the legal tradition and betrayal—that is, the handing over—of a child from her biological father to another man, a tradition and betrayal enforced in the name of protecting the tradition of the family—the raising of children by their parents.

Finally, *Michael H.* is about the tradition and the betrayal of the concept of liberty protected by the due process clause. For here, Justice Scalia, preaching about the great traditions that the clause protects, and the obligations of previous precedents, believes he is following those traditions and those precedents at the same time that his colleagues on the Court argue that he is betraying them. As Justice Brennan succinctly states, "[i]t is ironic that an approach so utterly dependent on tradition is so indifferent to our precedents."[31] When one thinks of tradition in law, one thinks naturally of the principle of *stare decisis*—the development of law through precedent and reasoning by analogy. Yet is this particular tradition—this handing down of precedential rules from one case to the next—not also a form of betrayal? And is not every betrayal also the beginning of a new tradition? When a judge produces a reading of preceding cases, her reading is always similar to and different from what came before. Sometimes this is deliberate—sometimes it is simply a result of the alterations produced by reading authoritative materials in new contexts. As the tradition grows and develops, it alters itself. And as it alters itself, it is both true and false to itself. It is both a handing down and a modification, however slight or subtle, of what came before. It is the simultaneous production of similarity and difference. It is both tradition and betrayal.

When we think of the traditions of American constitutional law, we think of the landmark precedents of the Supreme Court—*Marbury v. Madison*,[32] *McCulloch v. Maryland*,[33] *Brown v. Board of Education*,[34] and *United States v. Darby*,[35] to name a few. Yet the curious interrelation of tradition and betrayal is present even here. *Brown v. Board of Education* is, from one standpoint, the beginning of a great tradition of protection of civil rights. But from another perspective, it was a betrayal of the Court's proper institutional role, and of the intentions of the framers of the fourteenth amendment.[36] The same could be said of *Darby*, and even of *Marbury* or *McCulloch*—betrayals that nonetheless spawned a grand and glorious tradition. Do these cases create traditions of constitutional law, or betray earlier ones? Or are these not two different ways of saying the same thing?

From these remarks, it should be clear that I, too, am unsatisfied with Justice Scalia's opinion in *Michael H.*, and in particular with his reliance on tradition, which smacks of sexual and cultural intolerance and an almost willful blindness to the many different layers of tradition and countertradition in American society. And it should also be fairly clear that one could use deconstruction to critique Justice Scalia's opinion on many different levels—showing how, in his attempt to protect traditional family values, he destroys the possibility of a bond between a child and her biological father.[37] One might also note that while the Court appears to be the protector of family values, it does so by allowing parent-child relations to be severed by legal technicalities. Here the supreme law of the land (the Constitution) is claimed to reflect general traditional values, but in fact destroys particular parental bonds. The acknowledgment of one story about family relations is at the expense and exclusion of other, less "respectable" but no less extant versions.

Of course, Justice Scalia does not believe that the behavior of Michael H. and Carole D. is commonplace in his America. He even states at the beginning of his opinion that he "hopes" that this case is "extraordinary."[38] But his "hope" is a curious one. It is less a hope than a command—an assertion of authority. It is he same type of "hope" a schoolteacher expresses when she states that she hopes that her students are not chewing gum behind her back. It is the not too disguised assertion of the need for the cultural hegemony of a particular point of view, achieved by assuming other views out of existence.

Indeed, one might point to the irony of Justice Scalia's statement that this case is extraordinary, when it is used to make a general point about how all cases construing the due process clause should be decided. This irony is particularly pointed since it is well known that other substantive due process questions—for example, those involving abortion[39] and gay rights[40]—have been much on the Court's mind in recent years. The effort to stop the spread of constitutionally mandated sexual freedom has been a rallying point for the Court's conservative wing. One might feel moved to express the hope that the situation in *Michael H.* was extraordinary only if one believed—or rather, feared—that the country would at any moment be overrun by a veritable army of fornicators, homosexuals, and other sexual miscreants.

Our deconstruction has hardly seemed to buttress the logic of Justice Scalia's opinion. And, given the embrace of deconstructive techniques by the political left, this might not seem a surprising result. Nevertheless, (and here is the point upon which I particularly insist) could we not turn right around and do the same thing with Justice Brennan's dissenting opinion? Does Justice Brennan's opinion become immune from deconstructive technique merely because it is more "politically correct" to the left?

First, one might note the irony of Brennan's call for listening to the marginalized voices and practices of the poor, appearing as it does in a case involving persons apparently enjoying fairly affluent lives in Southern California.[41] Justice Brennan tells us that the atmosphere surrounding Justice Scalia's opinion is "one of make-believe."[42] Yet Justice Brennan too, engages in his own manufacture of tradition, his own form of "make-believe." As he heaps scorn on "the suggestion that the situation confronting us here [in *Michael H.*] does not repeat itself every day in every corner of the country,"[43] Justice Brennan implicitly invokes a different tradition or countertradition, a tradition of children born to adulterous parents. We could find a source in popular culture for this tradition as well. It is depicted in the many fascinating accounts of American sexual mores on daytime television. Indeed, it is represented by one of the most popular plot devices in the modern American soap opera: X, married to Y, is in fact carrying Z's baby. In fact, this plot device greatly predates such epic dramas as *The Edge of Night* or *As the World Turns*—Christianity itself is based upon a similar scenario.

Second, Brennan's castigation of Scalia's use of tradition involves its own not too subtle dependence on tradition. Justice Brennan argues that

> certain interests and practices—freedom from physical restraint, marriage, childbearing, childrearing, and others—form the core of our definition of "liberty." . . . In deciding cases . . . therefore, we have considered whether the concrete limitation under consideration impermissibly impinges upon one of these more generalized interests.[44]

For Justice Brennan, tradition can only be described abstractly. Nevertheless, its specific content can be determined from case-by-case adjudication, from judgments of similarity and difference to what has gone before—in short, from the tradition of readings and rereadings of authoritative materials that constitute the practice of constitutional *stare decisis*. Hence, Justice Brennan accuses Justice Scalia of "reinvent[ing] the wheel,"[45] because Justice Scalia deliberately avoids reasoning from similarities to previous precedent.

Justice Scalia uses tradition as a substitute for value choices—as a sort of congealed or immanent source of values, for which the Justices are not responsible. Their responsibility only arises if they deviate from its commands. Yet Justice Brennan makes an identical argument about precedent—that Justice Scalia is constrained by his institutional role to obey the Court's past decisions, and that he is lawless, or inserting his own values into the Constitution, if he fails to do this.[46] Just as Justice Scalia asks us to look to the narrowest and most specific traditions of our culture, Justice Brennan demands of Justice Scalia that he follow the most specific holding available—the precedents closest to the case at hand—as the appropriate source of authority.[47] Thus, while Scalia takes a broad view of precedent and a narrow view of tradition, Brennan does precisely the opposite, with predictably opposite results.

Third, and most important, we might marvel at Brennan's manipulation of the concept of tradition, as he miraculously discovers that the traditions protected by the Constitution—adultery, homosexuality, and fornication—are precisely those traditions to which majoritarian society objects the most.[48] The general description of society's traditions proves the undoing of their most specific manifestations. It is tradition used against itself. Perhaps if Justice Brennan is right, the Constitution never fails to protect tradition, no matter what the Supreme Court decides.

In this way, both Justices Brennan and Scalia prove to be traditionalists of the first order. Justice Scalia seeks to enforce his view of "tradition," establishing the hegemony of his vision of culture, thus betraying other values and other traditions in the process. But Justice Brennan is equally a betrayer. For he seeks to use a general concept of tradition to subvert tradition, thus betraying it. If Scalia's use of tradition is a betrayal, Brennan's use of tradition against itself is a betrayal of a betrayal. And in so doing Brennan attempts to elevate a countertradition—which rejects Justice Scalia's views of socially appropriate behavior—to constitutional importance.

II. Deconstruction and Politics

From the above, it should be clear that one can perform a deconstruction of *Michael H.* in either direction. And this brings us to the central issue in understanding the relation of deconstruction to ethics and politics, and to questions of value in general. This text—whether by "this text" I refer to the plurality opinion, the dissent, the Constitution, tradition, the family, or the history and culture of American sexual and domestic values—is potentially reinterpretable and deconstructible. And this phenomenon raises an embarrassing question for deconstruction. What can deconstruction possibly tell us about our choice of values if all texts are deconstructible, and there is nothing outside of the text? What is the relationship of deconstruction to justice, if it can be used to deconstruct (for example) both apartheid and the anti-discrimination principle? In short, what is the source of moral authority to deconstruct in one way rather than another—what tells us that we must explode the logic of Justice Scalia's opinion but not Justice Brennan's?

These are difficult questions for deconstructive theory. To answer them we must recall an important feature of deconstructive practice. Deconstruction poses a continuous critique of a certain metaphysical error, an error usually referred to as "logocentrism." There are many different versions of logocentrism, but each involves a search for "presence" —for the most true, real, valuable, or appropriate. Priority and ordering, evaluation and categorization are the primordial logocentric acts. They tell us what is more real, more privileged, more valued, more important. And deconstruction intervenes in this picture to lay low what was once high, to reverse and resituate the conceptual priorities and orderings upon which all the various forms of logocentrism thrive.

Yet when we view deconstruction and its purported enemy, logocentrism, in this light, we arrive at a paradoxical conclusion. Deconstruction, in and of itself, has nothing particular to tell us about justice, or ethics, or any questions of value. For any such conclusions we might reach would be by their nature ordering, prioritizing, evaluative—in a word, logocentric. Deconstruction thus becomes important to questions of value to the extent that it is not fully deconstructive—to the extent that it depends upon and nourishes itself upon some form of preexisting logocentric practice.

The best way to see this point is by asking the following question: How do we know when it is appropriate to deconstruct? After all, we deconstruct Rousseau, or Saussure, or Justice Scalia's opinion, but we do not deconstruct laundry lists, or the backs of cereal boxes, or the instructions that the flight attendant gives you before a plane takes off. Yet, of course, as each of these are texts, they could all be deconstructed.

We deconstruct a particular text because we think that the text has a particular form of richness that speaks to us, either for good or for ill. Thus, one deconstructs Plato because Plato appears to have a vision of philosophy very different from deconstruction. One deconstructs Saussure because Saussure has got it almost right, but the point at which his theory misfires is very revealing. One deconstructs the concept of apartheid because apartheid is evil. One deconstructs Justice Scalia's opinion because it is misguided.

What do each of these examples have in common? I believe that in each case, one deconstructs because one has a particular ax to grind, whether it be a philosophical, ideological, moral, or political ax. One does not, in contrast, have any such feelings about a cereal box. On the other hand, one might well decide to deconstruct the back of a cereal box if one had already decided that one was going to investigate the culture of mass consumerism, or the role of the child in modern American society, or what have you. In other words, even in the case in which one deals with a seemingly insignificant text, one is choosing that text for a reason, and that reason is one's particular ax.

I should note parenthetically that having read a number of works of Jacques Derrida, I have noted that Derrida himself is quite circumspect about the texts he chooses to deconstruct, and in the way he goes about reading them. I mean this as the highest compliment. A deconstructor does not seize upon every word in the text as the source of a deconstructive reverie, nor does she choose a text at random.

Yet if one always deconstructs for a reason, then there is a *logos* or rationale behind such a decision, a method to this textual madness. The deconstructionist may appear crazy, but she is crazy like a fox. Her practice is a logocentric practice at its inception even as it seeks to subvert the logocentrism of the particular text.

Not only does a deconstructionist begin deconstructing for a reason, she also ends her deconstruction for a reason. The reason may be complex or simple. She may stop because she has demonstrated to her own satisfaction that Justice Scalia's opinion is incoherent, or that apartheid is evil, or because she realizes that she is beating a dead horse by looking at the back of cereal boxes. She may cease deconstructing because her editor told her that the article had to be twenty thousand words and no more, or because she has run out of bond paper, or even because she is in a hurry and needs to get to the grocery store before it closes. In theory, however, one could go on. One could go on forever. In fact, of course, we always do stop. We decide, at some point, that there is nothing more to be decided about this undecidable text. If we always have an ax to grind when deconstructing, at some point we do find it necessary to bury the hatchet.

Thus, curiously, both the starting and the ending of deconstruction are not simply given by the act of deconstruction. But if the beginning and ending of deconstruction are logocentric, if a practice of deconstruction can only exist because of this logocentrism—this starting and this ending—then why do we think that the portion in the middle—the deconstruction itself—is any less filled with, infected with, established throughout by, a certain form of logocentrism? Are we not still grinding our ax? Are we not testing the metaphors and signifiers with our instruments of deconstruction, just as a dentist might scratch the plaque off her patient's teeth in search of a cavity or fissure that could be exposed and corrected?

We thus see that deconstruction, as a political practice, or as a pragmatics (that is, a theory of use or action) cannot avoid logocentrism, either at its beginning, its middle, or its end. To deconstruct is always to engage in a form of logocentrism. It is always to obey a certain law of where to begin and where to end, which turns of phrase to subvert and which to leave untouched. For after we have ground our ax, it directs what we shall execute with it. Moreover, each deconstruction bears the traces of the intellectual roads *not* taken, the metaphors and arguments not questioned. Our deconstruction of Justice Scalia's opinion bears the traces of our failure to deconstruct Justice Brennan's dissent, or our failure to deconstruct the previous three Supreme Court cases on the issue of parental rights, or indeed, any of the other opinions appearing in the United States Reports. Our deconstruction of apartheid bears the traces of our failure to question the anti-discrimination principle, or a libertarian conception of free speech, or of the market, and so on.

Deconstruction, therefore, does not alleviate the need for the existence of a set of political commitments that preexist the deconstructive act. These commitments may change as one deconstructs, and the deconstructor may change with them—but they must already be present for the deconstruction even to get off the ground. Thus, deconstruction turns out to be instrumental, rather than a source of ethical or political value.

Indeed, it would be strange if deconstruction were a *source* of anything. One might object that describing deconstruction as guided by the preexisting commitments and values of the individual deconstructor mistakenly assumes a relatively autonomous subject who controls what to deconstruct and what to leave untouched.[49] Yet deconstruction also requires us to question the existence of this relatively autonomous self.[50] Perhaps, then, deconstruction has a distinctive politics which nevertheless escapes logocentrism—it would be a politics that denies the full coherence and autonomy of subjects, and sees subjects as largely or even wholly constructed by the intersection of various cultural and political forces. In contrast, viewing deconstruction as an instrument employed by a subject reasserts logocentric assumptions about the self that deconstruction is designed to explode.

Yet this is not an objection to my argument. Rather, it is my argument—that deconstruction, as actually performed by individuals is always and already parasitic on some form of logocentric practice. This is every bit as true of critics of the autonomy of the self as it is of critics of any other subject of deconstruction. The deconstructor of the self is still picking her targets—she is still writing about the illusion of the self and not about the errors of Justice Scalia's opinion, or the wickedness of apartheid. And this choice (for we can find no other word to describe it) is still the grinding of a particular ax whether its real motivations are conscious or unconscious, whether the self who makes this choice is wholly autonomous or wholly constructed. And the more cleverly and skillfully the deconstructor of the self argues her case, the more overtly she displays her mastery and her purposefulness in doing so—thus uncannily subverting her own position. In short, deconstructive technique must also apply what it de-emphasizes or denies—that is, the self. For only selves can put the self in question—there is quite literally no one else to do it. And only selves with preexisting commitments (political or otherwise) would engage in such a project. My conclusion thus remains untouched: Without preexisting values, purposes, or commitments, deconstruction cannot begin. With them, it can never be other than logocentric.

I am sure that I am not the first person to note the curious relationship between deconstruction and an earlier French import—existentialism. Both approaches envision a sort of freedom—for the existentialist it is the freedom to act, for the deconstructionist it is the freedom of the text to signify endlessly. If we see life itself as the general text, the textual freedom of the deconstructionist becomes quite similar to the pragmatic (action-oriented) freedom of the existentialist. By sufficient deconstruction one can transform the general text into what one wants it to mean, just as for the existentialist one can make one's life mean what one wants it to mean. But in both cases there is a price to pay. For the deconstructionist, the text always means more than what one wants it to mean, just as for the existentialist one's moral choices have consequences that one could not predict or did not wish but that one is nevertheless responsible for.

This symmetry and ultimate agreement is quite curious, because deconstruction and existentialism would appear to be based upon completely opposed theories of the thinking subject. Existentialism exalts the freedom of the subject, and deconstruction, like much poststructuralist thought, tends to de-emphasize or even efface the subject. But I suggest that this similarity is really not as surprising as it might at first appear. Both approaches are seeking answers to the same set of philosophical problems, albeit from different directions. Thus, both philosophical practices end at the same point—with the need for preexisting moral and political commitment in the face of an undecidable text—the general text, the text of life in which ethical choice is inscribed.

Notes

1. 109 S. Ct. 2311 (1989).
2. Id. at 2335-39; Cal. Evid. Code § 621 (West, Supp 1990).
3. *Michael H.*, 109 S. Ct. at 2340-41.
4. Id. at 2344 n.6.
5. Id.
6. Id. at 2342 & n.3.
7. Id. at 2349-50 (Brennan, J., dissenting).
8. See id. at 2341.
9. See id. at 2344 n.6.
10. Indeed, they have been historically abridged by statutes such as California's. Thus, Justice Scalia argues, there can be no tradition of protecting these rights, for although "[t]he protection need not take the form of an explicit constitutional provision or statutory guarantee, . . . it must at least exclude . . . a societal tradition of enacting laws *denying* the interest." Id. at 2341 n.2 (emphasis in original).
11. 381 U.S. 479 (1965) (state prohibition of sale of contraceptives held an unconstitutional abridgment of marital privacy).
12. As five of his fellow Justices pointed out. *See Michael H.* 109 S. Ct. at 2346 (O'Connor, J., joined by Kennedy, J., concurring in part); Id. at 2350 (Brennan, J., joined by Marshall and Blackmun, JJ., dissenting).
13. See D. Kennedy, *Birth Control in America: The Career of Margaret Sanger* (1970); M. Sanger, *An Autobiography* (1938).
14. John Hart Ely's arguments against using tradition as a source of fundamental values are still among the most powerful. See J. Ely, *Democracy And Distrust*, 63-69 (1980). Ely also quotes Gary Wills for the proposition that "[r]unning men out of town on a rail is at least as much an American tradition as declaring unalienable rights." Id. at 60 (quoting G. Wills, *Inventing America*, xiii [1978]).

15. 367 U.S. 497, 522 (1961) (Harlan, J., dissenting).

16. Id. at 542.

17. The T.J. Hooper 60 F.2d 737, 740 (2d Cir .), cert. denied, 287 US 662 (1932).

18. See e.g., R. Berger, *Government by Judiciary: The Transformation of the Fourteenth Amendment* 123-24 (1977).

19. See id. at 161-63.

20. See *Lynch v. Donnelly*, 465 U.S. 668, 675 (1983).

21. See *Marsh v. Chambers*. 463 U.S. 783, 787-88 (1982).

22. See *Allegheny v. ACLU*, 109 S. Ct. 3086, 3112-15 (1989).

23. *Webster's New International Dictionary of the English Language*, 2684 (2d ed. 1951).

24. Id. at 260.

25. Id. at 2698.

26. Id. at 902.

27. Id. at 2685.

28. Dante. *The Divine Comedy*. Inferno, Canto XXXII, line 110 (1. Sinclair trans. 1961).

29. Id. at Canto XXXIV.

30. There is a particularly interesting exchange, alternatively amusing and disturbing, in the movie *Pillow Talk* (Universal-International 1959), a veritable icon of 1950's cultural sensibilities. Rock Hudson plays a bachelor with a seemingly inexhaustible supply of girlfriends who shares a party line with Doris Day. He teases Day about another man she is dating (who is actually Hudson, although Day does not realize this). Hudson suggests to Day that, "[t]here are some men who just, uh, they're very devoted to their mothers. You know, the type that likes to collect cooking recipes, exchange bits of gossip." Hudson thus simultaneously establishes his own heterosexual manliness while suggesting the homosexuality of the other; moreover, this is done through the use of insulting stereotypes about gays. Yet this, in turn, is merely a ruse designed to goad Doris Day into permitting heterosexual overtures by the other man (who is really Hudson). One wonders what went through Hudson's mind as he played his lines. Watching this movie today, the ironies of self-reference seem potentially endless.

31. *Michael H. v. Gerald D.*, 109 S. Ct. 2333, 2350 (1989) (Brennan, J., dissenting). Justices O'Connor and Kennedy, although concurring in most of the plurality opinion, specifically refuse to endorse fully Justice Scalia's arguments concerning tradition for this very reason. Id. at 2346 (O'Connor, J., concurring in part). In particular, Justice O'Connor states that she would not "foreclose the unanticipated by the prior imposition of a single mode of historical analysis." Id. at 2347. Of course, the whole point of Justice Scalia's theory of tradition is that it does foreclose certain future decisions by the judiciary—it is specifically designed to rein in what he sees as dangerous opportunities for judicial discretion, and moreover, "to prevent future generations from lightly casting aside important traditional values." Id. at 2341 n.2. And yet Justices O'Connor and Kennedy, no less traditionalists in their own ways, recognize that flexibility is necessary in the application of tradition to constitutional issues. Fixed rules set out in advance are, surprisingly, the enemy of tradition and respect for tradition. For a sophis-

ticated and subtle defense of precedential reasoning based on the values of tradition, see Kronman, *Precedent and Tradition*, 99 Yale L.J. 1029 (1990).

32. 5 U.S. (1 Cranch) 137 (1803).

33. 17 U.S. (4 Wheat) 316 (1819).

34. 347 U.S. 483 (1954).

35. 312 U.S. 100 (1941).

36. See R. Berger, supra note 18; Wechsler, *Toward Neutral Principles of Constitutional Law*, 73 Harv. L. Rev. 11 (1959).

37. We should note that this is not a case in which a putative father was attempting to avoid his paternal obligations or child support. The disapproval that one might have for unmarried fathers (or divorced fathers) who abandon their children is totally misplaced here. Nor is this a case of an absentee father who indicated no previous interest in his biological offspring, and who suddenly was seized with the desire (whether real or merely strategic) to make up for lost time. Rather, here was a situation in which, at least on its face, a father was attempting to preserve a bond to his child, and to strengthen an already existing parent-child relationship.

38. *Michael H. v. Gerald D.*, 109 S. Ct. 2333, 2337 (1989).

39. See, e.g., *Webster v. Reproductive Health Servs.*, 109 S. Ct. 3040 (1989).

40. See *Bowers v. Hardwick*, 478 U.S. 186 (1986).

41. *Michael H.*, 109 S. Ct. at 2351 (Brennan J., dissenting).

42. Id. at 2359.

43. Id.

44. Id. at 2350.

45. Id. at 2352.

46. Id. at 2352.

47. Thus, according to Justice Brennan, the proper question to ask is "whether the specific parent-child relationship under consideration is close enough to the interests that we already have protected to be deemed an aspect of 'liberty' as well." Id. He argues that *previous* cases have held that "although an unwed father's biological link to his child does not, in and of itself, guarantee him a constitutional stake in his relationship with that child, such a link combined with a substantial parent-child relationship will do so." Id. The issue in each case is whether the biological father "act[s] as a father toward his children." Id. (citing *Lehr v. Robertson*, 463 U.S. 248, 261 [1983] [quoting *Caban v. Mohammed*, 441 U.S. 380, 389 n.7 (1979)]. Interestingly, Justice Brennan's doctrinal definition of fatherhood is parasitic on the traditional role of the father in the unitary family.

48. See id. at 2352-53; *Bowers v. Hardwick*, 478 U.S. 186, 199 (1986) (Blackmun, J., joined by Brennan. Marshall and Stevens, JJ., dissenting).

49. See Schlag, "Le Hors de Texte, C'est Moi"—The Politics of Form and the Domestication of Deconstruction, 11 Cardozo L. Rev. 1631 (1990).

50. Id.

9

CRITICAL LEGAL STUDIES

Mark Tushnet is one of the leading figures in a movement known as critical legal studies (CLS). CLS has criticized both liberal and conservative approaches to the law and has advocated that constitutional theory be more self-critical and more aware of the social and economic contexts in which law is practiced and interpreted. Like critical race theory and feminist legal theory, CLS aims to expose the emptiness of abstract rights rhetoric as applied to those who because of poverty, discrimination, and marginalization are unable to exercise the actual freedoms those rights are supposed to protect. Like deconstruction, CLS claims that rights are not based on neutral, objective foundational considerations but rather on the interests of those in power.

CLS inherited legal realism's scepticism about the role of legal rules in adjudication. The law, according to CLS, is the result of struggles between different visions and conflicting interests, and it lacks the consistent, principled nature often attributed to it. Proponents of CLS argue that judges are not constrained by precedent or principle. As Mark Tushnet wrote in his book Red, White, and Blue, *"[i]n a legal system with a relatively extensive body of precedent and well-developed techniques of legal reasoning, it will always be possible to show how today's decision is consistent with the relevant past ones, but, conversely, it will also always be possible to show how today's decision is inconsistent with the precedents." According to this view, the law is radically indeterminate.*

In his contribution to this anthology, Tushnet surveys the main approaches to constitutional theory and argues inductively that no theory of constitutional interpretation determines—or even significantly constrains—judges' decisions. Even if some theory could provide such a constraint, he claims, there would still be no incentive for judges to follow that particular theory in their decision making.

In Tushnet's present view, the focus on constitutional theory should be replaced by attention to the judgment of individual judges since they must rely on their own judgment in reaching decisions. Judges with the right sort of character are likely to exercise good judgment. But how do we determine whether to have confidence in the character of any given judge? Tushnet argues for the importance of looking at judges' experience as an indicator of their character.

A critic of CLS could respond that, even if no theory will yield one right answer in every case, some theories can provide some constraints in some cases. Nonetheless, the role of theory still might be very limited and might leave judges largely to their own discretion, making it crucial to pay attention to judges' experience and character as Tushnet suggests.

S.J.B.

Constitutional Interpretation, Character, and Experience

Mark Tushnet

Over the past two decades the topic of constitutional interpretation has received considerable attention. Provoked by the need to defend the Warren Court's accomplishments, as they saw them, against intellectual assaults first from the proponents of "legal process" theory and then from political conservatives, liberal legal scholars tried to justify the Warren Court's decisions by a general theory of constitutional interpretation.[1] As a critic of liberal constitutional theory, I have tried to understand the intellectual structure of these explanations. By "liberal" constitutional theory, I mean a theory whose aim is to explain how constitutional restraints on government action can promote liberty in a democracy. Liberal constitutional theory confronts two dilemmas. First, constitutional restraints on government necessarily infringe the democratic liberty of citizens to enact whatever policies they prefer. Second, a constitutional specification of restraints on government must be interpreted by someone, yet it seems difficult to understand how a liberal constitution could constrain those who were called upon to interpret it. I believe that liberal constitutional theory has not adequately resolved these dilemmas.

On reflection, I have concluded that my critique of liberal constitutional theory was fundamentally flawed because it misunderstood the point of the liberal defense of judicial review. After describing the path that led me to that conclusion, I will outline my present understanding of the relation between constitutional theory and the practice of judging. Then I will summarize the results of a study of two episodes in which Supreme Court justices appear to have taken theoretical considerations explicitly into account as they deliberated. The study shows that constitutional theory served, not as a strong constraint, but as a broad framework within which the justices concluded that they could exercise sound judgment. Yet, if judgment replaces theory in our understanding of judicial review, how are we as citizens to be confident that the justices' judgments are indeed sound? My answer begins by noticing that the justices I examined had a range of experience in national politics that gave them confidence in their own judgments, and continues by suggesting that this sort of experience serves as an indication that the justices had characters in which the citizenry ought to be confident. Finally, I examine some issues that attention to character as the ground of judicial review raises.[2]

I. The Apparent Structure of Theories of Constitutional Interpretation

The fundamental problem of constitutional theory was, or so it used to seem to me, stated by James Madison in Federalist 51: "In framing a government which is to be administered by men over men, the great difficulty lies in this: You must first enable the government to control the governed; and in the next place oblige it to control itself."[3] As I saw it, this problem was rooted in a particular liberal conception of the relation between government and citizenry, which found its sources in Hobbes and Locke.

Here is a thin sketch of the way in which constitutional theory seemed to me related to liberal political theory. For Hobbes the problem of social order was to create a system in which people, essentially equal in their physical capacities, could avoid the disastrous war of all against all. In the state of nature each was vulnerable to attacks from others, and self-protective measures, while possible, meant that the level of productive investment for the future would be lower than was desirable. As Hobbes put it in one of the greatest rhetorical passages in political theory:

> In such condition there is no place for industry, because the fruit thereof is
> uncertain: and consequently no culture of the earth; no navigation, nor use
> of the commodities that may be imported by sea; no commodious building; no
> instruments of moving and removing such things as require much force; no
> knowledge of the face of the earth; no account of time; no arts; no letters; no
> society; and, which is worst of all, continual fear, and danger of violent
> death; and the life of man, solitary, poor, nasty, brutish, and short.[4]

For Hobbes and his successors,[5] the solution was to create government.
An immediate difficulty loomed, however. In Madison's terms, if the
government was strong enough to control the citizenry, why would it—
or the men who occupied positions of governmental power—not simply
become an aggressor against the rest? Instead of each being vulnerable
to attacks from everyone else, those not in the government would be
vulnerable to attacks from those in the government.[6]

Locke offered the constitutionalist solution. Government power
would be limited by establishing a system of protected individual
rights. Now, the government would be limited not only by the risk of
rebellion if it threatened to return people to a situation no better than
the state of nature, but also by the individual rights that people reserved to themselves when they created the government. The difficulty, within this version of the Lockean system, was to determine how
the government would in fact respect individual rights. Madison and
Hamilton in *The Federalist* expressed the basic misgiving: Simply
stating what the individual rights were would erect mere "parchment
barriers" that an aggressive government could readily breach.[7]

Designing a constitution then became the next step. Perhaps the
Constitution's framers' most creative insight was that they could take
advantage of people's inevitable aggressiveness to protect rather than
threaten individual rights. By setting ambition against ambition, the
separation of powers held out the prospect of creating a government
powerful enough to protect citizens against each others' aggression—
solving the Hobbesian state of nature problem—yet limited enough to
preserve individual liberty—solving the constitutionalists' problem.

I confess that I often think that, on the level of political theory, the
framers had, by this point, solved the problems that confronted Hobbes
and Locke. For reasons both political and theoretical, though, the
framers did not think so. Popular dedication to the idea of a bill of
rights specifying limits on government power ran so deep that the
Constitution's opponents used the absence of such a specification in the
original Constitution as a basis for organizing opposition. The Constitution's opponents were not satisfied that purely political mechanisms
would, in practice, protect liberty. James Madison, and other of the
Constitution's proponents disagreed, but they understood that they
faced a serious political problem. They responded by promising to pro-

pose constitutional amendments, now the Bill of Rights. This political compromise produced two other mechanisms to protect liberty: A bill of rights spelling out individual liberties, and judicial review both to police the boundaries between the branches and to enforce individual rights.

Having done so, however, the framers had re-created the Hobbesian problem. True, legislators and executive officials might not be in a position to trample on individual liberties, but what of the judges? Under the guise of policing the boundaries and protecting individual freedom, the judges might advance their own interests—their "ambitions," in Madison's terms—and thereby infringe everyone else's freedom. The problem was exacerbated by the fact that the judges would not be checked, at least directly, by what Madison called "the republican principle, which enables the majority to defeat [the] sinister views [of a minority] by regular vote."[8]

At this point liberal constitutional theories must deal with the second dilemma, that constitutional interpreters no less than the political branches must be constrained if the Constitution is to protect democratic liberty. The various theories serve to constrain the judges as they interpret the Constitution, and thereby limit their ability to violate liberty. The difficulty, then, was to explain how the theories of interpretation actually constrained judges. There were, as I saw it, two problems. The first, to which most attention is paid in constitutional theorizing, is that no theory of interpretation, when fully elaborated, actually offered the prospect of constraining judges. As I put it, talented judges, forced somehow to adhere to any specified theory of interpretation, could come out wherever they wanted anyway.

This essay cannot provide a full-scale defense of that proposition. Nonetheless, an outline of the argument may provide an important backdrop for the remainder of the essay.[9] The argument's structure is inductive: Consider several of the most prominent theories of constitutional interpretation and show that they license either too many or too few constraints on judges' actions, and conclude that it is unlikely that any other theory would be free of the same difficulties. The major contemporary theories of constitutional interpretation are these: (1) A theory of original understanding, according to which judges should give the Constitution's words the meaning they were generally understood to have when they were adopted; (2) a democratic theory of "representation-reinforcement," according to which judges should ensure that the ordinary political processes of a majoritarian democracy operate to allow everyone a fair chance of affecting political outcomes; (3) a moral theory, according to which judges should interpret the Constitution to advance the moral and political good as it is best understood today; and (4) a precedent-oriented theory, according to which judges should develop constitutional principles that yield acceptable results when applied to cases not yet before the courts. Each of these theories is subject to serious challenge within the Lockean-Hobbesian framework.

The theory of original understanding faces evidentiary and foundational difficulties. When scholars have investigated the original understanding of provisions like the First Amendment's establishment clause or the Fourteenth Amendment's equal protection clause, they typically have been unable to come to conclusions about original understanding that a moderately skeptical critic would find persuasive. The establishment clause's history, for example, suggests that some in the founding era understood the clause to be aimed at avoiding government coercion in religious matters, while others understood it to support strict separation of organized churches and the government, and still others had different understandings. Coming to a defensible conclusion about original understanding, strong enough to override the political preferences of contemporary majorities, seems impossible except for those already committed to a particular outcome.

Beyond the question of what to conclude from ambiguous evidence, it is often unclear what evidence to take into account, and how much weight to give it. As a legal matter, the Constitution and its amendments were adopted when they were ratified by the people. Yet, we have far more evidence about the understandings held by drafters and propounders than by ratifiers. The ratification evidence is both spotty and much more ambiguous than even the drafting evidence. Again, confident conclusions about what understandings were embedded in the Constitution is almost impossible in the most interesting cases.

Finally, original understanding theories confront a difficulty that characterizes nearly every other theory as well. Investigations into original understanding sometimes can produce firm conclusions so long as the understandings are stated at a rather high level of generality: "Equal consideration of everyone," for example, or "Separation of church and state." Courts, however, face much more concrete issues: Does a particular affirmative action program violate the equal protection clause? Is a prayer at a junior high school graduation ceremony a violation of the establishment clause (or, is it coercive)? The general understanding rarely sheds sufficient light on the particular problem.

The foundational difficulties may be even more troubling. Why should people today be bound by the understandings held by people in the past? One answer is simply a definitional stop: The Constitution must be interpreted according to original understanding because that is the only way to interpret legal documents. Those who find the original understandings unacceptable will not be persuaded by that. Another answer is that only the original understandings have the democratic legitimacy that could properly limit the political preferences of today's majority. That, however, is implausible. Changes in the society's composition make it difficult to accept the contention that the limits a group of white men placed on government ought to continue to limit what today's governments do.

Further, critics of original understanding theories argue that there are indeed other sources of democratic legitimacy for limits placed on government. These are the other prominent constitutional theories. Adherents of original understanding theories find those theories wanting. Yet, if their position prevails, we might be left with no significant limits on majoritarian power, which is itself troubling within the Lockean framework. In escaping from the threat of judicial subjectivity, original understanding theories may leave us in the grip of the tyranny of the majority.

"Representation-reinforcing" theories attempt to give judicial review a contemporary democratic warrant. According to these theories, courts can invalidate laws that obstruct the fair operation of the democratic system. Notably, they can invalidate unjustified exclusions from the franchise, and they can enforce rules allowing all views to be propounded in the political arena. When developed in detail, however, these theories too prove inadequate. Their most notable failing is that they do not handle questions of racial and gender discrimination at all well, without a great deal of manipulation that drains them of intuitive appeal. After all, today there are no formal exclusions of African-Americans and women from the franchise. Considered as interest groups, African-Americans and women can participate fully in political bargaining. There seems to be no formal problem in democratic representation that calls for special judicial attention to the interests of African-Americans and women, and yet many people believe that such attention is justified.

The main attempt to repair representation-reinforcement theories augments their attention to formal exclusion by saying that courts can invalidate laws when interests are informally excluded or not taken as seriously as their numbers would suggest. In explaining why informal exclusions matter, these theories suggest that the problem lies in the realities of contemporary politics: Excluded groups cannot in fact organize effectively to protect their interests. Once informal obstacles to effective organization come into play, however, many more groups than African-Americans and women may be entitled to special judicial protection. In particular, there is a strong case for interpreting the Constitution to protect consumers against the price-raising effects of economic regulation. In short, representation-reinforcing theories either license too little judicial review, failing to explain why laws adversely affecting African-Americans should receive special scrutiny, or too much judicial review. This reproduces the basic Lockean-Hobbesian problem.

The third prominent interpretive theory asks judges to enforce the best political-moral philosophy they can. Drawing on the historical tradition of natural law reasoning, this theory at least has the advantage of directing attention to what most people care about—whether laws promote the good, whether a constitutional interpretation is "right" morally. It has the disadvantage of running up against a deep strain of moral skepticism in modern society, at least among cultural elites. The fundamental problem, though, is not that meta-ethical skepticism is correct. Rather, the problem is that we live in a society characterized by wide differences among the people about what the good is, even if most of us agree that there is a good.

Once again, the "level of generality" problem arises. We might be able to come to some agreement about the content of the good, on a rather high level of generality. But, even with that agreement, the inferences we will draw about particular policies and laws will inevitably be controversial. Restrictions on the availability of abortions, or on affirmative action programs, may be right or wrong according to some moral or political theories, and we might even find some areas of agreement across such theories, but no one has yet discovered enough agreement to support invalidation of politically contentious laws. Here the difficulty is expressed by saying that judges who rely on moral theory are simply enacting their "merely personal" views.

Finally, there are precedent-oriented theories, frequently called theories about "neutral principles." Their animating idea is that judges can be constrained by forcing them to enforce only those principles which yield acceptable results in a range of imaginable cases to which the principles would be applied, not just in the case before them. The critique of these theories rests on the jurisprudence of American legal realism. In its best form, that jurisprudence contends that legal principles cannot constrain in the necessary way. Here the limits of this essay are particularly confining, because the full-scale defense of that conclusion requires a great deal of elaborate detail. The basic idea, though, is that legal arguments typically have two elements (in addition to the facts): A set of "background rules" and a set of "rules in play." Neutral principles theories focus on the "rules in play," that is, the rather limited number of rules that the parties bring to judges' attention as relevant to the problem at hand. Judges can be constrained by the rules in play, in the sense that sometimes only a limited number of conclusions can fairly be drawn from those rules. The legal realists argued, however, that the constraint disappeared once a judge located an appropriate background rule and put it in play. Of course, locating the right rule to transfer from the background to the foreground, so as to escape the constraining force of the rules in play so far, is not always easy. Good judges will be able to find them; less talented judges will not. Even worse, the lawyers for one party may be able to put a background rule in play and, because the lawyers for the other side are simply not as talented, the first side will prevail. Here, then, the apparent constraint of the legal rules disappears, submerged into the effects of differences in ability among judges and in the distribution of legal talent among parties. The Hobbesian metaphor of the war of all against all may have its greatest force, once the legal realist critique is developed, against precedent-oriented theories of constitutional interpretation.

There is one final standard argument for judicial review, that judges are "better" because they are immune from the political concerns that plague legislators. With legal realist critique in hand, the difficulty with that argument should be apparent. Judges may be loosely constrained by the culture of legality—and free, within those constraints, to respond to personal views—just as legislators would be loosely constrained—and free, similarly, to respond to political concerns. Something more than the culture of legality is needed to explain why we ought to be more troubled by legislators' responsiveness to political concerns than by judges' enforcement of personal values.

I noted earlier that a second problem lay behind the difficulty, to which most attention has been given in constitutional theory, that no theory seemed to provide enough constraints on judges. That problem, though neglected in the literature and simply flagged in my own work until recently, seems more important than the first. Suppose we had a theory of interpretation that, if adopted by the judges, really would constrain them in the way my construct of liberal political theory seems to demand. Still, what reason is there to believe that judges will adopt that theory? Here we seem to need a theory of judicial incentives. The most that constitutional theory had to offer at this point was the constraint of professional criticism. That is, if judges began to depart from the relevant theory's demands, scholarly criticism would bring them back into line. Although this picture was, for obvious reasons, attractive to legal academics, it remained unclear to me why scholarly criticism would have those effects. Certainly the experience of the Warren Court belied this picture. Constitutional law changed, of course, but not because of scholarly criticism. Indeed, the Warren Court persisted on its path despite heavy scholarly criticism. Furthermore, it was the scholars who came into line, only to discover that the Supreme Court had changed the law again, in response to obvious political influences.[10]

At this point, then, the connection between liberal political theory and theories of constitutional interpretation seemed to have dissolved. In their different ways, Philip Bobbitt and Richard Fallon offered a reconstruction of the connection.[11] They began by conceding the first criticism levelled against theories of constitutional interpretation: No single theory, indeed, could constrain. But, they argued, a set of theories provided a repertoire of rhetorics that, taken together, did restrain the judges. Examining how judges went about the task of interpretation, Fallon concluded that there was a hierarchy of interpretive approaches, which he argued came to have normative weight. Bobbitt was less explicit, but his map of ways of talking about the Constitution at least suggested a similar hierarchy.

Bobbitt and Fallon offered descriptions of judicial practice that were clearly more accurate than those implicit in constitutional theorizing before them.[12] Yet, two difficulties remained. First, their descriptions were not completely accurate, especially when coupled with their claims or suggestions about a hierarchy of approaches. Notably, most of the Supreme Court's jurisprudence of constitutional criminal procedure had, at least until recently, almost no connection whatever to general theories of constitutional interpretation. Second, and more important, the basis for their normative claims remained unclear. Although Fallon in particular tried hard to connect his factual claims to normative conclusions, still the fact that judges seemed to behave in certain ways, to give some approaches priority over others, does not readily explain why we ought to give their behavior normative weight. The closest one can come, I think, is that such behavior, when engaged in consistently, helps constitute a culture of legality that places some limits on what properly socialized judges do. The difficulty then is to explain why legislators do not find themselves limited by the culture of legality in the same way—that is, to explain why judicial review is necessary.

In the end, the approach offered by Bobbitt and Fallon seems unsatisfactory as a normative matter. Nonetheless, they brought out more clearly than their predecessors that we could regard theories of constitutional interpretation as rhetorics of justification. Bobbitt in particular was attracted to the idea that the theorist could do no more than identify how participants in the culture of constitutional interpretation talked. In this version the descriptive task is completely divorced from the normative one, which is relegated to some other domain. Quandaries in constitutional theory occur, on this view, because participants erroneously believe that they could achieve a resolution by deploying agreed-upon strategies of reasoned argument, when actually what they are doing is constituting a way of being in the world—the discourse of constitutionalism—through their discursive strategies. The controversy itself, rather than the possibility of its resolution, is the constitutional form of life.[13]

I remain troubled by this conclusion, because it seems to me quite problematic to treat law as a set of rhetorical devices without any intrinsic normative quality. But, Bobbitt and Fallon convinced me to reject the Hobbesian-Lockean argument I had been attracted to. At this point, my interests in constitutional theory came to interact with my historical interests. For several years I have been examining the work of Thurgood Marshall in detail. He was, I concluded, a great lawyer and judge, yet he was completely unconcerned with the questions of constitutional theory to which I and other theorists paid attention. Of course, as Bobbitt's and Fallon's work made clear, one could find the theoretical rhetorics of justification in Marshall's opinions, but the rhetorics did not seem to do the work that Bobbitt and Fallon attributed to them.

It seemed useful, then, to examine how judges really responded to constitutional theory. The following section summarizes a study of the role the theory of original understanding in two important cases in the 1940s and 1950s. Based on that information, and reflection on the work of Thurgood Marshall and Earl Warren, I offer a different and in some ways quite boring resolution of the problem of judicial constraint.

II. How Judges Use Constitutional Theory

Judges sometimes refer to theoretical concerns in their opinions, but the references rarely suggest that the judges were truly motivated by those concerns. For example, when Justice O'Connor cited John Hart Ely's theory of representation-reinforcing review in *City of Richmond v. J.A. Croson Co.*, it seemed more an adornment than a central part of her argument.[14] Even Justice Scalia, perhaps the most theoretically oriented member of the present Court, presents a rather truncated version of his constitutional theory. Justice Scalia combines a modest originalism with vigorous rule formalism, yet his excursions into constitutional history have been relatively superficial[15] and he has never adequately explained why he selects one rule to apply formalistically rather than another.[16] How, then does constitutional theory actually work as judges consider what to do, if it does not figure directly in their decision about what to do?

I doubt that that question can be answered by examining only the justices' published opinions. Because most opinions are now drafted by law clerks,[17] the opinions may not represent the work of the Justice making the decision. Even more, opinions are a form of persuasive writing, whose author must be sensitive to what moves his or her audience. Yet, what moves the audience need not be what moves the author. For example, Justice Felix Frankfurter is often characterized as a proponent of a theory of judicial restraint: Courts, Frankfurter is said to have believed, should be cautious in overturning decisions by democratically elected legislatures unless they have clear constitutional justifications.

Yet, when Frankfurter's actual practice is examined more closely, he seems to have been somewhat less cautious than this description suggests. The reason, I will argue, is that Frankfurter needed only to discover that the materials for determining original understanding were not compelling, in order to license him to exercise his judgment, a judgment unguided by the materials to which liberal constitutional theories direct attention.

During the Supreme Court's deliberations in *Brown v. Board of Education*, Justice Felix Frankfurter asked his law clerk Alexander Bickel to examine the drafting history of the Fourteenth Amendment to determine what its framers believed they were doing about segregated education.[18] Before Frankfurter received Bickel's memorandum, he was immobilized in *Brown* because he did not have a legal theory on which to rest what he believed to be the best possible decision. After receiving the memo, Frankfurter was unblocked, and lent his full support to Chief Justice Earl Warren's actions. Yet, why the memorandum had that effect is puzzling. With some pushing and shoving, the information Bickel disclosed can be used to support the Court's decision that segregation in the 1950s was unconstitutional. However, Bickel had not shown that the framers of the amendment specifically intended to authorize the Supreme Court to invalidate segregation when the Court found it appropriate to do so. If Frankfurter had been looking for affirmative support for the Court's impending decision in the framers' understanding, he would have been disappointed. Because the memorandum was not terribly strong, I believe that Frankfurter must have had something other than a search for original understanding in mind.[19]

Frankfurter's approach can be gleaned from an earlier excursion into original understanding theory. In *Adamson v. California*, decided seven years before *Brown*, Justice Hugo Black wrote an important dissent arguing that the framers of the Fourteenth Amendment intended that it have the effect of protecting people against violations of the Bill of Rights by state governments.[20] Provoked by Black's confidence in original understanding and apparently believing that Justice Stanley Reed's majority opinion did not adequately deal with Black's argument, Frankfurter wrote a concurrence. Notably, however, he did not offer a different interpretation of the framers' understanding. Frankfurter's primary point was that "between the incorporation of the Fourteenth Amendment into the Constitution and the beginning of the present membership of the Court," only one Justice of the Supreme Court —the first Justice Harlan, "who may respectfully be called an eccentric exception"—"ever indicated the belief that the Fourteenth Amendment was a shorthand summary of the first eight Amendments."[21] What mattered to Frankfurter, that is, were the views of the justices of the Supreme Court, not those of the framers of the Fourteenth Amendment.

In addition, Frankfurter argued that "it would be extraordinarily strange for a Constitution to convey such specific commands in such a roundabout and inexplicit way" as through the general words of the Fourteenth Amendment. He did refer to what the words meant to "those conversant with the political and legal history of the concept of due process, those sensitive to the relations of the States to the central government as well as the relation of some of the provisions of the Bill of Rights to the process of justice,"[22] and rejected Black's reliance on what he called "remarks of a particular proponent of the Amendment, no matter how influential."[23] He did not notice that statements by influential supporters of the proposal, quoted extensively by Black, might tell him something about what the words conveyed to people in 1868. Finally, Frankfurter made a policy argument. "[E]ven the boldest innovator would shrink," according to Frankfurter, from requiring every state to begin criminal proceedings with indictments, or to provide jury trials for all civil cases over $20.

Frankfurter's opinion involved original understanding theory only in a weak sense. His main concern was that incorporation would "tear up by the roots much of the fabric of law in the several States."[24] For Frankfurter, originalism offered an extremely loose check on judicial discretion. Judges should try to arrive at a sound policy, where policy is construed broadly to include concern for federalism, and should depart from that policy only if the language of the Constitution, as understood when it was adopted, compels them to.

Frankfurter expanded on this view of original understanding when he responded to an essay by Charles Fairman on the original understanding issue in *Adamson*, which concluded that Black was wrong.[25] Although Fairman's research was consistent with Frankfurter's position, its method, which examined statements of supporters and opponents of the Amendment, was not. Frankfurter wrote Fairman after the article was published, "[T]his business of trying to find the scope of the Fourteenth Amendment in this or that pamphlet or this or that individual expression of hope of what was accomplished by the Amendment is . . . no way of dealing with a 'constituent act' like the Fourteenth Amendment." For him, it was "decisive" that "it couldn't possibly have been contemplated by the submission of the Amendment or its ratification that half the States would uproot their whole system of criminal justice."[26]

Frankfurter expressed similar concerns about framers' understanding, spiced by his personal animosity to Justice Black, during the Court's consideration of *Sweatt v. Painter*, a challenge to segregation in Texas's law school system.[27] The state's brief in *Sweatt* exposed the Court for the first time to extensive materials about what the framers of the Fourteenth Amendment believed about segregated education. Texas showed that the framers of the Amendment were, to say the least, not troubled by segregation. Frankfurter could not rely on original understanding, and when Justice Black referred confidently to the purposes of the Amendment, Frankfurter replied testily that it was "futile to talk about what the 14th [Amendment] 'intended,'" and that the university cases "should be decided aside from any doctrinaire [views] or intentions as we construe them of the 14th Amendment" because "no one knows what was intended."[28]

By the time the Court had to decide *Brown*, Frankfurter knew that original understanding was unhelpful. In the Court's discussions in *Brown*, after Black said that the "basic purpose" of the Fourteenth Amendment was "to protect [against] discrimination"—seemingly consistent with the modest originalist method Frankfurter espoused in *Adamson*—Frankfurter sputtered, "How does Black know the purpose" of the Amendment? Frankfurter said that he had read "all of its history and he can't say it meant to abolish segregation," which was not quite what Black had argued.[29] Frankfurter's exchanges with Black in *Adamson* and later cases indicated, though, that Frankfurter did not really require support from original understanding for what he believed was the right course. Rather, all he needed to know was that original understanding did not preclude him from doing what seemed best.

Frankfurter's reaction to Bickel's memorandum confirms this interpretation.[30] The memorandum itself simply recited facts without drawing a conclusion. Frankfurter drafted, but did not circulate, a cover memorandum that revealed his views. In the memorandum Frankfurter indicated that Bickel's research showed that "the legislative history . . . is, in a word, inconclusive, in the sense that the 39th Congress as an enacting body neither manifested that the Amendment outlawed segregation in the public schools or authorized legislation to that end, nor that it manifested the opposite."[31] As Frankfurter saw things, original understanding mattered only to the extent that it might clearly bar the Court from doing what the justices believed appropriate. He did not require a license from the framers of the Fourteenth Amendment, aside from the words they placed in the Constitution; he merely needed to be sure that they did not prohibit him from acting. Originalism thus did constrain constitutional interpretation, but not much. Only in what might well be rare instances where original understanding ruled out an interpretation would judges be limited in what they did.

In *Adamson* and *Brown*, Frankfurter saw original understanding in the same terms. In both cases Black relied on original understanding to justify what he believed the Court ought to do. In *Adamson* Frankfurter refused to go along with the affirmative case Black made; more would be needed, he thought, to show that the framers intended to deprive the Court of the judicial discretion it would ordinarily exercise. In *Brown*, Frankfurter refused to find sufficient the framers' statements directly about segregated education, all of which pointed toward the conclusion that they believed it to be constitutional; again, more would be needed to show that they intended to deprive the Court of its discretion. In short, original understanding theory placed only a very loose frame around judicial discretion. It seems to me problematic to contend that such a loose frame is sufficient to satisfy the requirement of liberal constitutional theory that those who interpret the Constitution's limits on democratic choice, and therefore on the people's liberty, be constrained enough that liberty is indeed protected.

III. Judicial Experience and Character as Constraints

The preceding materials suggest a more general point, though the nature of the available evidence makes solid conclusions hard to draw.[32] I no longer believe that constitutional theory constrains, or is supposed to constrain judges. Rather, as Bobbitt argued, it serves primarily to provide a set of rhetorical devices that judges can deploy as they believe effective. Yet, this conclusion leaves the Lockean argument for constraint on governors, including judges, incomplete. If Frankfurter's approach to constitutional theory is more broadly held by judges, as I believe it is, why should we as citizens accept their judgments finding unconstitutional what we believe to be sound policy?

For Frankfurter and those like him, the answer was that the public should accept the justices' judgments about constitutionality because the justices were people of good judgment. Put so bluntly, this assertion may be either banal or inadequate. As we explore the question of judgment further, however, it may become more interesting and, arguably, more satisfactory.

Judicial review inevitably raises questions of comparative competence. Here the comparative question is, Why should the justices' sense of their own good judgment prevail over the judgment exercised by legislators and executive officials? The answers will vary depending on historical circumstances, and the circumstances in which Frankfurter operated are illuminating. When Frankfurter's view of a Justice's job crystallized as he worked at that job, Frankfurter sat on a Court whose members had already had substantial experience on the national political scene before they were appointed to the Court.[33] When *Brown* first came to the Court, its members included three former Senators (Black, Burton, and Minton), a former leader of the House of Representatives and Secretary of the Treasury (Vinson), two former Attorneys-General (Jackson and Clark), two former Solicitors-General (Reed and Jackson), and two of the nation's leading law professors, Frankfurter and Douglas, both of whom had been quite active in political affairs during the New Deal and, with Frankfurter, earlier.

The experience of these men had two effects. First, because they had operated at the highest level of national politics, they knew who the actors in the other branches were. They would neither idealize members of Congress as paragons of representation, nor cynically deprecate them as mere tools of special interests out to advance their personal careers. This knowledge allowed the justices to be straight-forwardly realistic about the judgmental capacities of members of Congress and the executive branch. As political realists, they became confident that their own judgment was sounder than that of others in the political system. They need not have believed that their judgment was dramatically better, but only enough better to justify displacing decisions made elsewhere.

Second, the justices may have taken seriously the selection process that put them on the Court. Having worked in national politics, they knew that there were many people qualified, in some minimal sense, to be on the Court. Yet, they knew, the political process had chosen them from this larger pool. They might have concluded that the reason they were chosen was precisely because the President and the Senate viewed them as having sounder judgment than alternative candidates. As they understood themselves, these men had become politically prominent not because they catered to the desires of their constituents or pressure groups, but because they exercised judgment, which the public then ratified by re-electing them or approving their appointment to the Supreme Court.[34] Having reached the Court because the public endorsed their capacity to exercise judgment, these justices believed that they ought to act on the Court as they had acted in politics.

Even so, an additional question arises. When justices exercise the power of judicial review, they are setting their judgment against that of other political actors. But, the justices must know that they too are not infallible. In the face of disagreement about the course recommended by sound judgment—that is, whenever the issue of judicial review arises—why were these justices confident that they were less likely to have erred than Congress?

To some extent, the fair answer may be that the justices had not thought through the implications of their reliance on good judgment. Like most people who reach high office, they tended to be self-confident, a character trait that might have blurred their vision of the underlying issues of democratic theory. Then, too, they may have been diverted by the attention that constitutional theory received among legal academics. If the justices had to worry only about constitutional theory, and if they were satisfied when they took theory to set a frame around their judgment, they may have concluded that whatever they did within that frame was justified—because no one was giving them advice or guidance on how to exercise judgment.

More important, perhaps, is that these justices relied on the fact that they had operated at the highest levels of national politics. In that way they could indeed connect judicial review and democratic governance. Not, of course, that the justices were direct representatives of the people in the way that members of Congress were. Rather, when the justices exercised judgment, they "represented" the people because they had been tested in the crucible of national politics and had been chosen for the Court because the people believed in their capacity to make sound judgments.

These justices read their job descriptions to entail exercising judgment. Constitutional theory mattered only if it compelled the conclusion that their judgment should be limited; where the justices were left with choices, constitutional theory did not tell them what to do. Seen in this way, Frankfurter was not the apostle of judicial restraint on the level of constitutional theory, because he had no general theory that guided his exercise of judgment. And, his true successors were people like Earl Warren and Thurgood Marshall, who, like Frankfurter, had reached the Supreme Court because they had sound judgment and then, once on the Court, continued to exercise the capacity for judgment that had led them there.[35]

Seeing Frankfurter aligned with Warren and Marshall may illuminate more contemporary issues. I have argued that, as these justices understood their work, their prior experience at the highest levels of national politics justified them in relying on their judgment in making constitutional law. Today, however, matters are rather dramatically different.

As conservatives began to attack the Supreme Court, liberal scholars began to believe that they could no longer rely solely on the capacity for judgment to defend the justices' actions. They therefore began to elaborate constitutional theories to justify the Warren Court's decisions. Moreover, conservatives believed that the problems endemic to constitutional adjudication derived precisely from the fact that Justices were exercising judgment. For conservatives, too, constitutional theory, particularly originalist theory, became attractive.

More important, however, conservatives appear to have concluded that the people appointed to the Supreme Court had developed bad habits of mind when they operated in national politics. For conservatives, the Warren Court, composed of politicians, converted constitutional law into ordinary politics; Earl Warren, conservatives believed, never abandoned politics after he left the California governor's office. What was needed, they believed, was to transform constitutional law back into law again. To do that, people with a different cast of mind were needed. Prior judicial experience became almost a prerequisite for nomination to the Supreme Court.[36] Somewhat less dramatically, the Republican nominees tended to have less experience on the national political scene; perhaps the feeling was that, not having reached prominence because their capacity to exercise sound judgment had been tested, the nominees would be more strongly guided by external sources of authority.

When Warren Burger joined the Supreme Court, its members had less substantial experience in the national political arena than the members of the Court had when *Brown* was decided. Burger had been an Assistant Attorney General and then a federal judge. Potter Stewart was a politician in Ohio and then a federal judge. William Brennan was a relatively unknown state supreme court judge, although he was the protégé of Arthur Vanderbilt, one of the country's leading state judges in the 1950s. John Marshall Harlan was a leading member of the New York bar before he became, briefly, a federal judge. Only Byron White, who had been Deputy Attorney-General, Abe Fortas, a private practitioner who was a close adviser to Lyndon Johnson, and Thurgood Marshall were large figures on the national political scene when they were appointed to the Supreme Court.

By 1992, the Court had been transformed in more than its political orientation. White was then the only Justice who had played a major role in national politics. Chief Justice William Rehnquist and Justice Antonin Scalia had been Assistant Attorneys-General, although Scalia also had been the chair of a relatively obscure federal oversight panel dealing with administrative law. The fact that President Nixon stumbled over Rehnquist's name in a conversation shortly before he nominated Rehnquist to the Court indicates the relative unimportance of Assistant Attorneys-General.[37] Justices Harry Blackmun, John Paul Stevens, and Anthony Kennedy were federal judges when they were appointed to the Supreme Court; they had been private practitioners uninvolved in the national political scene before that. Justices Sandra Day O'Connor and David Souter were state court judges without any national reputation.[38] Of the Justices recently appointed to the Court, only Clarence Thomas, who had served as chair of the federal Equal Employment Opportunity Commission and who had been a prominent spokesman for conservative judicial positions, was a figure with some national stature before his appointment to the Court. Aside from Thomas, almost none of the Justices on the Court in 1992 had been mentioned in national newspapers before their appointments to the Court—except in stories speculating about potential nominees.

This dramatic transformation in the kind of person appointed to the Supreme Court had its roots in the Warren Court's actions. By 1992, the justices, except for White, had been appointed by Republican presidents, most of whom had to have their nominees confirmed by Democratic Senates. The divided nature of the process imposed some limits on presidential choices, and undoubtedly played a part in leading presidents to nominate sitting judges to the Supreme Court. Judges already had one obvious professional qualification for the position, and the fact that most Republican nominees had not been active in national politics meant that they did not have track records their opponents could take advantage of. The three failed Republican nominations, and the intensely controversial Thomas nomination, came when the nominees did have that kind of track record. In addition, Republican presidents sometimes saw the chance to nominate a Justice as a political opportunity—to name the first woman to the Supreme Court, for example—but found it difficult to locate a distinguished nominee whose nomination satisfied all the political constraints on the choice.[39]

More important, though, Republicans had campaigned against the Warren Court for enforcing the justices' personal political preferences rather than the law. The rhetoric was of "strict construction," of "applying the law, not making it." Republicans could distinguish their justices from the Democrats' by making judicial experience a prerequisite for appointment to the Supreme Court. The nominees' claim that they would apply the law—rather than act politically—might be more credible than the same claim made by politically active nominees.

That might account for the prevalence of judges among the Republican appointees, but not for their relative lack of distinction.[40] Although one can do no more than speculate, the Republicans' choice probably resulted from a complex strategy. The Democrats' nominees had substantial political experience on the national scene. After 1980 Republicans were interested in reducing the national government's role in public affairs. By appointing relatively undistinguished people to the Court, Republican presidents could diminish the public image of the Court as an important institution of government. Appointing people whose primary experience was outside Washington had the same effect.

Further, the Warren Court justices were men who saw their service on the Supreme Court as just another job on the national political scene, like the others they had held. And, to the degree that the job was like the others, they would behave as justices as they had in their other political jobs. In contrast, for the Republican nominees, the appointment was not the culmination of a career of distinguished public service; it was a sharp jump up the scale. Under these circumstances, some of the Republican appointees have found their job a humbling experience. All accepted the principle that the Court should take a smaller role than the Warren Court had. This combination of experience and principle, personal humility and political orientation, meant that they were unlikely to act as aggressively as the Warren Court had.

Yet, having a view of the job in which the exercise of judgment played a far smaller role than it did in the eyes of Frankfurter, Warren, and Marshall, the justices on the present Court must nonetheless make decisions. Although it is too early to tell, I suspect that the Court is likely to divide into two groups. As my mention of formalism suggests, one group may feel the pull of constitutional theory, which will take the place of judgment in their decisional universe. It seems reasonably clear that Justice Scalia already has this view, and will be the leader of the group if it emerges. The other will find exercising judgment increasingly attractive despite what they thought they had learned from the Warren Court experience. Significantly, the joint opinion of Justices O'Connor, Kennedy, and Souter in *Planned Parenthood of Southeastern Pennsylvania v. Casey* expressly and dramatically defended the role of judgment in constitutional adjudication: "The inescapable fact is that adjudication of substantive due process claims may call upon the Court in interpreting the Constitution to exercise the same capacity which by tradition courts have always exercised: Reasoned judgment."[41] In part they will do so because it is always difficult to foreswear the power that exercising judgment brings. But in part they will do so because they are likely to discover that constitutional theory does not work, and that in the absence of theory judgment is all that remains.

The politics behind the Court's present composition raises even more starkly the question of how to justify judicial review that rests solely on the exercise of judgment. For, I have argued, the Warren Court's justification for judgment was that its members' capacity to make sound judgments had been validated by their prior experience in national politics. Neither the members of the present Court nor, more important, the public can rely on prior experience to validate the exercise of judgment.

There may, however, be a way out of this dilemma. So far I have focused on experience as validating the exercise of judgment. Perhaps experience is not the desideratum in itself but only an indicator of something more important. What may matter is another apparently banal feature of public officials, their character. I do not mean those relatively unimportant character traits—public civility, an ability to act in public in the manner consistent with the audience's expectations— that are ordinarily described as "judicial temperament." Rather, I mean character in the deeper sense of having a public and private life inseparably intertwined, so that exercising bad judgment in the judge's public capacity is as unthinkable as exercising bad judgment in his or her personal life. This suggestion makes experience important because how a person performed before being appointed to the Court offers us information about his or her character in this deeper sense.

Experience is only an indicator of character. There are others. As Amélie Oksenberg Rorty puts it, "a person's ethical character is a relatively stable configuration of deeply entrenched and widely ramified traits and dispositions. . . . They do not depend solely on the chance of circumstance to elicit them: The cognitive dimensions of such traits structure a person's interpretations of situations in such a way as to elicit a typical self-sustaining response."[42] How judges or nominees have acted under pressure, including the pressures of the nomination process itself, indicates character. So does the way they react to disappointment. And, finally, how judges or nominees treat their opponents, with respect or disdain, connects character in the narrow sense with the broad traits we ought to seek in our judges. If my focus on character is correct, though, we should avoid trying to assess judges with reference to the content of their decisions. We might want judges who have shown themselves to be stalwart and compassionate in their dealings with colleagues, but we ought not look at a judge's decisions to see if they "are" compassionate—or, perhaps better, express compassion—because that would introduce a substantive evaluative standard that the focus on character aims at avoiding.

Scholars and the public understandably reduce their attention to a nominee's character after confirmation, because life tenure makes continued focus on character in the narrow sense seem pointless. Nonetheless, we can gain or lose confidence in a judge's judgment by examining how his or her job performance expresses the judge's character. Again, the issue would not be whether the judge's decisions satisfy some substantive requirement, but whether they are offered to the public in a generous and open spirit. As we gain a better grasp of the judge's character, we may become more willing to accept his or her exercise of judgement. We may come to accept the exercise of judgment by people who were appointed to the Court without having "enough" experience: Their performance may validate our confidence in their judgment. With one obvious exception,[43] those justices on the present Court who are not captured by the illusion that theory can constrain them by dictating results seem to have done so.

IV. Conclusion

As I indicated at the outset, I have offered only a sketch of a way of thinking about judicial performance that might be more adequate than my earlier belief that constitutional theory had to be the core of an evaluation of that performance. Focusing on character rather than theory does have one feature that is, for me, an obvious advantage: It enables us to discuss judicial performance in a way that prescinds from the simple-minded normative evaluation of results that too often fully describes constitutional scholarship. It makes coherent an evaluation like, "Justice Frankfurter was a great judge even though many of his most important decisions were simply wrong." And, because I believe that scholars ought to be able to make such evaluations, an approach like the one sketched here is attractive.

Plainly, the idea that character in a deep sense matters needs to be developed beyond my suggestion that experience is an element that we can use to evaluate character. For example, I have little doubt that, in the end, questions of how one evaluates character in the deep sense will turn out to be quite as contestable as are normative evaluations of the Court's work. Further, attention to character opens up lines of inquiry that I believe would be fruitful. Constitutional scholars would have to confront the puzzle of Felix Frankfurter's character—gracious and generous to his law clerks, mean-spirited when speaking of some of his colleagues—to understand constitutional law itself. And, the example of William Douglas suggests either that we might still want to hold substantive criteria of evaluation in reserve to deal with judges who do not have the requisite character, or that character in the sense of being an integrated person need not entail that the subject is a nice person.[44] Still, I believe that we could learn a great deal about judging before we reached that point. Paying attention to character makes more sense to me now than paying attention to theory does.

Notes

1. The introductory comments here track the argument in Mark Tushnet, RED, WHITE AND BLUE: A CRITICAL ANALYSIS OF CONSTITUTIONAL LAW (1988).

2. I develop my views and discuss some of the recent literature on judicial character in Mark Tushnet, *The Degradation of Constitutional Discourse*, GEO. L.J. (forthcoming).

3. THE FEDERALIST PAPERS No. 51, at 322 (Clinton Rossiter ed. 1961).

4. Thomas Hobbes, LEVIATHAN: ON THE MATTER, FORME AND POWER OF A COMMONWEALTH ECCLESIASTICALL AND CIVIL 100 (Michael Oakeshott ed. 1962).

5. I insert my last qualification: That I am offering my understanding of the relation between liberal political theory and constitutional theory, not something I put forward as a correct interpretation of Hobbes or Locke.

6. For Hobbes, governmental aggression may have been limited by human nature: The government could attack–that is, could extract taxes–up to the point where the citizens concluded that they were no better off under a government than in the state of nature. But, the human capacity to consume being limited, perhaps the people in the government could not use as much as they might possibly extract, and therefore would not extract up to the "state of nature" limit. In these circumstances, people would be better off even with a rather aggressive government.

7. THE FEDERALIST PAPERS, No. 48, *supra* note 3, at 308.

8. *Id.*, No. 10, p. 80.

9. What follows is a short summary of the argument in Mark Tushnet, RED, WHITE, AND BLUE, *supra* note 1.

10. Perhaps the most symbolic expression of this phenomenon is Erwin Chemerinsky, *Foreword: The Vanishing Constitution*, 103 HARV. L. REV. 43 (1989).

11. P. Bobbitt, CONSTITUTIONAL FATE: THEORY OF THE CONSTITUTION (1982); Richard Fallon, *A Constructivist Coherence Theory of Constitutional Interpretation*, 100 HARV. L. REV. 1189 (1987).

12. I should note, however, that prior theorists were less clear about whether they were in fact trying to describe judicial practice than to offer criteria for evaluating it.

13. This is suggested by Bobbitt's occasional citations to Wittgenstein.

14. 488 U.S. 469 (1989).

15. For a recent discussion, see L. Benjamin Young, Jr., Note, *Justice Scalia's History and Tradition: The Chief Nightmare in Professor Tribe's Anxiety Closet*, 78 VA. L. REV. 581 (1992).

16. For my views on Justice Scalia's jurisprudence, see Mark Tushnet, *Scalia and the Dormant Commerce Clause: A Foolish Formalism?*, 12 CARDOZO L. REV. 1717 (1991).

17. See David O'Brien, STORM CENTER: THE SUPREME COURT IN AMERICAN POLITICS 128 (1986).

18. See, e.g., Richard Kluger, SIMPLE JUSTICE 599 (1975). For more detail on my examination of these materials, see Mark Tushnet, *Judges and Constitutional Theory: A View from History*, 63 U. COLO. L. REV. 425 (1992); Mark Tushnet, with Katya Lezin, *What Really Happened in* Brown v. Board of Education, 91 COLUM. L.REV. 1867 (1991).

19. As I have argued elsewhere, Tushnet with Lezin, supra note 18, at 1894, I believe that Frankfurter faced some difficult psychological problems created in large measure by his colleague and friend Robert Jackson, who insisted that a decision to invalidate segregation would be political rather than legal, and that Bickel's historical work let Frankfurter devote his attention to the "legal" problem of devising an appropriate remedy.

20. 332 U.S. 46 (1947).

21. Id. at 62.

22. Id. at 63.

23. Id. at 64.

24. Id. at 67.

25. Charles Fairman, *Does the Fourteenth Amendment Incorporate the Bill of Rights? The Original Understanding*, 2 STAN. L.REV. 5 (1949).

26. Frankfurter to Fairman, Jan. 27, 1950, Felix Frankfurter Papers, Harvard Law School, reel 3:15.

27. 339 U.S. 637 (1950).

28. Conference notes on *Sweatt v. Painter*, William O. Douglas Papers, Library of Congress, Box 191, file: Argued Cases #44; Conference notes on *McLaurin v. Board of Regents*, id., file: Argued Cases #34.

29. Notes on 12-13-52 Conference, Douglas Papers, Box 1149, file: Original Conference Notes re Segregation Cases.

30. Some of the following paragraphs are drawn directly from Tushnet, *Judges and Constitutional Theory, supra* note 18.

31. Dennis Hutchinson, *Unanimity and Desegregation: Decisionmaking in the Supreme Court, 1948-1958*, 68 GEO. L. J. 1, 40. The cover memorandum Frankfurter actually circulated did not include this statement of Frankfurter's conclusions.

32. Richard Fallon has suggested to me that at any time the rhetorical structures may be sufficiently "rigid" to preclude some results. I am skeptical about that; the structures he and Bobbitt describe seem to be flexible enough to accommodate anything (as virtually any pluralist account would be). Of course my skepticism is subject to the Wittgensteinian arguments mentioned above, which I believe to be misplaced in an unabashedly normative discourse like constitutional law.

33. For a somewhat different elaboration of this analysis, see Mark Tushnet, "The Warren Court as History," in THE WARREN COURT IN HISTORICAL AND POLITICAL PERSPECTIVE (Mark Tushnet ed., forthcoming).

34. Black may have been the most conscious of the relation between constituency and judgment, having appealed to Ku Klux Klan sentiments in his early election campaigns and then repudiating those sentiments as he moved in national politics. See Tony Freyer, HUGO L. BLACK AND THE DILEMMA OF AMERICAN LIBERALISM 61, 69-71, 82-84 (1990).

35. Warren, like Black, came to repudiate an earlier misjudgment, in Warren's case his support of the internment of Japanese-Americans during World War II. See G. Edward White, EARL WARREN: A PUBLIC LIFE 75-76 (1982).

36. Of the fourteen Republican nominees since 1968 (including the failed nominations of Haynsworth, Carswell, Bork, and Ginsburg), only Justices Powell and Rehnquist were not judges at the time of their appointment. Of the twelve nominees by Roosevelt and Truman, only two (Rutledge and Minton) were judges at the time of appointment. None of the four Kennedy-Johnson appointees were judges when appointed, although Thurgood Marshall had been a judge on the Second Circuit for four years before he became Solicitor-General.

37. See "Reliving the Watergate Years with Some New Tapes," NEWSWEEK, June 17, 1991, p. 32.

38. Technically Souter was a federal judge when he was appointed to the Supreme Court, but he had not heard any cases in that capacity.

39. I thank Bill Eskridge for this final point.

40. Justice Scalia is arguably the most distinguished of the recent appointees, but that is so largely because of the competition. Legal academics try to claim him for their own, without recognizing that he had been a second-rank scholar at a first-rank law school before he started on the path to the Supreme Court. His

leading publications were *The ALJ Fiasco–A Reprise,* 47 U.CHI. L. REV. 57 (1979); *Vermont Yankee: The APA, the D.C. Circuit, and the Supreme Court,* 1978 SUP. CT. REV. 345; *Procedural Aspects of the Consumer Products Safety Act,* 20 UCLA L. REV. 899 (1973) (co-authored with Frank Goodman), and *The Hearing Examiner Loan Program,* 1971 DUKE L.J. 319. Compared to the pre-appointment scholarship of his academic predecessors on the Court, Frankfurter and Douglas, this is thin indeed. Scalia had also published a number of extremely short comments, mostly in his capacity as head of the Administrative Conference or as chair of a bar association on administrative law.

41. 112 S.Ct. 2791, 2806 (1992).

42. Amélie Oksenberg Rorty, *The Advantages of Moral Diversity,* 9 SOC. PHIL. & POL. 38, 40-41 (1992).

43. See Tushnet, *The Degradation of Constitutional Discourse, supra* note 2.

44. Although, with Douglas, one would have to be quite attentive to the way his personality, and the contexts in which he operated, changed over time.

10

SCEPTICISM

Recent debates about constitutional interpretation have focused on whether the Constitution has a determinate meaning and on who should be given the power to decide what that meaning is. The focus on the meaning of the Constitution has, according to Robin L. West, eclipsed the discussion of the Constitution's value. The constitutional scepticism explored by West is not scepticism about what the Constitution means, but, rather, normative scepticism about whether the values embodied in it are the right ones.

West's contribution to this anthology differs from the previous selections, and from nearly all writing on constitutional interpretation, in suggesting that the Constitution, properly interpreted, may turn out to be morally flawed. If so, we may find ourselves in the awkward position of defending certain laws and public policies as being required by justice, while having to acknowledge that they are constitutionally impermissible.

Does West's normative constitutional scepticism provide any guidance for judges who share this view? Judges and other officials who openly refuse to go along with constitutional requirements they consider unjust will surely jeopardize their professional standing. However, to those interested in progressive reform, West points out that "the Constitution is merely difficult, not impossible, to change." Rather than forcing our political initiatives to fit the constraints of the Constitution, she argues, we should bear in mind that the Constitution is not a static document and can be revised, whether radically through the process of amendment or more subtly and incrementally through judicial interpretation itself.

S.J.B.

Constitutional Scepticism

Robin L. West

Introduction: Constitutional Meaning and Value

Interpretive constitutional debate over the last few decades has cen-
tered on two apparently linked questions: whether the Constitution can
be given a determinate meaning, and whether the institution of judicial
review can be justified within the basic assumptions of liberalism. Two
groups of scholars have generated answers to these questions. The
"constitutional faithful" argue that meaning can indeed be determi-
nately affixed to constitutional clauses, by reference to the plain meaning of the document,[1] the original intent of the drafters,[2] evolving
political and moral norms of the community,[3] or the best political or
moral philosophical theory available[4] and that, because of that determinacy, judicial review can indeed be brought within the rubric of
liberalism. Taking issue with the constitutional faithful is a group who
might be called "constitutional sceptics." Scholars in this group see, in
every constitutional phrase or doctrine, the possibility of multiple interpretations, and in the application of every constitutional method
the possibility of multiple outcomes. It follows from this indeterminacy
that judicial review cannot be easily justified by reference to liberal assumptions, because the power of the interpreting judge irreparably compromises the stability and rationality of the "Rule of Law" so central
to liberal ideals.[5]

   As important as the debate over constitutional determinacy may be,
its prominence in modern constitutional theory over the last thirty
years has carried with it serious opportunity costs. Specifically, the
prominence of the debate over the Constitution's *meaning*, whether it
can be said to have one, and the implications for the coherence of liberalism that these questions of interpretation seem to raise, has pushed
to the background an older and possibly more important debate about
the Constitution's *value*. By asking relentlessly whether the Constitution's meaning can be made sufficiently determinate to serve the Rule of
Law—by focusing almost exclusively on whether constitutionalism is
possible within liberal theory and whether liberalism is possible,
given an indeterminate Constitution—we have neglected to ask wheth-

er our Constitution is *desirable*. Does it further the "good life" for the individuals, communities, and subcommunities it governs?

We might pose these evaluative questions in any number of ways. Has the Constitution or the Bill of Rights well served the communities and individuals they are designed to protect? Are the visions of individualism, community, and human nature on which the Bill of Rights rests, and the balances it strikes between rights and responsibilities, or civic virtue and freedoms, noble conceptions of social life, true accounts of our being, hospitable to societal and individual attempts to live the good life? More specifically, does the First Amendment, for example, well serve its core values of free expression, individual actualization, and open political debate? Assuming that it does, are those values good values to have? Are they worth the damage to our social cohesion, our fragile sense of fraternity with others, and our attempts at community that they almost undeniably cause? Are the Fourteenth Amendment's sweeping and majestic guarantees of "liberty" and "equal protection of the law," appearances notwithstanding, in fact unduly stingy? Do they simply, and cruelly, fail to guarantee a liberty that would meaningfully protect against the most serious constraints on peoples' liberties, or an equality that would even begin to address the grotesque material inequities at the very heart of our social and economic life? Do those guarantees perversely *protect*, rather than guarantee against, those constraints and inequities? Similarly, but from a quite different political orientation, are Fourth Amendment guarantees simply not worth their cost in law enforcement? Is it unwise to let eighteen-year-olds vote? Is the Second Amendment the height of foolishness?

These questions—about the value, wisdom, decency, or sensibility of constitutional guarantees—do of course receive some attention in contemporary legal scholarship, but nevertheless, it seems fair to say that in spite of the legal academy's supposed obsession with "normativity," normative questions about the Constitution have not been at the heart of constitutional discourse of the last thirty years. By contrast, normative questions of precisely this sort constitute the great bulk of scholarship in other areas of law. Scholars question the value of the holder in due course doctrine in commercial transactions, the negligence doctrine or strict liability in tort law, the rules governing acceptance of unilateral contracts in contract law, and insanity defenses in criminal law. But normative questions are neither the subject of constitutional "grand theory" nor, more revealingly perhaps, the subject of doctrinal constitutional scholarship. Instead, while theoretical constitutional scholarship centers on questions about the *meaningfulness* of the Constitution and its implications for the possibility or impossibility of liberalism, doctrinal constitutional scholarship centers on questions of the Constitution's *meaning*, rather than questions of its *value*. Thus, for example, rather than debate whether the First or the Fourteenth Amendment is a good idea, doctrinalists debate what the First Amendment or the Fourteenth Amendment means, and theorists debate whether they have any meaning and what it means to assert that they do or do not have meaning. In short, neither theoretical nor doctrinal constitutional scholarship places the value, rather than either the meaningfulness or the meaning, of the Constitution at the heart of constitutional analysis.

That we lack an explicitly normative debate about the Constitution's value might be evidenced by the visible effects of that absence in our substantive constitutional arguments. Let me cite a few examples, simply to convey the flavor of what I suggest is missing. One debate between constitutional scholars arising over the last few years, and of great interest to political progressives, concerns the constitutionality under the First Amendment of the attempts made by some cities and universities to control, through disciplinary sanctions, the intimidation and subordination of racial, ethnic, and sexual minorities by use of "hate speech." Those contributing to the small explosion of scholarly writing on this topic have generally taken one of two polar positions: one group of scholars and litigators (generally liberal) argues that hate speech regulations are simply unconstitutional under the First Amendment[6] while a second, more or less minority (and generally progressive), position argues that they are constitutional, either by virtue of the similarity between hate speech regulations and traditionally accepted limits on the First Amendment, or because of limits we should imply into that amendment through the "penumbral" and balancing, or counterbalancing, effect of the Fourteenth Amendment's equality clause.[7] The position that seems to have no adherents is that hate speech regulations are desirable, for progressive reasons, but are nevertheless unconstitutional, but shouldn't be, and that this shows that, at least from a progressive perspective, the First Amendment is morally flawed. But again, this position seems to have no adherents. Instead, those who think hate speech regulations are a good idea generally think they are constitutional while those who think they are not a good idea generally find them unconstitutional. No one seems to find them both desirable and unconstitutional, and hence exemplary of a problem with the First Amendment. No one, in other words, is led by a commitment to the desirability of hate speech regulations and a fair reading of the Constitution to take a progressive and morally sceptical stance toward the Constitution.

A second and structurally similar example involves the constitutionality of anti-pornography ordinances. Despite the wide range of conflicting feminist and libertarian positions on this issue, no one advances the apparently logical, and initially plausible, position that these ordinances are eminently desirable, but unconstitutional, revealing a serious problem with the First Amendment. Instead, those who view these ordinances as unconstitutional generally view them as objectionable,[8] while those who view the ordinances as desirable generally find them constitutional as well.[9] Again, no one is led by a commitment to the value of anti-pornography regulations and a fair reading of the Constitution to take a morally sceptical stance toward the Constitution, or at least toward the First Amendment.

Although this paper focuses primarily on the absence of progressive sceptical arguments about the Constitution's value, the same point holds regarding the absence of sceptical stances toward the Constitution reflective of other political or moral commitments. Thus, one finds few people arguing that the Constitution does indeed protect a woman's right to an abortion and, therefore, over-protects privacy, because abortion rights are morally unjustifiable. Few argue that the Constitution protects the individual's choice of sexual lifestyle and, therefore, over-protects individual choice, because homosexuality is an immoral way to live. No one seems led by a conservative commitment to the value of regulating private morality and a fair reading of the Constitution as prohibiting that regulation to the conclusion that the Constitution is morally and politically flawed. On the other hand, no one seems to believe that the Constitution does indeed fail to protect reproductive or gay rights, but that these rights should be granted, and that this shows the Constitution's inadequacy. Again, those who view abortion rights as desirable generally view them as constitutionally protected, and those who view them as unprotected generally view them as undesirable. No one seems led by virtue of their political views on abortion or sexuality combined with a fair reading of the Constitution to the conclusion that the Constitution is flawed.

The absence of these arguments in the legal literature evidences the more basic privation noted above: There is no general tradition, at least in the legal literature, of *normatively* sceptical constitutionalism from a liberal, progressive, conservative, or any other developed political or moral perspective. Regardless of political viewpoint, constitutional scholars are peculiarly reluctant to see either the Constitution or a particular constitutional guarantee as being at odds with our political or moral ideals, goals, or commitments. We tend to see the Constitution as an inappropriate object of criticism, and this may be even more true today than it was thirty, forty, or fifty years ago. Even in post-critical, post-modern, post-structuralist, post-feminist times, we lack a developed body of legal scholarship that takes a morally critical stance toward the Constitution and the rights it purports to protect.

The main purpose of this paper is simply to draw attention to this absence and initiate movement toward reversing the trend. By elaborating a progressive argument against constitutionalism I hope to show, by example, that we should develop normative arguments, grounded in politics and morality, for and against constitutional fidelity. My second aim, however, is to try to account for the absence of normative constitutional debate. Why isn't there a recognizable body of constitutional scholarship criticizing the Constitution, on moral or political grounds? Why do so few advocates endorse the positions noted above: That hate speech regulation or anti-pornography ordinances are desirable but unconstitutional; that the Constitution protects abortion rights, but shouldn't; that the Constitution does, but shouldn't, protect reproductive or gay rights; or doesn't, but should, allow the regulation of private morality?

There is, of course, a "psychoanalytic" or "socioanalytic" explanation for the absence of constitutional doubt in the literature. Theorists, like the rest of the culture, and across the political spectrum, may find it sociologically or psychologically difficult to view the Constitution as morally problematic, or indeed even morally flawed. Either because there is so little else that binds us together as a civic culture, or, perhaps, simply out of a psychic need to identify some sort of authority in our lives who will love us as well as authoritatively guide us, we all may have a hard time seeing the Constitution itself—rather than its erroneous interpretation by a pernicious, dishonest, overly-conservative, or unduly activist Court as being "the problem," the obstacle to the attainment of some desired political or moral goal. We have trouble seeing the Constitution as part of the problem rather than part of the solution, and as a consequence, we tend, both in popular consciousness and at the level of theory to blur constitutionality with morality to see the Constitution as more or less in line with moral and political virtue. It may be that because we have this difficulty, we are disinclined to oppose the Constitution itself, rather than its erroneous interpretation, to some moral ideal, to some cherished utopian vision, or more baldly, simply to some political ambition. Although this explanation may have some merit, it also sounds a bit dated, and even nostaligic: Whatever may have been the case in the past, it is difficult to believe that in the fractured, relativist, nihilist, minimally *pluralist* moral climate in which we presently live and argue, that we are all still afflicted with an irrational and deeply emotional affection for a foundational legal document.

The explanation advanced in this paper for our continuing constitutional fidelity is considerably less global: At least one reason for our modern reluctance to generate constitutional criticism, I will argue, might stem from the preemptive logic of the "interpretation debate" that has dominated scholarship over at least the last two decades. As mentioned at the outset, the absence of normative debate can be viewed as a simple "opportunity cost" of the prominence of interpretive debate.

Thus, whatever may be the effects of our psychic or social attraction to the Constitution, the logic of the interpretation debate alone, I will endeavor to show, has made sceptical arguments regarding the Constitution's value extremely difficult to even articulate, much less debate, even among political radicals who almost assuredly bear no excessive patriotic, civic, or psychic loyalty to the United States Constitution. I will try to show that our focus on questions of constitutional interpretation and methodology has minimally diverted our attention from questions of constitutional value, but the logic of that debate has also made questions of constitutional value difficult, for various reasons, to even raise.

The first section of this paper sketches one possible basis for a morally sceptical stance toward the Constitution. The sceptical position is grounded, again, not in the "indeterminacy thesis," but instead in a rejection of the *morality* (rather than coherence) of the liberalism that informs constitutional decisionmaking, and in an affirmation of a progressive and egalitarian political and moral orientation. This section argues, very simply, that our Constitution is fundamentally and possibly irreversibly at odds with progressive egalitarianism, and that because of that it is a seriously flawed document.

The second section examines why, with only a few exceptions, notably Derrick Bell's[10] and Alan Freeman's critical race theory,[11] Mark Tushnet's "rights critique,"[12] and Mary Becker's[13] feminist analysis of the Bill of Rights, this form of constitutional scepticism, what might be called "progressive constitutional scepticism," has not been elaborated in constitutional scholarship, despite the large numbers of constitutional writers and advocates who unquestionably hold egalitarian and progressive moral and political commitments. My argument will be that the logic of the dominant interpretive debates precludes articulation and elaboration of sceptical evaluative argument. The conclusion then examines the costs, to progressivism as well as to constitutional discourse and theory, of the absence of this form of constitutional scepticism.

I. Progressive Constitutional Scepticism

Progressives have both substantive and methodological reasons to be sceptical about the Constitution's value. I define "progressivism," *in part*, by its guiding ideal: Progressives are loosely committed to a form of social life in which all individuals live meaningful, autonomous, and self-directed lives, enriched by rewarding work, education, and culture, free of the disabling fears of poverty, violence, and coercion, nurtured by life-affirming connections with intimates and co-citizens alike, and strengthened by caring communities that are both attentive to the shared human needs of its members and equally mindful of their diversity and differences. Much of this guiding ideal, however, is shared by liberals. What *distinguishes* progressives from liberals is that while liberals tend to view the dangers of an over-oppressive state as the most serious obstacle to the attainment of such a world, progressives, while agreeing that some obstacles emanate from the state, argue that *for the most part* the most serious impediments emanate from unjust concentrations of *private* power—the social power of whites over blacks, the intimate power of men over women, the economic power of the materially privileged over the materially deprived. From a progressive perspective, it is those concentrations of private power, not state power, that presently riddle social life with hierarchic relationships of mastery and subjection, of sovereignty and subordination. Hence, it is those concentrations of private power that must be targeted, challenged, and reformed by progressive political action. That action, in turn, will often involve state intervention into the private spheres within which hierarchies of private power are allowed to thrive, and that simple fact will commonly pit the progressive strategy of ending private domination against the liberal goal of minimizing the danger of an oppressive state.

This difference between progressives and liberals largely accounts for the degree of conflict between their respective analyses and goals. For example, liberals and progressives generally agree, and lament, that the freedom of gays and lesbians to form and maintain nurturing intimate relationships is threatened by discriminatory state action. At the same time, progressives, far more than liberals, are sensitive to the degree to which that freedom is threatened by the continuing and seemingly unshakable hegemonic rage of an intolerant, abusive, and often violent minority of heterosexual private citizens. That hegemonic rage, not just state action, must somehow be challenged and transformed if gays and lesbians are to thrive. Similarly, liberals and progressive feminists agree, and lament, that the freedom of women to engage simultaneously in well-compensated work, in public life, and in a rewarding home and family life is threatened by discriminatory state law. Still, the dramatic and well-publicized split between liberal feminists and progressive feminists reflects the extent to which progressive feminists, unlike liberal feminists, realize that women's lives and freedom may be endangered more by private, intimate, economic, and social systems of power and control than by pernicious or discriminatory state action: By, for example, a family structure that saps women's time, energy, and self-esteem with unequal distributions of demanding and unpaid domestic labor; the social acceptability of private sexual violence and coercion in marriage and intimacy that threatens women's safety and drains women's sense of self-possession and self-will; and the prevalence of unequal compensation for work of comparable responsibility and difficulty that deprives women of material security, self-esteem, and independence. If we call these systems of private coercion, intimate violence, and economic disempowerment "patriarchy," then it seems that patriarchy exists and perpetuates itself to a considerable degree independent of "state action," discrimination or otherwise. Awareness of, and concern about, that social fact distinguishes progressive from liberal feminists.

Similarly, from a progressive perspective, African Americans and other ethnic minorities are hindered in their search for meaningful freedom and full civic equality, not so much by discriminatory state laws or actions as by the continuing and escalating presence of a virulent white racism in virtually all spheres of private, social, and economic life. Awareness of, and concern about, that complex social fact in large part distinguishes progressive "critical race theorists" from their one-time liberal allies. To take one final example, the poor in this society are hurt not nearly so much by pernicious or discriminatory state actions as by concentrations of private economic power. Again, concern over the centrality of this social fact distinguishes progressive from liberal politics on issues of class. Generally, what defines a progressive political perspective is simply the awareness that the greatest obstacles to enjoyment of the good life valued by liberals and progressives alike are not actions of any sort taken by states or state officials, but concentrations of *private* power, whether of a patriarchal, racist, homophobic, or capitalist sort.

If that progressive insight is basically correct, then at least two problems exist with the scheme of individual rights and liberties protected by the Constitution. First, the Constitution does not prohibit the abuse of private power that interferes with the equality or freedom of subordinated peoples. The Constitution simply does not reach private power, and therefore cannot possibly prohibit its abuse. Even the most far reaching liberal interpretations of the Reconstruction Amendments—the only amendments that *seemingly* reach private power—refuse or fail to find either a constitutional prohibition of private societal racism, intimate sexual violence, or economic coercion or a constitutional imperative that the states take affirmative action to eradicate it. Justice Harlan's famous liberal dissent in *Plessy v. Ferguson*,[14] for example, made painfully clear that, even on his reading of the amendment (which, of course, would have outlawed Jim Crow laws), the Fourteenth Amendment does not challenge the sensed or actual cultural and social superiority of the white race. More recently, Justices Brennan and Marshall's argument in their dissent in *City of Richmond v. J.A. Croson Co.*,[15] that the state *may* remedy private discrimination if failure to do so would enmesh the state in those discriminatory practices, did not suggest that the Constitution *requires* the state to address private discrimination. Similarly, virtually no liberal judges or commentators have read the Constitution and the Reconstruction Amendments to require that states take affirmative action to address the unconstitutional maldistribution of household labor, with its serious, well-proven, and adverse effects on women's liberty and equality. No liberal court or commentator reads the Constitution to require that states or Congress take action to protect against homophobic violence and rage, or to protect against the deadening, soul-murdering, and often life-threatening effects of homelessness, hunger, and poverty. The Constitution apparently leaves untouched the very conditions of subordination, oppression, and coercion that relegate some to "lesser lives" of drudgery, fear, and stultifying self-hatred. For that reason alone, the Constitution appears to be fundamentally at odds with progressive ideals and visions.

The incompatibility, however, of progressivism and the Constitution goes deeper. Not only does the Constitution fail to prohibit subordinating abuses of private power, but, at least a good deal of the time, in the name of guaranteeing constitutional protection of individual freedom, it also aggressively *protects* the very hierarchies of wealth, status, race, sexual preference, and gender that facilitate those practices of subordination. Thus, the Constitution seemingly protects the individual's freedom to produce and consume hate speech, despite its propensity to contribute to patterns of racial oppression. It also clearly protects the individual's right to practice religion, despite the demonstrable incompatibility of the religious tenets central to all three dominant mainstream religions with women's full civic and political equality. It protects the individual's freedom to create and use pornography, despite the possible connection between pornography and increases in private violence against women. It protects the privacy and cultural hegemony of the nuclear family, despite the extreme forms of injustice that occur within that institution and the maldistribution of burdens and benefits visited by that injustice upon women and, to a lesser degree, children. Finally, it protects, as a coincidence of protecting the freedom and equal opportunities of individuals, both the system of "meritocracy" and the departures from meritocracy that dominate and constitute the market and economy, despite the resistance of those systems to full participation of African Americans and hence despite the subordinating effects of those "markets" upon them. Very generally, the Constitution, incident to protecting the ideational, economic, and familial spheres of individual life against the intrusive effects of benign and malign legislative initiatives, protects that realm of private, intimate, social, and economic culture that creates and then perpetuates a spirit of intolerance toward, alienation from, and active hatred of subordinated persons. By so doing, the Constitution not only fails to protect against that subordination, but it also fails to exhibit neutrality toward it: It nurtures precisely those patterns and practices that are most injurious to the economic opportunities, the individual freedoms, the intimacies, and the fragile communities of those persons already most deprived in the unequal and unfree social world in which we live.

Finally, this incompatibility of the Constitution with progressive ideals is neither momentary nor contingent. It is not a product of false or disingenuous interpretation by a particular court or Justice hostile to progressive politics. Rather, the Constitution's incompatibility with progressive ideals stems from at least two theoretical and doctrinal sources that lie at the heart of our constitutional structure: First, the conception of liberty to which the Constitution is committed and, second, its conception of equality.

First, as is often recognized, the Constitution protects a strong and deeply liberal conception of what Isaiah Berlin has termed the "negative liberty"[16] of the individual to speak, think, choose, and labor within a sphere of noninterference from social, community, or state authority. As is less often recognized, however, the Constitution creates and protects these spheres of noninterference not only in preference to, but also *at the cost of*, the more positive conceptions of freedom and autonomy necessary for progressive change. The cultural, intimate, private, and economic spheres of noninterference protected by the Constitution are the very spheres of private power, control, and coercion within which the positive liberty of subordinated persons to live lives of meaning is most threatened. Thus, the Constitution protects the rights of producers and consumers of racial hate speech and pornography so as to protect the negative liberty of those speakers and listeners. By doing so, it not only fails to protect, but also actively threatens, the positive freedom of women and African Americans to develop lives free from fear for one's safety, the seeds of racial bitterness, the "clouds of inferiority,"[17] the interference with one's movements, and the crippling incapacities to participate fully in public life occasioned by the constitutionally protected cultures of racism and misogyny. The negative liberty of the individual heralded and celebrated by liberalism is not only inconsistent with, but also hostile to the positive liberty central to progressivism, simply because protection of "negative liberty" necessarily creates the sphere of noninterference and privacy within which the abuse of private power can proceed unabated. The Constitution is firmly committed to this negative rather than positive conception of liberty, and is thus not only not the ally, but also a very real obstacle, to progressive ideals.

Second, the Fourteenth Amendment's mandate of equality, rather than being a limit to the Constitution's celebration of liberty, is also a bar to progressive progress, the heroic efforts of progressive litigators, judges, and commentators to prove the contrary notwithstanding. The "equal protection of the laws" guaranteed by the Fourteenth Amendment essentially guarantees that one's membership in a racially or sexually defined group will not adversely affect one's treatment by the state. As such, the mandate powerfully reinforces the liberal understanding that the only attributes that matter to the state are those shared universally by all members of the community: The possession of equal dignity, the power to form one's own plan of life, and the universal aspirations to autonomy and so forth. Precisely this understanding of equality, grounded in the liberal claim and promise of universality and equal treatment, however, renders the Equal Protection Clause an obstacle to progressive progress. The need to acknowledge and compensate for the individual's membership in profoundly non-universal subordinate groups—whether racially, sexually, or economically defined—is what distinguishes the progressive political impulse from the liberal. It is precisely that membership in non-universal groups, and the centrality of the non-universal attributes that distinguish them, that both liberalism and the liberally defined constitutional mandate of equality are poised not simply to ignore, but also to oppose. It is, then, both unsurprising and inevitable that the Fourteenth Amendment's Equal Protection Clause is understood as not requiring, and indeed forbidding, the state and public interventions into private, intimate, and economic spheres of life needed to interrupt the patterns of domination, subordination, and inequality that continue to define the lives of those within these protected private realms.

Methodologically, the Constitution is also hostile to political and moral progressivism, simply because it elevates one set of moral values above others, relegating non-constitutional ideals or visions to the sphere of the "merely political." The Constitution's peculiar status as a bridge between liberal morality and aspirations and positive law, although much heralded by liberal philosophers and constitutionalists, poses a triple danger to progressive ideals. First, because the Constitution is indeed *law*, and law in the ordinary as well as extraordinary sense, it imprints upon the liberalism on which it rests the imprimatur of positive legal authority. One set of political convictions hence receives not only the persuasive authority derived from its merits, but also the political, willed authority of the extant, empowered, positive sovereign. These ideals simply *are*, as well as ought to be; and they *are* in a way that makes compliance mandatory. Second, because the Constitution is law in the extraordinary as well as ordinary sense, the positive political authority imprinted upon the liberal morality of the

Constitution is of a higher, permanent, and constitutive sort. It severely constrains moralities and aspirations with which it is inconsistent in the name of the community from which it purportedly draws its sovereign authority. Thus, it is not just "the law" that is hostile to non-liberal moral aspirations, such as progressivism. It is also, more deeply and meaningfully, "we the people"—all of us, the inter-generational community of citizens—for whom the Constitution speaks and from whom it draws its authority that is hostile to the ideals with which it is inconsistent. Third, because the Constitution is also undeniably a moral as well as legal document, the authority it embodies is exercised not only coercively—telling us who we must be—but also instructively—telling us who we ought to be. It defines and confines not just our options—as does any law, higher or lower—but our aspirations as well. For all three reasons, the Constitution is not just a peculiarly authoritarian legal document, but is also authoritarian in a peculiarly parental way. Like a parent's authority over the identity of his or her children, the Constitution both persuades us *to be* a certain way and it constitutes us *in* a certain way. It creates us as it defines a morality to which we will and should subscribe.

For all of these reasons, the Constitution is methodologically as well as substantively hostile to progressive politics. The moral authoritarianism at its core is in many ways conducive to the reverence for the individual and distrust of the mass so central to liberalism, but it is inimical to the egalitarian, inclusive, and largely communitarian methods—the grass roots politics at the local level and the participatory democracy at the national and state level—that must form the foundation of genuine progressive change. Effective political challenges to the subordination of some groups by others must rest on a fundamental change of human orientation in both the dominated and oppressing groups: The dominated must come to see their interests as both shared with each other and opposed to the interests of the stronger; and the stronger must come to embrace empathetically the subordinated as sufficiently close to their own identities to be "of their concern." Neither progressive end—the mounting of sufficient power within the ranks of the subordinated through cross-group organizing or the challenge to the received self-identity of the strong—is attainable through the legal, coercive imposition of a particular moral paradigm that characterizes constitutional methodology. In fact, the moral and legal authoritarianism at the heart of our constitutional method will almost invariably frustrate it.

These three attributes of our Constitution—its commitment to negative liberty at the cost of positive liberty, its individualist and universalist, rather than particularist and anti-subordinationist understanding of equality, and its moral authoritarian methodology—are just three possible grounds for scepticism about the Constitution's compatibility with progressive politics. If progressive politics are necessary for moral progress, then these three attributes are also grounds for scepticism about the compatibility of the Constitution with moral progress in this country.

This list is obviously not exhaustive. Other reasons grounded in progressive morality may exist for doubting the wisdom of the constitutional project. At the same time, the whole of the Constitution is certainly not adverse to progressivism, and some features of the Constitution, at least when properly viewed, may promote progressive projects. Nevertheless, it seems fair to say that *at least* the twin concepts of liberty and equality with which the Constitution is aligned, as well as our constitutional method, are not neutral toward progressive politics and ideals and collectively constitute a potent political, moral, and even social force against the realization of those aspirations.

II. The Absence of Progressive Constitutional Scepticism

Why is it that neither this progressive case against the value of the Constitution, nor any of its implications for particular issues, has a sizeable number of adherents in the legal profession, or has received more than occasional elaboration in constitutional scholarship? Although I have labelled the sceptical stance toward constitutionalism outlined above "progressive," it is by no means only those who think of themselves as political progressives who align themselves with some part of a progressive agenda. Political orientations generally are not monolithic, and progressivism in particular can be embraced in part by persons at virtually all points along the political spectrum. Thus, a sizeable number of liberals making up the mainstream of constitutional discourse, the vast majority of critical legal scholars, a probable majority of feminist legal theorists, most critical race theorists, and at least a few conservative legal theorists subscribe to some subset of "progressive" political commitments. The question posed above might be framed in this way: Of the scores of constitutional writers favoring progressive political commitments, why do only a handful *also* believe that these progressive initiatives are truly unconstitutional, revealing a serious moral failing in our constitutional scheme? Why are almost all of these more or less progressive writers, activists, and thinkers seemingly convinced that their beliefs are consistent with the Constitution? In contrast to whatever scepticism, nihilism, or simple pessimism progressives hold toward the Court, the public, Congress, and our public institutions, why are they so relentlessly optimistic about the Constitution itself? Why do so few think that, because of its deep incompatibility with progressive political and moral goals, the Constitution, although desirable at times, generally does more harm than good, and that we would be better off without it?

Perhaps the main reason is purely strategic. From a jurisprudential perspective, the absence of normative debate about the Constitution reflects a seemingly perverse refusal to apply the lessons of legal positivism to the document applied as a matter of course in other areas of the law: We actually find it difficult to separate the Constitution "as it actually is" from our moral ideals of "what it should be," although we have few difficulties separating the law of negligence, the holder in due course doctrine, or the consideration doctrine from our ideals of what tort, commercial, or contract law should be. We have not achieved the positivist "separation of law and morality" in the constitutional sphere that we seem to embrace almost automatically in most other areas of law. But this may not be as surprising, or inconsistent, as it first appears. The positivist insistence on the separation of "the law" on the one hand and its merit or demerit on the other—the separateness of the actual and the ideal—ensures a clear perception of the law's true nature, a logical prerequisite to meaningful criticism and hence reform. Only by first understanding what the law is, the positivist argues, can we determine what it should be, and only after we see what it should be can we reform it. But, perhaps what is distinctive about the constitutional context is that there simply is no realistic chance of "reforming" the Constitution, and hence no sensible reform-based motive for insisting on the positivist separation of the Constitution "as it is" from the Constitution "as it ought to be." Given the permanence, the higher status, and the "constitutiveness" of constitutional law, what one achieves through insistence on the moral inadequacy of the Constitution is not the clear-headedness essential to its enlightened reform stressed by the classical legal positivists, but rather one's own exclusion from the community whose audience is sought.

From a purely strategic perspective then, there may simply be no gain and considerable cost from the positivist insistence on separating the constitutional "is" from the constitutional "ought." The Constitution is simply not amenable to the gradualist, piecemeal, liberal reform that positivism facilitates. Criticizing the Constitution may too closely resemble criticizing the earth for revolving around the sun. Although neither as natural nor as unchangeable as the law of the earth's rotation, the law of the Constitution is considerably more resistant to change than the criminal codes or private law regimes to which Bentham and his positivist followers directed their critical and reformist attentions. The costs of asserting the incompatibility of the Constitution with one's own moral and political values are high, and obvious. Once the unconstitutionality of a favored reform is conceded, marginality is virtually assured. Given the dominance of lawyers in constitutional discourse and their continuing commitment to change the world through law, the absence of a critical perspective that fails to achieve meaningful reform and delegitimizes the very values according to which the law is found wanting may not be so surprising.

Strategy alone, however, does not tell the entire story. After all, many, if not most, constitutional theorists are not litigators, or even aspire to be litigators. No matter how many of the last generation of grand constitutional theorists were one-time law clerks, there are now many contemporary constitutional theorists who have no secret or express urge whatsoever to tie their constitutional views to a potential argument for effectuating a desirable legal change. The absence of normative scepticism from constitutional discourse must have causes other than the strategic desire to back the winning horse, coupled with the obvious truism that an argument that concedes unconstitutionality to argue the immorality of the Constitution will lose in court every time.

In this section I will argue that the absence of normative scepticism from constitutional discourse is also attributable, at least in part, to the logic of the poles of the interpretive debates concerning the Constitution's meaning, its meaningfulness, or meaninglessness that currently dominate constitutional scholarship. Both the constitutional faithful—those who insist upon the determinacy of constitutional meaning and hence legitimacy of constitutional review within the framework of liberalism—and the constitutional sceptical—those who challenge the determinacy of the Constitution and hence the compatibility of judicial review with liberal theory—are, for different reasons, unlikely to pursue sceptical arguments about the Constitution's value, even if they adhere to the progressive political or moral premises on which that scepticism might be grounded. Thus, the absence of progressive scepticism about the Constitution might reflect the degree to which the now standard debate over interpretivism has captured the terms of constitutional discourse. Whatever the case concerning the wisdom of refraining from constitutional critique for strategic reasons, there is no good reason, I will argue, to allow the debate over interpretation to preempt debate over constitutional value. To the degree that the absence of a morally sceptical stance regarding the Constitution reflects a commitment to one or the other of the poles of debate over meaning, we should put aside, if we cannot resolve, the latter, so that we can again focus our attention on the former.

A. The Progressive Critique and Liberal Constitutional Faith

All members of the constitutionally faithful[18] pole of the debate adhering to the determinacy of constitutional meaning and to the compatibility of the constitutional enterprise with liberal premises will be disinclined to express progressive critiques of constitutionalism. For those purposes, the constitutionally faithful should be divided into two subgroups: the "traditional liberals" and a possibly larger group with mixed political commitments who might be called "progressive liberals."

First, of the sizeable number of the constitutionally faithful who are traditional or classical liberals, the disinclination to see whatever merit there is in the progressive case against the Constitution is fairly easy to explain. The traditional liberal, simply by virtue of his or her politics, will be relatively inattentive to the harms of subordination occasioned by the private sphere and insulated by constitutionalism. The progressive critique of the Constitution will, therefore, have no strong intuitive appeal. For this group, the constitutional commitment to the insularity of the private sphere converges perfectly with the political belief that the private sphere is the sphere of autonomy, growth, and self-actualization, rather than the "hellhole" of violation and subordination described by progressives. There is a perfect fit, in other words, of the coercive morality of the Constitution and the aspirational morality of traditional liberal politics. When the Constitution is correctly interpreted, it aligns with correct liberal moral commitments. There is simply no merit to the progressive critique.

This characterization of "traditional liberalism," however, obviously does not fairly describe the broad political commitments of persons within the "constitutionally faithful" camp of the interpretation debates. A sizeable number of the constitutionally faithful are committed to some aspect of progressive politics. The hard question, then, is not why the traditional liberal is blind to the progressive critique of constitutionalism, but why those who are committed to constitutional determinacy and method *but also* sympathize with at least some progressive goals and methods, nevertheless shy away from attacking directly the morality of the Constitution. For them, the refusal to see the unconstitutionality of politically desirable progressive proposals as arguments against the Constitution must stem not from politics, but from a view of the Constitution as rooted in a higher, deeper, more "constitutive," or simply "prior" *morality*, and not simply a more coercive legal command. Hence, for this group, the unconstitutionality of proposals based on a politics incompatible with the constitutional mandate carries with it the moral justification of their demise. For the constitutionally faithful theorist who views some progressive proposals as politically wise, their unconstitutionality implies not the limits of the morality or justification of the Constitution, but rather the limits of the morality of the proposals themselves. It may be a politically and hence morally "good thing" to limit access to hate speech or pornography, but it must be a constitutionally and hence super-morally "better thing" to restrain our desires to do the (merely) politically right thing. For the constitutionally faithful, the Constitution provides a higher norm both positivistically and morally, and therefore the "lower" moralities with which it conflicts must simply give way. Their virtue cannot suggest fault with the Constitution itself.

The logic of constitutional faith, one might assume, eventually brings about a concrete reordering of moral and political priorities and a reordering of epistemological perceptions of the social world as well. To accommodate the moral and legal commitment to the priority of the constitutional norm in the face of an unconstitutional but desirable political proposal, the faithful constitutionalist must either elevate to new heights the stakes of departing from the constitutional norm or denigrate the evil the unconstitutional progressive proposal was designed to remedy. It is, then, not surprising that, in the hate speech and antipornography examples, the negative liberty of individual consumers of that speech achieves almost mystical status for faithful constitutionalists, while the harms caused by hate speech and pornography are trivialized. This simultaneous elevation of individual liberty and trivialization of group harm in turn affects the way the faithful constitutionalist sees the world. The harms occasioned by pornography, hate speech, and unequal distributions of domestic labor all become not just trivial, but even invisible. Their evil is "trumped" out of existence by the perceived evil of limiting a negative right. There is then no disabling conflict between the constitutional morality to which the faithful constitutionalist is definitionally committed and the political morality that may conflict with constitutional morality. The "moral dissonance" always present in the faithful constitutionalist's position is reduced to nothing through the altering of the perceptual landscape.

The constitutionally faithful theorist also harboring some commitment to progressive political methodology similarly risks moral dissonance created by the methodological incompatibility of the communitarian and collectivist methods of progressivism and the authoritarian methods of constitutionalism. As the faithful theorist reduces the risk of substantive dissonance by reorienting his perceptions of the social world to trivialize the private harms occasioned by subordination in the private sphere, he is inclined to minimize the risk of methodological dissonance by simply reorienting his perceptions of the virtues and vices of progressive methods. The vast majority of constitutionally faithful liberals harboring at least a fondness for the participatory democracy central to progressivism effect the accommodation between the Constitution's methods and the methods of progressive politics by simply attributing to participatory democracy the same majoritarian vices that constitutional methodology is perfectly poised to correct when directed against democratic excesses of a conservative or reactionary political hue. Whether the democratic wish being frustrated is the conservative desire to punish flag-burners or dispensers of contraception, or the progressive desire to punish or penalize hate speech or pornography, the constitutionally faithful liberal will argue that democracy has outreached its moral justification. In both cases she can readily conclude that constitutional methodology is perfectly designed to identify and rectify the excess. It just doesn't matter whether the democratic desire has come to fruition through the progressive methods of coalition building, consciousness raising, and democratic participation or through the politics of reaction and hate-mongering. In either case, the peculiar dangers to the individual and to the private sphere posed by majoritarianism are present, and in either case, the Constitution and the courts are poised with methodological perfection to eliminate them.

This muting of the sceptical voice among liberal and progressive-liberal constitutionalists is unfortunate. As I will argue below, there are real costs from the muting of progressive doubts about the moral or political value of the Constitution. But it is also unfounded, and it is unfounded even within the assumptions of the very liberal tradition that presumably inspires constitutional faith. The muting of scepticism is unfounded because there simply is no connection between the determinacy of the Constitution, the hallmark of constitutional faith, and the Constitution's *morality*. The notion that there is some connection, implicit in volumes of liberal writing on the Constitution and explicit in the remainder, rests on the fallacious argument that because the Constitution's *in*determinacy would imply its illegitimacy, and its illegitimacy in turn would imply its immorality, therefore, the Constitution's determinacy must imply both its legitimacy and morality. Not only is this wrong, but it is also profoundly illiberal. Conceding the necessity of determinacy to liberal legitimacy, it does not follow that the Constitution's determinacy is a *sufficient* condition of its ultimate political morality, for two reasons. First, determinacy may be a *necessary* but not a sufficient condition of legitimacy. Even a fully determinate Constitution might be illegitimate for reasons independent of its determinacy. Second, and more importantly, legitimacy may be a necessary but not a sufficient condition of morality. Even a fully "legitimate" constitutional enterprise—legitimate, for example, within the contours of either liberal or republican political theory—may be immoral for reasons independent of its legitimacy.

In other words, only through conflation of determinacy with legitimacy, and then legitimacy with morality, does interpretive faith in the determinacy of the Constitution become moral faith in its ultimate justification. No conceivable grounds, however, justify that double conflation. Determinacy no more exhausts political legitimacy than political legitimacy exhausts moral justification. The mistaken notion that it does reflects either the profoundly illiberal view of the state as fully justified if "legitimate"—rather than as fully justified if, and only if, truly liberatory—or the equally illiberal view that that which has traditionally been valued must continue to be valued, regardless of our changing appreciation of the burdens and harms it inflicts, or, using the Deweyan phrase for the "nerve" of liberalism, regardless of our changing "intelligence" about the effect of that object on our felt, experienced lives.

B. The Progressive Critique and Constitutional Scepticism

Constitutional sceptics[19]—those who doubt the determinacy of constitutional phrases, and hence the compatibility of the Constitution with liberal political theory—are also disinclined to embrace a progressive normative critique of the Constitution, even if they subscribe to progressive political and moral goals and methods. This fact alone is surprising because constitutional sceptics for the most part are members of the critical legal studies movement, a legal academic movement that itself may be defined by a commitment to progressive, left-wing, or radical politics. Thus, one may legitimately assume that most constitutional sceptics subscribe to most if not all of the progressive political commitments described above, and would therefore be inclined to assert the moral and political desirability of progressive political proposals designed to remedy abuses of power within the private, intimate, or social sphere. Yet, even from the sizeable number of progressive, feminist, or critical constitutional writers committed to the indeterminacy thesis and clearly supportive of progressive causes, one finds very little scholarship critical of the Constitution. The question remains, why?

The main reason may be strategic; but again, strategy alone cannot be the whole story. Although there may be others, one additional reason for the lack of criticism of the Constitution from constitutional sceptics may be that the logic of constitutional *scepticism* precludes moral *criticism*: For constitutional sceptics, neither the meaning nor the method of the Constitution is sufficiently determinate to be pernicious. If a text has potentially contradictory meanings, it can hardly be faulted for its substantive political implications, for it quite literally has none. Thus, for the sceptic, the Constitution's apparent incompatibility with progressive causes can hardly be attributed to the Constitution. Instead, the impulse to attribute these outcomes to the Constitution, the sceptic argues, rather than to its human interpreters and appliers, evidences the bad faith that the indeterminacy thesis is in part designed to uncover. The Constitution and the liberal tradition it purports to serve are sufficiently malleable to be susceptible to non-liberal, illiberal, conservative, tyrannical, or progressive interpretations. That it has received any particular interpretation or application, therefore, is a function not of its content, but of the constraining influences of the interpretive community or the political predilections of the interpreting judge. It follows that there is no reason, intrinsic to the constitutional text, for the Supreme Court's persistently non- and anti-progressive application and interpretation of the Constitution. Although the Court has generally read the Constitution to burden and limit the reach of affirmative action programs, for example, nothing in the document mandates that result. Consequently, the political inclinations of the judiciary, or the communities from which that group is drawn, must explain their interpretation. The Constitution itself can be read either to permit or to invalidate such plans. Similarly, the Constitution neither permits nor forbids hate speech ordinances. That it is read in such a way by liberal commentators and the Supreme Court, is not attributable to the language, content, or history of the Constitution, but rather to the constraints of the politics of the judge or community responsible for the interpretation.

The progressive critique of constitutional methodology is also obscured by the indeterminacy critique at the heart of constitutional scepticism. The authoritarianism of constitutionalism so antithetical to progressive political methodology simply disappears if the Constitution has no definitive meaning: If the indeterminacy claim is sound, the Constitution cannot be authoritative. A text that can mean either A or not-A can hardly be characterized as authoritative. If the indeterminacy thesis is right, the authoritarianism of constitutionalism cannot be attributed to the Constitution itself, although it might be attributable to the institutional forms, such as judicial review, responsible for its implementation. Not surprisingly, of the constitutional sceptics drawn to progressive political methods, few find any serious basis for moral, as opposed to epistemological, scepticism.

Here again, though, the inferences seem flawed. Constitutional scepticism no more obviates the need for normative constitutional criticism than constitutional faith undercuts its credibility. First, even if the Constitution is contradictory in precisely the way claimed by the sceptics—so any legal rule that is intended to specify results by reference to its content can be manipulated to reach contradictory results—it does not follow that the constitutional *tradition*, as opposed to the constitutional *document*, fails to render determinate results—results which, if history is a guide, are profoundly hostile to progressive politics. The indeterminacy thesis shows merely that the constitutional text, coupled with liberal theory, does not entail determinate results. But it does not follow that constitutional results are indeterminate. It only follows that it is not the text—the law—that does the determining. If we understand the constitutional tradition to be that which determines outcomes, and understand that tradition to include the politics of the community, the predilections of the judge, and in short the hegemonic and choice-denying inclinations of the judge's social context, then not only are constitutional outcomes determined, they are despairingly over-determined. They are over-determined, furthermore, by the very social and private forces of racism, misogyny, and classism that render progressive interpretations of the same document untenable. The felt determinacy of the Constitution and its felt incompatibility with progressivism hold *regardless* of the indeterminacy of the document and of liberalism itself.

Furthermore, it is worth noting that, to the extent that the indeterminacy critique is motivated by a European and existentialist impulse to unmask the otherwise denied responsibility of the judge for her political choices, the consequences of that critique are deeply paradoxical and self-defeating. On the one hand, the indeterminacy thesis, if true, precludes the judge from avoiding responsibility for the political and moral consequences of her decisions by cloaking them in the garb of a disingenuous legalism. On the other hand, however, the same critique exonerates the Constitution's authors. Peculiarly, the same indeterminacy critique that highlights the human responsibility of the present interpretive community or judge simultaneously obscures the equally human responsibility of the text's authors. Texts no less than interpretations have consequences, and one would expect a movement committed to demystifying the human authorship of, and hence responsibility for, institutional facts to be sensitive to the very real consequences of chosen words, and hence the responsibility for those consequences of the text's drafters. The indeterminacy critique muddles that responsibility as it denies the meaningfulness of the written text. It accordingly confuses the authority upon which that responsibility is predicated, and hence the moral dangers implied by the subsequent deference to textual authoritarianism so central to traditional constitutional method.

Whatever the merits of these arguments, however, it seems fair to say that constitutional sceptics view indeterminacy as obviating the need for progressive normative critique, just as constitutionally faithful liberals view constitutionalism as undermining the justification of progressive critique. For one group the critique is obviated; for the other its justification is undermined. All of this happens with no examination of the merits. The logic and framework of interpretive debates over the Constitution's meaning and meaningfulness have obscured debate over the Constitution's ultimate value by making the debate either illegitimate or moot. We might, therefore, be wise to consider putting aside our doubts about constitutional determinacy to look afresh at questions of constitutional value.

Conclusion: Progressive Politics and Constitutional Discourse

The absence of a tradition morally sceptical toward the Constitution from a progressive perspective has weakened progressivism, weakened our constitutional debates, weakened constitutional interpretation, and consequently, possibly weakened the Constitution itself. Progressivism is injured in at least two ways. First, there are obvious adverse political consequences if it is both true and unacknowledged that our constitutional guarantees of individual rights and liberties fail to guard against abuses of private power and affirmatively protect the spheres in which those abuses occur. The second type of damage, however, is more subtle and possibly more serious. The lack of a clear understanding of the obstacle to progressivism posed by constitutional guarantees further denigrates the "outlaw" position of the disadvantaged in this society simply because the advocacy of measures deemed both anti-communitarian and anti-individualist through their unconstitutionality is not consistently coupled with a critique of the Constitution that delegitimizes those initiatives. The tendency of all subordinated persons toward self-belittlement by trivializing the nature of their injuries is geometrically enhanced by the self-perception that their injuries do not exist because their infliction is constitutionally protected. To insist on the injustice of it is to injure, in a profound—because constitutional—sense, the entire community of which both the dominant and subordinate are a part. The understanding of the harms suffered by subordinated persons in the private realm is thereby frustrated when those injuries are perceived as having been the occasion of unconstitutional, and hence deeply immoral, legislative initiatives. The battle for passage of a progressive statute or ordinance, such as a hate speech regulation or an anti-pornography ordinance, destined to be found unconstitutional becomes the occasion not of greater public consciousness of the uniqueness, nature, and intensity of the suffering, but rather an occasion for obliterating difference by blurring the harm sustained by hate speech or pornography with other injuries sustained by other factions seeking ends at odds with constitutional guarantees. Greater understanding of the degree to which the Constitution frustrates progressivism would at least clarify the nature of the problem and might potentially demystify and hence dethrone and "untrump" constitutional morality.

A clearer understanding of the systemic threat to progressivism posed by constitutionalism that might be gained through a sustained debate over the value of constitutionalism might also enhance the quality of constitutional dialogue. Mainstream liberal constitutional discourse is presently characterized by an almost obsessive refusal to acknowledge or examine the nature of the costs of constitutional rights and liberties because of the logic and structure of rights themselves: The right exists to preclude precisely such cost-benefit analyses. Because there is no social cost that a right does not theoretically "trump," from a liberal perspective there is simply no reason to assess the costs of rights, and plenty of reason not to: Assessment only threatens societal respect for the right in question. Nevertheless, this refusal to address the consequences of rights ultimately leaves them groundless, as well as dangerous. The right must implicitly, if not explicitly, rest on some intuition that in the long run the benefits of having a right—whether self-actualization, autonomy, intimacy, privacy, meritocratic treatment, or economic self-determination—outweigh any costs incurred by its possession. Failure to examine the wisdom of this balance in light of our expanding knowledge of the experience of persons most vulnerable to the harms occasioned by those rights, and failure to countenance the possibility that perhaps the balance ought to be restruck, does not constitute "liberalism" in its best light; far from it. Instead, it constitutes a deeply conservative, traditionalist, and even reactionary posture toward the possibility of change and a profoundly illiberal rejection of the use of pragmatic knowledge to come to grips with an evolving social world.

The absence of a sustained tradition of normative constitutional scepticism also hurts the Constitution, in precisely the way that John Stuart Mill warned: Unexamined institutions, ideas, and cultures become fossilized, non-vital, superstitiously worshipped, and then perversely discarded echoes of their original impulses.[20] This is surely as true of liberal ideals, institutions, and cultures as it is of the unexamined and uncriticized conservative traditions and religions that Mill ridiculed.

Finally, we should remember that the Constitution is merely difficult, not impossible, to change. It can be changed fundamentally through amendment, interstitially through judicial interpretation, and in fact if not form through patterns of practice occasioned through changes in consciousness. The strategic impulse to insist upon the constitutionality of unconstitutional progressive initiatives, because of the sense that the Constitution itself cannot be changed, may be unduly pessimistic. Reform through critique is not utterly beyond the pale in constitutional dialogue or doctrine. Although the Constitution may be fundamental law, it is a fundamental charter of our self-understanding, as well, only if we permit it to be. Although a changed self-understanding is surely not a sufficient condition of change in a fundamental law, it is undeniably a necessary one. Failure to achieve it because of a sense of futility does nothing but render the immutability of an anti-progressive Constitution a self-fulfilling prophecy.

Notes

1. See, e.g., *Planned Parenthood v. Casey*, 112 S. Ct. 2791, 2874 (1992) (Scalia, J., joined by Rehnquist, C.J., White & Thomas, JJ., concurring in the judgment in part and dissenting in part). "The issue is whether [abortion] is a liberty protected by the Constitution of the United States. I am sure it is not. I reach that conclusion . . . because of two simple facts: (1) the Constitution says absolutely nothing about it, and (2) the longstanding traditions of American society have permitted it to be legally proscribed."*Id.*

2. For examples of originalist interpretation and defenses of originalism, see Raoul Berger, FEDERALISM: THE FOUNDER'S DESIGN (1987); Raoul Berger, *Against an Activist Court*, 31 CATH. U. L. REV. 173 (1982); Raoul Berger, *New Theories of "Interpretation": The Activist Flight from the Constitution*, 47 OHIO ST. L.J. 1 (1986); Robert H. Bork, *Original Intent: The Only Legitimate Basis for Constitutional Decision Making*, 26 JUDGES' J. 12 (Summer 1987); Robert H. Bork, *The Constitution, Original Intent, and Economic Rights*, 23 SAN DIEGO L. REV. 823 (1986); Antonin Scalia, *Originalism: The Lesser Evil*, 57 U. CIN. L. REV. 849 (1989).

3. For an example of "consensualist" interpretation, see *Penry v. Lynaugh*, 492 U.S. 302 (1989).

4. Those adopting this view include Bruce Ackerman, Ronald M. Dworkin, and John H. Ely. *See generally* Bruce Ackerman, RECONSTRUCTING AMERICAN LAW (1984); Bruce Ackerman, SOCIAL JUSTICE AND THE LIBERAL STATE (1980); Bruce Ackerman, WE THE PEOPLE (1991); Ronald M. Dworkin, TAKING RIGHTS SERIOUSLY (1977); John H. Ely, DEMOCRACY AND DISTRUST: A THEORY OF JUDICIAL REVIEW (1980).

5. See, e.g., Mark Tushnet, RED, WHITE, AND BLUE: A CRITICAL ANALYSIS OF CONSTITUTIONAL LAW 6-11 (1988); Paul Brest, *The Misconceived Quest for the Original Understanding*, 60 B.U. L. REV. 204, 224-37 (1980). For an impassioned argument against the "indeterminacy thesis" on this ground, see Owen Fiss, *Objectivity and Interpretation*, 34 STAN. L. REV. 739, 742-62 (1982).

6. See, e.g., George P. Fletcher, *Constitutional Identity*, 14 CARDOZO L. REV. 1, 26-27 (1992); Suzanna Sherry, *Speaking of Virtue: A Republican Approach to University Regulation of Hate Speech*, 75 MINN. L. REV. 933 (1991); Nadine Strossen, *Regulating Racist Speech on Campus: A Modest Proposal*, 1990 DUKE L.J. 484.

7. J. Peter Byrne, *Racial Insults and Free Speech Within the University*, 79 GEO. L.J. 399 (1991); Richard Delgado, *Campus Antiracism Rules: Constitutional Narratives in Collision*, 85 NW. U. L. REV. 343 (1991); Charles Lawrence, *If He Hollers, Let Him Go: Regulating Racist Speech on Campus*, 1990 DUKE L.J. 431 ; Mari Matsuda, *Public Response to Racist Speech: Considering the Victim's Story*, 87 MICH. L. REV. 2320 (1989).

8. See Ronald Dworkin, *Liberty and Pornography*, 38 N.Y. REV. BOOKS, Aug. 15, 1991, at 12; Barry W. Lynn, *"Civil Rights" Ordinances and the Attorney General's Commission: New Developments in Pornography Regulation*, 21 HARV. C.R.-C.L. L. REV. 27, 48-56 (1986).

9. Catharine Mackinnon, *Not a Moral Issue*, 2 YALE L. & POL'Y REV. 321, 336-40 (1984); Catharine Mackinnon, *Pornography, Civil Rights and Speech*, 20 HARV. C.R.-C.L. L. REV. 1, 22-32 (1985).

10. Derrick A. Bell, AND WE ARE NOT SAVED: THE EXCLUSIVE QUEST FOR RACIAL JUSTICE (1987).

11. Alan Freeman, *Antidiscrimination Law: The View From 1989*, 64 TUL. L. REV. 1407 (1990); Alan D. Freeman, *Race, Class and the Contradictions of Affirmative Action*, 7 BLACK L.J. 270, 270-74 (1982); Alan D. Freeman, *Race, Rights and the Quest for Equality of Opportunity: A Critical Legal Essay*, 23 HARV. C.R.-C.L. L. REV. 295, 316-25 (1988); Alan D. Freeman Et Al., *A Hurdle Too High: Class Based Roadblocks to Racial Remediation: A Panel*, 33 BUFF. L. REV. 1, 4-10, 15-17 (1984).

12. Mark V. Tushnet, *An Essay on Rights*, 62 TEX. L. REV. 1363(1984) .

13. Mary E. Becker, *The Politics of Women's Wrongs and the Bill of "Rights": A Bicentennial Perspective*, 59 U. CHI. L. REV. 453 (1992).

14. 163 U.S. 537, 552 (1896) (Harlan, J., Dissenting)

15. 488 U.S. 469, 528 (1989) (Marshall, J., joined by Brennan & Blackmun, JJ., dissenting)

16. Sir Isaiah Berlin, *Two Concepts of Liberty*, in FOUR ESSAYS ON LIBERTY 118 (1969).

17. Martin Luther King, Jr., WHY WE CAN'T WAIT 83 (1963).

18. See *supra* text accompanying notes 1-4.

19. See *supra* text accompanying note 5.

20. J. S. Mill, ON LIBERTY (1859).

Suggestions for
Further Reading

So many works on constitutional interpretation have been published in recent years that any selected bibliography is bound to be somewhat arbitrary. However, we think the following selections are good starting places for students and researchers interested in learning more about the approaches represented in this book.

General

A useful collection from the perspective of legal and political theory is *Modern Constitutional Theory: A Reader*, 2nd ed., edited by John H. Garvey and T. Alexander Aleinikoff (St. Paul: West Publishing, 1991). For the perspective of literary theory, see *Interpreting Law and Literature: A Hermeneutic Reader*, edited by Sanford Levinson and Steven Mailloux (Evanston, Ill.: Northwestern University Press, 1988). Two recent symposia are in *Southern California Law Review* vol. 58, nos. 1-2 (January 1985) and *The University of Chicago Law Review* vol. 59 (Winter 1992), the latter of which is reprinted as *The Bill of Rights in the Modern State*, edited by Geoffrey Stone, Richard A. Epstein, and Cass Sunstein (Chicago: University of Chicago Press, 1992). Two excellent books by prominent legal scholars who take approaches that differ from those in this anthology are John Hart Ely, *Democracy and Distrust: A Theory of Judicial Review* (Cambridge: Harvard University Press, 1980); and Laurence H. Tribe and Michael C. Dorf, *On Reading the Constitution* (Cambridge: Harvard University Press, 1991).

Chapter 1

Frederick Schauer further develops his views on interpretation in *Playing by the Rules* (New York: Oxford University Press, 1991). Schauer analyzes and defends the role of meaning in interpretation in "An Essay on Constitutional Language," *UCLA Law Review*, vol. 29 (April 1982), pp. 797-832; "Easy Cases," *Southern California Law Review*, vol. 58, nos. 1-2 (January 1985), pp. 399-440; and "Formalism," *Yale Law Journal*, vol. 97 (March 1988), pp. 509-48. For comments on Schauer's views, see "Symposium on Law and Philosophy," *Harvard Journal of Law and Public Policy*, vol. 14 (Summer 1991).

Chapter 2

An excellent collection of articles by advocates and critics of originalism is *Interpreting the Constitution: The Debate over Original Intent*, edited by Jack N. Rakove (Boston: Northeastern University Press, 1990), which includes classic articles by William Brennan, Edwin Meese, Robert Bork, Paul Brest, and Henry Monaghan, as well as a helpful bibliography. The most extended defense of originalism is Robert Bork's book, *The Tempting of America: The Political Seduction of the Law* (New York: Macmillan, 1990).

Chapter 3

Richard Epstein's main works on constitutional law are *Takings: Private Property and the Power of Eminent Domain* (Cambridge: Harvard University Press, 1985) and *Forbidden Grounds* (Cambridge: Harvard University Press, 1992). The classic discussion of analogies in common law is *An Introduction to Legal Reasoning* by Edward H. Levi (Chicago: University of Chicago Press, 1949).

Chapter 4

A recent collection on pragmatism is *Pragmatism in Law and Society*, edited by Michael Brint and William Weaver (Boulder: Westview Press, 1991), which includes Posner's article "What has Pragmatism to Offer Law?", comments on Posner's work by Stanley Fish, and criticisms of pragmatism by Ronald Dworkin. Posner's main work on constitutional interpretation is *The Problems of Jurisprudence* (Cambridge: Harvard University Press, 1990), which also includes discussions of law and economics as well as many other topics. For a liberal version of pragmatism, see Stanley Fish, *Doing What Comes Naturally* (Durham: Duke University Press, 1989).

Chapter 5

Three very influential books written by Ronald Dworkin are *Taking Rights Seriously* (Cambridge: Harvard University Press, 1978); *A Matter of Principle* (Cambridge: Harvard University Press, 1985); and *Law's Empire* (Cambridge: The Belknap Press of Harvard University Press, 1986). For a recent application of Dworkin's theory to the abortion controversy, see his "Unenumerated Rights: Whether and How *Roe* Should be Overruled," *The University of Chicago Law Review*, vol. 59 (Winter 1992), pp. 381-432, which is followed by criticisms by Richard A. Posner. For a comprehensive introduction to and critique of Dworkin's theory, see Stephen Guest, *Ronald Dworkin* (Stanford: Stanford University Press, 1991).

Chapter 6

An up-to-date collection on critical race theory is *Critical Race Theory: A Reader*, edited by Kimberlé Crenshaw, Neil Gotanda, and Kendall Thomas (New York: New Press, 1993). For more work by Patricia Williams, see *The Alchemy of Race and Rights* (Cambridge: Harvard University Press, 1991). The founder of critical race theory is considered by many to be Derrick Bell, whose books include *And We are Not Saved: The Elusive Quest for Racial Justice* (New York: Basic Books, 1987) and *Faces at the Bottom of the Well: The Permanence of Racism* (New York: Basic Books, 1992). For discussions of racist hate speech, see Mari J. Matsuda, Charles R. Lawrence III, Richard Delgado, and Kimberlé Crenshaw, *Words That Wound: Critical Race Theory, Assaultive Speech, and the First Amendment* (Boulder: Westview Press, 1993).

Chapter 7

Three excellent recent collections of articles by feminist legal theorists are *Feminist Legal Theory: Readings in Law and Gender*, edited by Katharine T. Bartlett and Rosanne Kennedy (Boulder: Westview Press, 1991); *At the Boundaries of Law: Feminism and Legal Theory*, edited by Martha Albertson Fineman and Nancy Sweet Thomadsen (New York: Routledge, 1991); and *Feminist Jurisprudence*, edited by Patricia Smith (New York: Oxford University Press, 1992). For an elaboration of Martha Minow's work on difference, see her book, *Making all the Difference: Inclusion, Exclusion, and American Law* (Ithaca: Cornell University Press, 1990). For an alternative feminist theory that focuses on dominance, see the writings of Catharine A. MacKinnon, especially *Feminism Unmodified: Discourses on Life and Law* (Cambridge: Harvard University Press, 1987) and *Toward a Feminist Theory of the State* (Cambridge: Harvard University Press, 1989).

Chapter 8

For other articles on deconstruction and constitutional interpretation, see J. M. Balkin, "Deconstructive Practice and Legal Theory," *The Yale Law Journal*, vol. 96 (1987), pp. 743-86; David Couzens Hoy, "Interpreting the Law: Hermeneutical and Poststructuralist Perspectives," *Southern California Law Review*, vol. 58, nos. 1-2 (January 1985), pp. 136-76; Pierre Schlag, "The Problem of the Subject," *Texas Law Review*, vol. 69 (1991), pp. 1627-43; and the symposium on "Deconstruction and the Possibility of Justice" in *Cardozo Law Review*, vol. 11 (1990), which includes an article on law by Jacques Derrida.

Chapter 9

For an elaboration of Mark Tushnet's approach, see his *Red, White, and Blue: A Critical Analysis of Constitutional Law* (Cambridge: Harvard University Press, 1988). A survey of critical legal studies by one of its most prominent proponents is *The Critical Legal Studies Movement* by Roberto Unger (Cambridge: Harvard University Press, 1986). Three useful collections of work in critical legal studies are *The Politics of Law: A Progressive Critique*, 2nd ed., edited by David Kairys (New York: Pantheon Books, 1990); "Constitutional Law from a Critical Legal Perspective: A Symposium," *Buffalo Law Review*, vol. 36 (Spring 1987); and the articles in *Stanford Law Review*, vol. 36 (January 1984). For some criticisms of this approach, see Andrew Altman, *Critical Legal Studies: A Liberal Critique* (Princeton: Princeton University Press, 1990).

Chapter 10

Although her contribution to this anthology is on constitutional scepticism, Robin L. West is best known for her work on feminist legal theory. See, for example, her article, "Jurisprudence and Gender," in *Feminist Legal Theory: Readings in Law and Gender,* edited by Katharine T. Bartlett and Rosanne Kennedy (Boulder: Westview Press, 1991), pp. 201-34. As West points out in this anthology, virtually no theorists have advocated constitutional scepticism. Two notable exceptions are James P. Sterba, "The U.S. Constitution: A Fundamentally Flawed Document," in *Philosophical Reflections on the United States Constitution: A Collection of Bicentennial Essays,* edited by Christopher B. Gray (Lewiston, N.Y.: Edwin Mellen Press, 1989); and Mary E. Becker, "The Politics of Women's Wrongs and the Bill of 'Rights': A Bicentennial Perspective," *The University of Chicago Law Review,* vol. 59 (Winter 1992), pp. 453-517. Compare also Henry Monaghan, "Our Perfect Constitution," *NYU Law Review,* vol. 56 (May-June 1981), pp. 353-96.

About the Book and Editors

Current controversies over abortion, affirmative action, school prayer, hate speech, and other issues have sparked considerable public debate about how the U.S. Constitution should be interpreted. Such controversies, along with the changing composition of an often deeply divided Supreme Court, have led to a resurgence of interest in theories of constitutional interpretation.

This anthology, edited by Susan J. Brison and Walter Sinnott-Armstrong, presents some of the most exciting and influential contemporary work in this area. Written by ten of the country's most prominent legal scholars, the selections represent a wide variety of interpretive approaches, reflecting different political orientations from the far right to the far left. These theorists have drawn on a variety of other disciplines, including literature, economics, history, philosophy, and politics, and have in turn influenced these fields.

The selections were chosen for their accessibility, originality, variety, and importance. Together they provide an excellent introduction to constitutional interpretation as well as a valuable collection for experienced scholars in the field.

Susan J. Brison is assistant professor of philosophy at Dartmouth College and writes in the areas of philosophy of mind and philosophy of law. She is currently writing a book on free speech and conflicts of rights.

Walter Sinnott-Armstrong is associate professor of philosophy at Dartmouth College. He is also author of *Moral Dilemmas* (1988) and coauthor with Robert Fogelin of *Understanding Arguments: An Introduction to Informal Logic, Fourth Edition* (1991).

About the Contributors

J. M. Balkin is professor of law as well as the Graves, Dougherty, Hearon & Moody Centennial Faculty Fellow at the University of Texas School of Law.

Robert H. Bork is John M. Olin Scholar in Legal Studies at the American Enterprise Institute.

Ronald Dworkin is professor of jurisprudence at Oxford University and professor of law at the New York University School of Law.

Richard A. Epstein is James Parker Hall Distinguished Service Professor of Law at the University of Chicago School of Law.

Martha Minow is professor of law at the Harvard University School of Law.

Richard A. Posner is a judge on the United States Court of Appeals for the Seventh Circuit and senior lecturer at the University of Chicago School of Law.

Frederick Schauer is Frank Stanton Professor of the First Amendment and Professorial Fellow of the Joan Shorenstein Barone Center on the Press, Politics and Public Policy at the John F. Kennedy School of Government at Harvard University.

Mark Tushnet is associate dean and professor of law at the Georgetown University Law Center.

Robin L. West is professor of law at the Georgetown University Law Center.

Patricia Williams is professor of law at the Columbia University School of Law.

Cases Cited